Essentials of *Applied* Quantitative Methods for Health Services Managers

James B. Lewis, ScD
Associate Professor of Health Management & Policy

Robert J. McGrath, PhD
Assistant Professor of Health Management & Policy

Lee F. Seidel, PhD
Professor of Health Management & Policy

Department of Health Management and Policy
College of Health and Human Services
University of New Hampshire
Durham, New Hampshire

JONES AND BARTLETT PUBLISHERS
Sudbury, Massachusetts
BOSTON   TORONTO   LONDON   SINGAPORE

World Headquarters

Jones and Bartlett Publishers
40 Tall Pine Drive
Sudbury, MA 01776
978-443-5000
info@jbpub.com
www.jbpub.com

Jones and Bartlett Publishers
Canada
6339 Ormindale Way
Mississauga, Ontario L5V 1J2
Canada

Jones and Bartlett Publishers
International
Barb House, Barb Mews
London W6 7PA
United Kingdom

Jones and Bartlett's books and products are available through most bookstores and online booksellers. To contact Jones and Bartlett Publishers directly, call 800-832-0034, fax 978-443-8000, or visit our web site, www.jbpub.com.

Substantial discounts on bulk quantities of Jones and Bartlett's publications are available to corporations, professional associations, and other qualified organizations. For details and specific discount information, contact the special sales department at Jones and Bartlett via the above contact information or send an email to specialsales@jbpub.com.

This publication is designed to provide accurate and authoritative information in regard to the Subject Matter covered. It is sold with the understanding that the publisher is not engaged in rendering legal, accounting, or other professional service. If legal advice or other expert assistance is required, the service of a competent professional person should be sought.

Production Credits
Publisher: Michael Brown
Editorial Assistant: Catie Heverling
Editorial Assistant: Teresa Reilly
Senior Production Editor: Tracey Chapman
Senior Marketing Manager: Sophie Fleck
Manufacturing and Inventory Control Supervisor: Amy Bacus
Composition: DSCS/Absolute Service, Inc.
Cover Design: Kristin E. Parker
Cover Image: © Kheng Guan Toh/Dreamstime.com
Printing and Binding: Malloy, Inc.
Cover Printing: Malloy, Inc.

Library of Congress Cataloging-in-Publication Data

Lewis, James B. (James Bradley), 1950-
    Essentials of applied quantitative methods for health services managers / James B. Lewis, Robert J. McGrath, and Lee F. Seidel.
        p. ; cm.
    Includes bibliographical references and index.
    ISBN-13: 978-0-7637-5871-4 (pbk.)
    ISBN-10: 0-7637-5871-X (pbk.)
    1. Health services administration.   2. Quantitative research.   I. McGrath, Robert J., 1967-   II. Seidel, Lee F.
III. Title.
    [DNLM: 1. Health Services Administration.   2. Statistics as Topic.   3. Program Evaluation. WA 950 L674e
2009]
    RA971.L495 2009
    362.1068—dc22

                                                                                                    2009023884

6048

Printed in the United States of America
13 12 11 10 09   10 9 8 7 6 5 4 3 2 1

Table of Contents

Preface

Health services managers require a varied repertoire of skills and expertise, including both qualitative and quantitative elements. The purpose of this book is to bring numerous quantitative methods from other fields, including industrial engineering, operations research, finance, and general systems analysis into the health services arena, and enhance the quantitative skill set of health administration students. The content and "tone" of the book are the result of working with undergraduate and graduate health management students at the University of New Hampshire, as well as elsewhere. The book builds upon our experience that many students lack confidence in their quantitative abilities, and as a result develop a somewhat incomplete set of skills.

The book assumes a basic understanding of algebra, statistics, and financial and managerial accounting as well as familiarity with economics, healthcare organizations, and health services management. Based upon these foundation competencies, quantitative methods are presented within a health services administration context. Every effort has been taken to avoid clouding these methods behind algebraic or quantitative curtains. When doubts exist, we have simplified our presentation. This book is not meant to take the place of more advanced texts in any of the techniques of quantitative analysis presented here. Although the array of quantitative methods presented in the text is somewhat eclectic, the topics selected share the characteristic of being routinely used by health services managers. Intentionally, the book includes basic concepts and foundations—it is essential that students grasp these basics before moving on to applying more advanced analytical tools. As such, the book is not intended to expand a student's ability to perform health services research.

Our experience also suggests that learning and being able to use quantitative methods require learning experiences designed as loops, not straight lines. Basic points, terms, and calculations need to be repeated to be effectively incorporated into the student's repertoire. Assuming that students possess complete recall of an earlier course in statistics, for example, is an instructional blunder that jeopardizes the effectiveness of a professor as well as the ability of students to learn.

v

Most of the quantitative applications presented can be completed using a general spreadsheet program. However, we have avoided particular software applications and instructions on how to use specific spreadsheet programs. After gaining a firm understanding of the mathematical concepts underlying the quantitative tools presented, students are encouraged to use suitable computer (or even calculator) programs; we feel it is important to gain this firm conceptual understanding first, however. In addition to introducing (or in some cases reviewing) quantitative concepts, the book provides students with an example of application of these tools within the context of completing an external assessment component of a strategic plan. It is hoped that this application provides students with a view of how the quantitative tools are used in practice.

Essentials in Quantitative Methods for Health Services Managers emerged from the interests of three professors searching for a more effective approach to teaching students how to use quantitative methods as health services managers. Students deserve special recognition for helping us through the years to appreciate the difference between teaching and learning quantitative methods and for assisting in determining effective teaching and learning strategies. Throughout this book practice as well as understanding is stressed. It is our conclusion that students are better able to incorporate these methods into their professional repertoires when they have had the opportunity to experience and apply these methods in a context related to their professional interests. Exercises have been incorporated into each chapter for students to use to experience a specific method. When we use this book, students are often required to turn in assigned exercises as their ticket into a specific class. Reading about a quantitative method is not the same as using the methods to solve a realistic health services management problem.

Ultimately, of course, developing the comprehensive repertoire of skills needed to be a competent manager of health services is a student's responsibility; doing this is a complex, ambiguous, and challenging endeavor that spans a career. No single collection of quantitative methods is sufficient to meet this challenge. Hopefully, however, this collection will assist many in developing their basic repertoire.

James B. Lewis, ScD
Associate Professor of Health Management & Policy

Robert J. McGrath, PhD
Assistant Professor of Health Management & Policy

Lee F. Seidel, PhD
Professor of Health Management & Policy

Department of Health Management and Policy
College of Health and Human Services
University of New Hampshire
Durham, New Hampshire

Chapter 1

The Role and Function of Quantitative Methods in Health Services Management

---

LEARNING OBJECTIVES

After studying this chapter, you should be able to:

1. Describe how health services managers analyze, design, and implement in a systems context.
2. Differentiate between efficiency and effectiveness as vital managerial interests.
3. Describe how quantitative methods fit into the repertoire of the health services manager.
4. Describe the general systems model in relation to health services.

LEARNING OBJECTIVE 1: EXAMINE HOW HEALTH SERVICES MANAGERS ANALYZE, DESIGN, AND IMPLEMENT IN A SYSTEMS CONTEXT

Health administration, as a profession, deals with the management of human, fiscal, physical, and information resources to meet the goals and objectives of healthcare organizations. Survival of the healthcare organization in a competitive environment, as well as characteristics of this survival, involve multiple factors, including the abilities of managers. The challenge is to provide healthcare organizations, and the communities, patients, and clients they serve, with competent managers able to perform the robust and challenging role of manager.

Being a competent manager in a healthcare organization means fundamentally different things depending upon specific role expectations, perspective, and circumstance. Within a healthcare organization, managers are assigned very different functions, each with potentially different definitions of core competency. Managers in the human resources department of a hospital face different management challenges than the managers in the hospital's planning and marketing department or the financial services department. Different types of healthcare organizations

1

may require different types of managers. Nursing homes may require managers with different skills and values than public health clinics. Healthcare organizations also may shift their definition of desired or needed management competency because of a shift in their objectives, in characteristics in their environment, or in both. A hospital in the process of affiliating with a regional healthcare system may require different management talents than the hospital intending to remain a solo institution. Definitions of management competency also may change based upon perceived or real changes in the field of management. The competencies expected of professional health services managers encompass a very wide breadth and depth of potential responsibilities, values, interests, and abilities. Health administrators need a broad repertoire of skills to function in this dynamic situation. More specifically, multiple perspectives also exist concerning the role and function of the health manager in a contemporary healthcare organization. Being able to use quantitative methods designed to assist managers make decisions is one essential part of this repertoire, regardless of the role and function of any health services manager. Figure 1-1 is one framework able to integrate many of these perspectives and is based upon the simple recognition that managers need the ability to analyze, design, and implement.

Analyzing, as a core managerial competency, is the ability to discover what is. It involves, for example, discovering the current market share of an organization. It involves discovering the actual total cost of a specific service rendered by the organization. It involves discovering who does what with what resources to provide a specific service. It involves using forecasting to discover the logical or reasonable future of the organization. The key and defining aspect of analysis is discovery. Sometimes discoveries shift the organization's goals and objectives. Other times discovery is used to determine whether the organization is meeting and how it is meeting its goals and objectives. To facilitate discovery, quantitative methods provide the manager an analytical road map. Each quantitative method has a unique analytical ability. For example, a method such as queuing theory can only be used to analyze specific types of waiting lines. When incorporated into the manager's repertoire, quantitative methods provide the manager with useful and robust tools.

Designing, as a core management competency, is the ability to identify and arrange resources in a manner commensurate with goals and objectives. If the goal is to provide a specific service, managers need to be able to design (or redesign) the mix of resources needed to provide the service. The goal of operating a short-stay surgical unit in a hospital requires that a manager identify and arrange the

Figure 1-1 General Management Competencies

resources needed to realize the goal, such as specialized equipment and staff. If the goal is for the organization to retain specific information, then managers must be able to design work processes to capture, report, and store the desired information. Design as a managerial competency often involves engineering because it encompasses the ability to break down desired capabilities, such as an organization's goals and objectives, into requisite components or parts. If the organization desires a new service, it is a manager's responsibility to design the service by first determining the different mix of human, fiscal, physical, and information resources needed to provide the service, and then specifying exactly how much of each will be needed to provide the service. Design of new work processes, or the redesign of existing ones, involves developing detailed plans so that when the plans are executed the desired capability has been incorporated into the organization. Design also involves developing these detailed plans as to what is needed as well as how the needed resources should be used. Design is performance oriented; the new or revised design must establish the desired performance capability.

Implementing, as a core management competency, is the ability to change the organization. The process of implementation may require the manager to change the behavior of specific employees. It may also involve the ability of the manager to accumulate and operationalize the resources necessary to achieve desired goals and objectives. Whereas design may be the management competency that determines what is needed, implementation is the management competency that installs new or revised elements in the organization. The manager's repertoire needs to include quantitative methods to assist implementing change within the organization. These methods include, for example, Program Evaluation Review Technique (PERT). The Program Evaluation Review Technique is a formal method used by managers to plan and control projects. It informs managers of the desired order and schedule of activities needed to be accomplished to realize the overall completion of a project or change within the organization, such as the opening of a new short stay surgical unit in a hospital.

LEARNING OBJECTIVE 2: TO DIFFERENTIATE BETWEEN EFFICIENCY AND EFFECTIVENESS AS KEY MANAGERIAL INTERESTS

Managing in the Health Services Organization

A healthcare organization is any organization that provides health and medical services to patients, residents, and clients, such as an acute care or specialty hospital, a nursing home, an ambulatory care organization, such as a university health services, public health clinic, and a home health agency. The defining characteristic in this definition of a healthcare organization is patient care; care provided by physicians, nurses and therapists to prevent and treat disease or infirmity. The mission of these organizations serves to distinguish them as healthcare organizations.

Services provided to patients could include a surgical procedure, diagnostic examination, specialized treatment, or disease prevention or screening program. These services also could be an appropriate meal, a safe and comfortable environment, or an accurate and timely bill for service. All healthcare organizations provide a range of services and specialize in providing individual patients a particularized array of services based upon a patient's needs or diagnosis. The central and defining element of all healthcare organizations is the provision of a personal and personalized experience, and high quality health or medical service. As such, a central expectation shared by all health administrators is the expectation that management practice will lead to the *efficient* provision of *effective* services to people in need of service.

The interests of managers and the interests of the healthcare organizations that employ health administrators as managers are difficult to distinguish. Both interests emphasize that patients receive needed services and that services are provided in an *efficient* manner. Healthcare organizations and health administrators rely upon physicians, nurses, and therapists to determine or diagnosis the needs of a patient accurately and to plan and execute an intervention or treatment that has some probability of success in maintaining or improving the health status of the patient. Clinical interests stress the needs of individual patients and the identification of appropriate service interventions. Decisions made by clinicians are based upon what they consider to be *effective* approaches, interventions that have some probability of clinical or medical success. The physician, nurse, or therapist has been educated and trained to select and apply current knowledge to assist patients. Clinical interests and perspectives are focused on the *effectiveness* of a service—the ability of a service to accomplish its predetermined objective. Although clinicians are not necessarily oblivious or insensitive to *efficiency*, their unique role and function stem from their commitment to provide effective service to patients. They alone have the expertise to determine a patient's needs (i.e., diagnosis) and to meet them (i.e., treatment) and are judged by their peers, specific systems, and patients based upon their ability to provide an *effective*, but not necessarily an *efficient*, service.

Efficiency as a Management Interest

Efficiency is the ratio measure of output over input. High efficiency is achieved when a service is rendered using the least amount of resources. Inefficient clinical practice, such as requiring more clinical tests than necessary to make an accurate diagnosis can lead to a highly inefficient healthcare organization. Using more medical supplies than needed or even stocking more medical supplies than needed are other examples of operational inefficiency. Using an excess number of people to prepare a meal or render a bill is inefficient; an excess amount of input resources are being used to produce a specific output. Unlike operational effectiveness which is primarily in the province of the clinician, operational efficiency lies within the dual province of both clinicians and managers. Health administrators are retained to analyze, design, and implement work processes in the healthcare organization that lead to desired levels of operational efficiency.

Inefficient work processes waste scarce resources. Efficient work processes provide services that maximize the opportunities created by the mix of resources used to produce the service. Managers are employed by organizations to ensure that desired levels of efficiency are attained, not by accident, but by design. Being interested in efficiency differentiates the health services manager from the health service clinician. Striving for maximum appropriate efficiency is a management value that requires a specific repertoire of skills—the ability to analyze current levels of efficiency, the ability to design and redesign services to achieve desired levels of efficient, and the ability to implement new or revised services.

Effectiveness as a Management Interest

Effectiveness means the ability to accomplish a defined task. For example, if a specific drug is able to cure a specific infection, then that drug can be considered effective. If a specific medical procedure or therapy is able to cure or alleviate a specific disease or infirmity, then the procedure is effective. To be effective, the procedure or drug must accomplish its intended purpose. Multiple factors may influence the effectiveness of planned intervention or treatment. For example, some patients may respond differently to the same drug. Sometimes the effectiveness of a procedure or treatment is influenced by the behavior of the patient, something not totally controllable by the clinician. Effective treatments are those treatments that have a probability of success; sometimes these probabilities may be 5%, 50%, or 95% depending upon the state of clinical and scientific knowledge and/or the existing health status of the patient.

Healthcare organizations rely upon clinically trained professionals to select the appropriate clinical services or treatments for specific patients from the array of services offered by the organization. Clinical professionals are expected to select appropriate services and, if not available in the healthcare organization, to refer the patient to another organization. In the healthcare organization, managers are not empowered to override or veto clinical judgments involving a patient's diagnosis or treatment. Clinical protocols are established by clinical professionals, not managers. At the operational level, the clinical staff determine how effective the organization will be in accomplishing its mission to provide a high-quality personal and personalized health or medical service to specific patients (to treat disease or infirmity).

At the strategic or macro level of organizational decision making and action; however, managerial interests involving organizational effectiveness emerge. For example, the costs and benefits of investing in new technology must be identified and examined from both a clinical and organizational perspective before the decision is made by the organization to acquire and implement it. Even though a new technology may enhance the effectiveness of the clinicians affiliated with the organization and thereby increase the organization's effectiveness, its acquisition and/or operational cost to the organization may prevent the organization from acquiring it. Managerial involvement in these types of strategic decisions is one example of how managers influence the effectiveness of the healthcare organization. Health administrators also are trained to use epidemiology and are expected to use epidemiology to analyze the health and medical needs of the communities and groups of individuals served or potentially serviced by the healthcare organization.

Efficiency and Managerial Competence

Just as clinical operational *effectiveness* is the responsibility of the clinical professional, operational and organizational *efficiency* is the primary responsibility of the health administrator as manager. As stated, efficiency means providing a needed service using no more resources than necessary; it is a ratio measure of output and input. Health administrators are employed in part to ensure that any service provided by the healthcare organization is supplied in an efficient manner. Being able to determine current levels of efficiency is an example of analysis as a managerial competency. Being able to design or redesign how the organization does something to enhance efficiency is an example of design as a managerial competency. Being able to change how the organization provides a service to enhance operational efficiency is an example of implementation as a managerial competency.

Striving to make the healthcare organization efficient is a dominating, unique, and defining value associated with management and managers and the field of health administration. Whereas the credit for effective clinical practice must be given to the clinical sciences and professions and the technologies they use, credit for efficient operations and the efficient use of resources must be given to health administrators and their ability to analyze, design, and implement.

LEARNING OBJECTIVE 3: DESCRIBE HOW QUANTITATIVE METHODS FIT INTO THE REPERTOIRE OF THE HEALTH SERVICES MANAGER

Theoretical designs to describe or illustrate the role and function of management abound. Models such as the Shewhart or Deming cycle (also known as the "Plan-Do-

Check-Act;" the PDCA approach), systems theory, chaos theory, management by objectives, and many more have been developed to organize management thinking and action. Indeed, the level of acceptance or "popularity" of these models has varied over time, as models come into and fall out of favor. One constant remains, however. It is clear that effective managers need to be able to do many things well.

Managers must be able to:

- Articulate organizational objectives.
- Assess opportunities and threats in the internal and external environments.
- Design effective and distinctive organizational strategies.
- Make decisions regarding the allocation of human, fiscal, physical, and information resources to implement these strategies.
- Motivate staff and colleagues to work collaboratively on accomplishing the strategies.
- Evaluate the effectiveness of the strategies.
- Modify the strategies and resource allocation decisions, as necessary.

Management should be viewed as both an art and a science; the principal focus of this book is on the latter aspect, specifically developing skills and tools in quantitative analysis. We do not wish to suggest that quantitative data should be the sole driver for management decision making; we are not advocating a cookie-cutter approach to management or a slavish dependency on numbers. However, effective managers use a variety of quantitative tools, skills, and techniques to complement their intuitive, subjective, and qualitative analysis.

Managers remain very interested in formal methods that can assist them to enhance the operational and organizational efficiency of the healthcare organization. Given their professional concern involving *efficiency*, managers are expected to know how to use specific methods to enhance the efficiency of healthcare organizations. Formal methods expand the ability of health administrators to analyze, design, and implement and constitute an essential element of the manager's unique and defining repertoire of skills. These methods, many of which are quantitative, and come from operations research, applied statistics, and industrial engineering, provide managers with specific protocols to analyze current levels of efficiency, design new services or redesign existing services to enhance efficiency, and implement change efficiency.

Most of the quantitative methods used by health services managers are based upon the fundamental ability of healthcare organizations and health administrators to count. For example, to determine service efficiency, healthcare organizations count or account for their resources and services. Healthcare organizations count:

- The number of laboratory tests performed
- The number of patient visits to an emergency room

- The number of meals served to nursing home residents
- The number and type of surgical operations
- The number of immunizations
- The number and type of employees used to provide specific services
- The costs associated with each service

Management actions designed to assess and improve the efficiency and effectiveness of a healthcare organization always begin by counting what is currently being done.

Although basic, counting may not be simple. Every healthcare organization provides a broad array of services. Not everything done in the healthcare organization can or should be counted. Healthcare organizations count those aspects of their operation necessary to assess service effectiveness and/or efficiency. For example, hospitals count the number of patients discharged and the number of days that patients spend in a hospital to calculate the average length of stay (ALOS) of their patients. Average length of stay is a traditional measure of hospital activity. Some hospitals compare themselves with other similar institutions to determine whether they are adhering to similar patterns of utilization. All hospitals generally compare their ALOS with national trends and take national trends into consideration when forecasting service utilization. When ALOS is calculated for a specific medical diagnosis, comparing results by attending physicians also may yield important information concerning the effectiveness and efficiency of clinical practice. Calculating the ALOS of a hospital, like so many similar calculations, begins with counting.

Ambulatory care clinics also count. For example, they count the number of patient visits per day, usually by time of day. This information can assist in determining whether the staffing in the clinic is appropriate for the demand for service. This information can also be used to design efficient staffing levels based upon demand levels that change based upon hour of the day, day of the week, and month of the year.

Other examples of counting include dietary departments in hospitals and nursing homes counting the number of meals prepared and served. Custodial services in all types of healthcare organizations usually count the number of square feet cleaned and the number of staff hours used to clean. Because efficiency is a ratio measure of output (e.g., square feet cleaned) and input (e.g., staff hours used to clean), counting enables the manager to analyze current levels of efficiency, design new approaches to enhance efficiency and implement any needed changes. Being more efficient requires knowing the amount of work accomplished as a measure of output and the amount of resources used to accomplish the work as a measure of input. Knowing input and output levels is a prerequisite for analysis and design or redesign.

Still other examples can be found throughout healthcare organizations. For example, medical laboratories count the number and type of medical test processed. This provides a statement of the laboratory's output. It also provides a statement of the tests physicians ordered to accomplish their diagnoses. Both can be used to assess efficiency and effectiveness. This list of examples also can include business offices in hospitals counting the number and type of health insurance claims processed, pharmacies counting the number and type of prescriptions filled, and hospitals counting the number of live births. Counting is the common attribute of each of these activities and a prerequisite to assess and improve service efficiency and effectiveness.

To count appropriately often requires using a unique classification or counting system. Diagnosis related groups (DRGs) help hospitals count appropriately the number and type of patients discharged. The classification system objectively assigns each discharged patient to a specific category. The number of patients in each category can then be counted by day, week, or year to yield an accurate listing of hospital actions by discharge diagnosis. Although used as a basis for reimbursement, DRGs were developed as an output measurement system for hospitals.

Healthcare organizations also count mistakes; in fact, this aspect of trying to assess and measure clinical errors has taken on considerable currency in the healthcare system. Examples of such mistakes include errors made in administering medications and blood transfusions, and mistakes made in surgery. Surgical deaths are counted. Postoperative infections are counted. Pathology reports that indicate unnecessary surgical resections are counted. Patient complaints are counted. Inaccurate patient bills are counted. Meals served cold are counted. Patients inappropriately transported to another healthcare organization are counted. Stock out conditions in inventory are counted. Single mistakes and/or patterns of mistakes can be used to determine where change (i.e., redesign) may be needed in the healthcare organization.

Similar to footprints on a sandy beach, the services provided by the healthcare organizations create a trail that can be counted. Once counted, the information expands the manager's ability to analyze the effectiveness and efficiency of the organization or a part of the organization. Service counts are a product of what services were offered by the organization (i.e., capacity) as well as the frequency these services were used (i.e., utilization). The difference between capacity and utilization is an important distinction.

Every healthcare organization offers a unique array of services and has a finite or limited service capacity. For example, a 100-bed hospital has the capacity to generate no more than 36,500 patient days in a typical year (i.e., 365 days × 100 beds). Some healthcare organizations have the capacity to perform surgery, others do not. These types of expressions indicate the capacity of the healthcare organization. For example, not all hospitals have the capacity to perform neurosurgery, and as such, would not create any service counts involving this type of surgical operation. Not all hospitals have the capacity to offer patients certain cancer treatments.

To assess efficiency requires knowing the capacity of the healthcare organization as well as how the capacity is used.

Utilization is the amount of capacity actually used and is usually reported for a specific period of time, such as an hour, shift, day, week, month, or year. The frequency of a service being rendered, aside from being dependent upon its availability, also reflects the need (and demand) for the available service. Often this need is a decision made by a clinician. A count of laboratory tests by type of test indicates the contribution a medical laboratory makes to the effective operation of the healthcare organization and effective medical care. This same count also can be used to assess service efficiency when combined with counts of the number and type of supplies used and the number and type of staff used in the laboratory as input measures. Counts that indicate utilization when combined with measures of capacity provide the ability to determine the amount and percent of capacity being used. A more complete identification of what is counted in health services organizations, as well as a discussion of how these counts are used, is found in Chapter 2.

As stated, improving the operation of any healthcare organization through the application of quantitative methods begins with the ability to count, often an ability delegated to an information system. What is counted and how it is counted is important, as it establishes the data library managers rely upon as they analyze and design. Formal analytical methods, techniques, and models designed to assess efficiency and effectiveness can only be used in conjunction with an adequate data library. Some quantitative methods have very specialized demands in terms of what needs to be counted to then use the specific method. As such, what is placed in a data library will influence the manager's ability to perform expected functions; namely, the improvement of the efficiency of the healthcare organization using an appropriate method, technique, or model.

LEARNING OBJECTIVE 4: DESCRIBE THE GENERAL SYSTEMS MODEL IN RELATION TO HEALTH SERVICES

Quantitative Methods and the Systems Model

Management, as a profession and field, has long searched for specific methods to assist managers analyze, design, and implement change as organizations strive to enhance their efficiency and effectiveness. Some methods, still in use today, trace their birth to the era of scientific management and the needs of large-scale production lines designed to efficiently produce physical products such as automobiles. In this era, the complex organization was conceptualized as a machine with the pieces of the organization thought of as cogs in the greater machine. Workers were considered cogs. Equipment was considered cogs. Managers were retained to design organizations as machines and ensure that cogs did what they were supposed to do in the most efficient way possible. Managers wrote procedures to tell human cogs how to do their specific job. Specific methods also were developed to determine the efficiency of individual cogs and assist managers design or redesign cogs and machines. Organizations that produced the best for least were considered survivors.

In this earlier era, division of labor was a new concept because workers were retained to perform one set of tasks necessary for the finished product, not as craftsman held individually responsible for an entire product. The need for people as managers also was new. Coordinating the cogs in the greater machine was a task expected of the manager to ensure efficiency. The thinking in this era emphasized that more efficient machines were more desirable than less efficient machines, that workers were merely extensions of the machine, and that science or engineering could be used to analyze operations and design or redesign work processes. Some of the quantitative methods used today by health administrators trace their conceptual roots to this era. Techniques drawn from industrial engineering, operations research, and operations management emphasize the production characteristics of the organization. Although the era of managers looking to classical bureaucratic theory and the principles of scientific management is over, many quantitative techniques remain available for health administrators to use to analyze, design, and implement within the healthcare organization.

Today, managers in general, and health administrators in particular, are more likely to rely upon general systems theory (Figure 1-2) for concept and direction. This theory suggests that healthcare organizations are one example of goal-directed systems with identifiable inputs, work processes that convert inputs into outputs, identifiable outputs, and feedback loops that serve to direct and control the system. To understand the complexity of activity within any organization, the general systems model provides the ability to assign activities or features of the organization to one of four categories: inputs or resources, conversion processes (i.e., what is done with the inputs), outcomes (what is desired), and feedback.

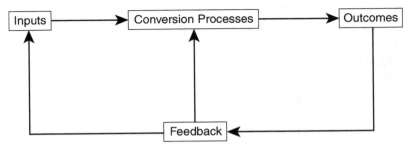

Figure 1-2 The General Systems Model

Organizations are considered open systems that are influenced by events and circumstances external to the organization. As open systems, organizations draw resources from their dynamic environment and provide back to their environment some valued product or service. In spite of this fundamental change in the way managers think about organizations and management, quantitative methods originally developed during the era of scientific manager are still used and considered central in the repertoire of methods that defines the unique abilities of the manager.

Elements of the General Systems Model

Using the systems model to improve the efficiency and effectiveness of the healthcare organization requires appreciation of the defining elements of the systems model.

Organizational Goals

Any system strives to attain its goals by accumulating sufficient resources and converting these resources into desired products or services. Goals express the intent of the system. Organizations, however, have multiple and sometimes conflicting goals. For example, maximizing organizational profit and providing services to anyone regardless of their ability to pay are potentially conflicting goals for any private healthcare corporation. Therefore, the use of the general systems model may be limited by the type and amount of goal ambiguity or conflict that exists in the healthcare organization. The first and most important analytical challenge faced in our quest for improved efficiency and effectiveness is to identify system goals.

Inputs Are Resources

Inputs are the resources needed to achieve a desired goal often expressed as a desired output or outcome. Inputs are needed to accomplish the desired goal of the system. Examples include:

- People, each with a skill deemed needed by the organization
- Time
- Supplies and materials
- Capital assets, such as buildings and equipment

Based on this definition it is reasonable to expect that different types of healthcare organizations, because of their different goals, have different input resources. For example, the input resources needed by a nursing home are different from the input resources needed by an acute care hospital or by a clinic. An organization's wealth may also determine its inputs. As many inputs can be purchased, the amount and type of input resources held by the organization may be a product of the financial position of the organization.

As they are used, most inputs resources are counted. Financial accounting counts expenses and revenues by category. Other processes count the number and type of workers employed and the numbers of hours worked. Still other systems count the supplies used.

Conversion Processes Add Value

Conversion processes convert inputs into outcomes. A surgical procedure is a conversion process. It takes a specific array of inputs (e.g., people such as a surgeon and nurses plus capital assets and equipment) and converts them into a desired outcome, such as the removal of a diseased gall bladder. Conversion adds value. A conversion process takes inputs and produces an outcome. In the process that transforms inputs into outcomes, value is added. Working with clinicians, health administrators strive for efficient as well as effective conversion processes.

System Modifiers Influence the System

System modifiers influence inputs and conversion processes. Examples of modifiers include need, demand, want, social values, and physical climate. A system modifier is something that influences a conversion process but is outside the direct control of the system. For example, how a hospital converts resources into patient days is influenced by the "need" for medical care. As "need" changes, such as with the advent of HIV infections, conversion processes are changed (e.g., blood is transfused using different procedures/universal precautions). Laws and regulation modify and influence conversion processes.

System modifiers can be as bold as a fundamental change in reimbursement policies or as subtle as a specific health profession striving for the autonomy, status, and income historically reserved for the physician. A system modifier also can be the cultural attributes of the specific organization when these attributes either cannot or will not be changed.

Outcomes and Outputs

Outcomes or outputs are the results created by the system. It is hoped that these results are the desired, intended, or expected goals of the system (or subsystem) under study. If results match expectations, the system is accomplishing its goals. If results do not match expectations, change may be required. Examples of outcomes include the improved health status of the population, the organization's financial position, the number and type of hospital patient days or discharges, the number and type of clinic visits, or the number of meals served. Outcomes or outputs are the units of service produced by the organization. Many outcomes or outputs are counted by the organizations. Outcomes involving the worth of an organization are counted using financial accounting. Statistics are generated by organizations that report their outputs and outcomes.

Subsystems and Suboptimization

For purposes of analysis, design, and implementation, large complex systems are usually conceptualized as having multiple layers or subsystems. For example, a human body as a system has one subsystem for circulation and another to control its nerve function. Subsystems serve systems. For example, dietary, imaging, medical information, and patient process subsystems in a hospital serve the acute care system, called a hospital, created by the interplay of numerous subsystems.

Within the hierarchical and interdependent arrangement created by subsystems within a system, suboptimization is expected. Suboptimization is the recognition that the ultimate goal of any subsystem is to meet the requirements of its larger system and that meeting these large and more important system requirements may mean that any individual subsystem may need to operate at less than its highest level of efficiency.

Managers analyze, design, and implement to maximize the performance of the organization as a system. Efficiency and effectiveness are measures of performance. To achieve the goals and objectives of the organization, subsystems are analyzed, designed, and implemented. Expectations placed on subsystems come from system goals and objectives. In some instances, managers expect to have inefficient subsystems so that the organization as systems can be efficient. Suboptimization occurs when subsystems perform below their potential so that the overall organization as a system meets its goals and objectives. In some instances, managers design subsystems to perform below their potential. In other words, suboptimization can be a design parameter used in designing subsystems.

A classic example of suboptimization is a hospital's emergency room. Service is expected to be available, and not necessarily used, 24 hour per day, 7 days per week. By definition, the emergency room is intended to be very inefficient. Staff are retained to be available and provide services when they are needed. The utilization of an emergency room typically is only a small percentage of its capacity. In most emergency rooms, input levels are high and output levels relatively low.

Feedback

Feedback is typically information the organization generates to adjust inputs and/or conversion processes to change the desired outcome or make the actual outcome more closely resemble its goals. Healthcare organizations produce multiple forms of feedback. Patient outcomes are feedback. Patient opinions about their service encounters are feedback. Market share is feedback. The Balance Sheet and Statement of Income and Expense are feedback, just as conversation between employees is a form of feedback. Generally, feedback is system or subsystem output information that is used to monitor, evaluate, adjust, or change the system or subsystem so that the organization is better able to achieve its stated goals and objectives.

PUTTING IT TOGETHER: QUANTITATIVE METHODS AND THE GENERAL SYSTEMS MODEL

The general systems model provides the framework for our examination of specific quantitative methods. This model focuses our attention on inputs, conversion process, outputs, feedback loops, and modifiers. It is sufficiently robust to capture the essence of all types of healthcare organizations and tells managers to analyze and design healthcare organizations as systems and subsystems. Efficiency and effectiveness are the two primary performance measures used in healthcare organizations. To be an effective healthcare manager requires the ability to view the healthcare organization as a system and to make the organization perform better on both performance measures. Quantitative methods exist to assist managers to analyze and design systems and facilitate implementation of change within the organization not as ends, but as means to enhance organizational effectiveness and efficiency.

A quantitative method is a specific tool, technique, or model that can be used by managers to help address specific situations or problems. Frequently, quantitative methods involve collecting information (or using information collected by others) and manipulating the information using mathematics and statistics. Examples include economic analysis, queuing theory, Program Evaluation Review Technique (PERT), and general system flow charting. Many quantitative methods involve using specific mathematical models to analyze systems. Some methods have very specific applications and specific rules governing their application. Methods included in this work have been drawn from many fields, including industrial engineering, operations research, and general management analysis. Selected methods have the ability to assist managers analyze systems, design, or redesign systems and implement desired change in systems.

Another way to explain quantitative methods for health services managers involves application. To be considered a quantitative method in this context, the tool, technique, or model must have broad application in the healthcare organization and serve the needs of managers. The method must be something that the health administrator working in the hospital, nursing home, or ambulatory clinic needs to use or know about.

Not all quantitative methods have applications in health services management. All statistics are not quantitative methods used by health services managers. Also, some quantitative methods are not purely mathematical. For example, in statistics students learn the rudiments of testing a hypothesis using a t and f test. These tests are statistical methods used under specific conditions to test a hypothesis based upon a sample. In contrast, often in a same statistics course, students learn basic linear regression. As taught in statistics, the t or f test is not a quantitative method for health service management; it is a statistical method. Its use in health services management situations is rather limited. In contrast, linear regression is a professionally recognized technique used often by health services managers in forecasting. General system flow charting is a specific method to analyze systems. It is not mathematical or statistical; however, it meets the criterion of being used in certain situations by health services managers.

A REPERTOIRE OF QUANTITATIVE METHODS: AN OVERVIEW OF THE REMAINDER OF THE BOOK

Health administrators as managers have unique repertoires. Health service managers know how to do things other people do not. Health services management is a profession based upon a unique body of knowledge, values, and skills. Managers employed by a healthcare organization need to know (as part of their defining repertoire) how to design efficient systems of health and medical care and how to improve the efficiency of existing systems of care. In other words, efficiency is important to health service managers. Tools, techniques, and models used to improve the efficiency of health and medical care systems are essential elements in the repertoire of health services managers. Most methods are related to "efficiency." However, this should not be misinterpreted to mean that health services management is only interested in or trained to improve is "efficiency." Efficiency as well as effectiveness are central values for the professional manager of health services.

Management, like many other fields, can be thought of as reasoned judgment. In applying reasoned judgment, managers need formal methods to assist them to define and resolve problems. Just as master chefs need and create recipes to govern their culinary creations, health services managers need formal methods to analyze and improve complex systems. Using quantitative methods, however, does not absolve the manager from the broader responsibility of being a manager; quantitative methods and tools merely aid the manager in making reasoned judgment.

This book expands a health services manager's abilities to analyze, design, and implement. It provides methods to analyze systems and complex work processes. It also provides methods to design and implement new or revised work processes or subsystems in healthcare organizations. Frequently, the tools, models, and techniques involve using mathematical approaches. This book is organized by area of application.

Section I, Foundation Competencies, provides basic skills needed to use the quantitative methods included in subsequent sections. For some, it will be well-known material. For others, it provides a needed review. The foundation competencies include: Chapter 2, Working with Numbers; Chapter 3, Flow Charting; and Chapter 4, Time Value of Money.

Section II, Forecasting Competencies, addresses many approaches that can be used to forecast. Chapter 5, The Art and Science of Forecasting, points out that although many aspects of forecasting are quantitative in nature, subjective and qualitative factors are also critical to the process. Chapter 6, Trend Forecasting Techniques, covers specific mathematical models to detect and extend trends for purposes of forecasting. Chapter 7, Regression Forecasting, covers the application of this statistical model to forecasting. Overall, this section establishes the health services manager's ability to understand and use basic analytical forecasting to construct logical and reasoned forecasts. Forecasting is presented as a core competency associated with the role of the heath services manager. Basic algebraic and statistical competencies are needed to complete this section of the book.

Section III, Designing and Analyzing Systems, provides health services managers with the ability to apply specific quantitative methods to specific types of service systems. Chapter 8, Analyzing Capacity and Resources, includes methods to estimate the capacity of service systems. Chapter 9, Managing Waiting Lines, addresses the application of single and multiple channel queuing theory as a method to describe waiting lines. These chapters require basic abilities involving algebra and statistics.

Section IV, Project Analysis, covers five types of applied quantitative methods related to projects. A project is defined as a one-time activity or significant modification to an existing service. Chapter 10, Decision Analysis, formalizes the decision-making process regarding a choice among projects. Chapter 11, Economic Analysis, presents approaches to cost-benefit, cost-effectiveness, and cost-utility analysis used by managers to select among different projects or different project approaches to achieve similar results. Chapter 12, Program Evaluation Review Technique (PERT), is a technique to define a new project and to establish an appropriate time schedule and project implementation control system. Chapter 13, Financial Evaluation of Projects, covers methods used to assess the financial implication of projects and includes specific methods related to the cost of capital, and project risk. Chapter 14, Quality Analysis, addresses quantitative aspects related to evaluating the quality level of a project or program. Overall, this section establishes the manager's ability to analyze, design, and implement projects within the healthcare organization. A basic understanding of economic concepts, financial accounting, statistics, and algebra are needed to complete this section.

Section V, An Application of Quantitative Methods, Chapter 15, Quantitative Analysis in Strategic Planning, provides an extended example of an application of quantitative analysis, including elements of database creation for use in strategic planning. The chapter presents a framework for organizing and evaluating the external environment of a healthcare organization.

This book expands the repertoire of the health services manager to analyze complex systems, and to be able to design and implement changes in systems. Applications are drawn from hospitals, nursing homes, and ambulatory care clinics. Traditional quantitative methods with limited management applications in these settings have been reserved for more advanced presentations. Application is of paramount importance. Throughout the book, repeated reference is made to the importance associated with the ability to effectively communicate results. No matter how perfect or insightful the analysis or design, if it cannot or is not effectively communicated to decision makers in the healthcare organization, the health services manager has failed. Quantitative methods are a robust tool in the skill repertoire of the health services manager and must be used skillfully.

SECTION I

Foundation Competencies

Chapter 2

Working with Numbers

LEARNING OBJECTIVES

1. To be able to calculate and use descriptive statistics.
2. To be able to compare different types of data using statistical inference and hypothesis testing.
3. To be able to present data effectively and efficiently in visual form.

REAL WORLD SCENARIO

James Walden is the CEO of Port City Hospital, a medium-sized hospital located in a moderately populated seacoast region in New England. It services a community of approximately 230,000 people, but has four competitor hospitals within a 30-mile radius. Over the past 10 years, civic development leaders have been transforming a closed air force base into a trade center and have been slowly attracting corporate entities to the area. In the past year, two major employers have relocated their corporate offices and/or large manufacturing centers to the trade center, adding an estimated 30,000 new persons to the area. In addition, another large insurance company has doubled its workforce in the same town as Port City Hospital, creating an additional 4000 jobs, at least two thirds of which they anticipate filling from outside the area. Within the hospital, Mr. Walden has been hearing increased concerns from physician and nursing leadership about workload increases. In looking at utilization data, Mr. Walden is curious if the hospital is realizing a growth pattern that is both different than previous years and different than other hospitals in the area. Knowing this might facilitate his decision to expand certain services or the hospital itself.

Numbers are a form of language. For managers, they facilitate the way we communicate about the functioning of organizations. They allow us to count, describe, compare, and predict. Mathematics and statistics—the calculation and manipulation of numbers—are the primary tools that facilitate these numerical "conversations."

Numbers and analysis also provide justification for action (or sometimes inaction). They are static and unbiased, and when used properly and transparently, they allow those interpreting their analysis to make reasoned and informed decisions. Health services managers utilize numbers extensively in their work, because most of what is done in any organization must be quantified. As the adage goes; if you can't measure it, you can't manage it.

This chapter reviews the basic forms of mathematical and statistical analysis used in health services administration, including various descriptive and inferential statistics. The chapter concludes with basic guidelines and examples of how to best present data in tabular and graphical form.

LEARNING OBJECTIVE 1: CALCULATING AND USING DESCRIPTIVE STATISTICS

Statistics is a term that usually invokes dread and discomfort in students and practitioners alike. This is probably because statistics holds a close relationship to mathematics, although the two are distinct. Statistics uses mathematical relationships between data to allow managers to make decisions about both the data itself and about the likelihood that sampled data represent a broader and more generalized trend or population. Statistics, however, need not be difficult. For managers, some simple categorizing of techniques can help focus statistical analysis in ways that are easily understood and applied.

Managerial statistics have three primary functions. The first function is to describe certain data elements, such as the number of births over a time period or the expenses incurred for a service unit. The second function is to compare two points of data, such as births from 1 year to the next or error rates between care sites. The third is to predict data, such as visit volume in future months. This chapter examines the first two, saving prediction for Chapters 5, 6, and 7, given its specialized nature. First, however, a discussion about the nature of data is in order. Data are quite simply numbers within a context. Green, although a very nice color, is only an adjective by itself. If, however, we record the eye color of a room of 20 people, and then code those colors with numbers—i.e., 1 for blue, 2 for brown, 3 for green—we have transformed the colors into points of data. Similarly, if we were to then count the number of people with green eyes, we have performed a statistical function—the calculation of a descriptive statistic.

A number of different types of analyses can be performed on data. When the time comes to conduct these analyses, students often face "analysis paralysis." Imagine, for example, that you find yourself in a new position, and you have been asked by your boss, Mr. Walden, to take a look at some utilization trends using data from the organization's data warehouse. You pull up the corresponding data files, and are faced with more than 30 variables (columns in a spreadsheet) and tens of thousands of records (rows in a spreadsheet representing individual patient visits). In the middle is a sea of numbers of various sorts that continue on as you scroll and scroll down the screen. In some organizations, there may be millions of data records in thousands of tables, which is intimidating to be sure. However, a data file with 10,000 rows and one with 20 are not all that different. Each can be described in similar ways. What is important is the data itself. Understanding what the numbers represent (the context) and how they were created will lead you down certain analytic paths and not others, allowing you to put some statistical methods aside for some data.

Measuring Data

Data come in only four varieties. Students of introductory statistics will no doubt recall the terms *nominal, ordinal, interval,* and *ratio.* All refer to measurement of data variables. Variables are simply data that can take on different values, depending on what is being measured. In the earlier example, the color of 20 people's eyes was recorded, thus creating the variable "eye color." In this instance it is a variable that is measured nominally. Nominal refers to data that exist in non-overlapping categories. They have no ranking and are mutually exclusive; for example, eye color, insurance type, gender, and ethnicity. Ordinal variables are slightly different in that they are still measured categorically, but the categories have a ranking. An example of this would be satisfaction scales, in which somewhat satisfied might be followed by very satisfied, etc. These are common in health surveys. The final two types are often taken together as interval/ratio variables. These are often termed *continuously measured variables*; examples include time and money. The difference here is that they are actually still categories, but the distance between categories is equal. Think of a time scale as derived in seconds—one second, two seconds, etc. We could derive smaller increments if we so wished, creating fractions of seconds as is often done in Olympic time trials and racing. The increments ultimately do not matter, however. What does matter is that the distance between them is equal. This allows mathematical calculations on these forms of data. The difference between interval and ratio data has to do with the presence of a meaningful zero when measuring a ratio variable, a distinction not important for this discussion.

At this point the insightful student might realize that examining measurement provides two distinct types of variables—those that have equal distances between measurement points and those that do not. Often, these distinctions are recognized by labeling nominal and ordinal data as categorical, and interval/ratio data as continuous. We too will follow this convention. Ordinal data present a unique measurement form. It is important to understand the type of data you are working with because each is analyzed differently.

Descriptive Statistics with One Variable (Univariate)

First, examine descriptive statistics in relation to categorical data. Table 2-1 provides data on 14 patients, recording their insurance type.

Insurance type is a categorical variable. The categories are not ranked, nor is there any relationship among them. Patients usually claim a type of primary insurance (or lack thereof) upon visit. To describe the data, we are limited to only a handful of techniques. The first is to simply count. Here we can count total patients or patients by the type of insurance they have. The second, which requires a bit of mathematics to be conducted first, is to create percentages for the number of persons falling into each category. A percentage is simply the number of persons in a category divided by the total number of persons, multiplied by 100. Not multiplying by 100 is also correct, although this provides a decimal fraction and not a percentage. For example, we may wish to know how many people reported having United as their insurer. One way to summarize this would be to count, which amount to three individuals in Table 2-1. To calculate a percentage, we would divide that 3 by 14, which gives us 0.21, or 21% of patients. Percentages and fractions provide slightly more information than do counts. Inherent in them is the context of the whole. If we tell you three patients had United insurance, you may still wonder if that is a lot, not many, or a modest amount; but if we say 21% of patients had United, you now have some sense of the entire group of patients, although we have not provided the total. Here, providing the total in addition to the percentage would provide both the count and the total, creating a more complete picture of the data being described. Listing counts and percentages of categorical data is also called creating frequencies from the data. We could graph the data at this point and obtain a visual representation of how frequently patients used various types of insurance as we have done in Figure 2-1. From a descriptive standpoint, this is the limit of analyzing a singular categorical variable.

Table 2-1 Insurance Type by Patient

1	United	8	BC/BS
2	Medicare	9	Medicaid
3	Medicaid	10	Uninsured
4	Medicare	11	Medicare
5	BC/BS	12	Uninsured
6	United	13	United
7	BC/BS	14	MBCA

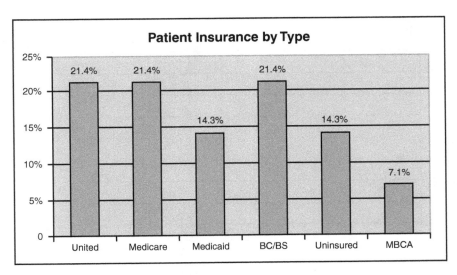

Figure 2-1 Patient Insurance by Type

The second type of data you may wish to describe are those measured as interval/ratio variables. These are also commonly referred to as continuous data. Again, these are actually categorical data as well, but the categories are of equal size. Examples include variables such as time, money, height, and weight. The equal distances between categories are what allow for mathematical analysis of these data. So, for example, adding one dollar to two dollars adds the same amount as adding one dollar to ten dollars. This allows us to calculate a number of descriptive measures that examine the centrality of the data and its spread, which are both useful for our purposes. We first examine measures of central tendency.

Measures of Central Tendency

As described, data that are collected across a number of observations vary from observation to observation; thus, the term *variable*. Plotting these data reveals both the spread and the clustering of individual observations. An example is given in Figure 2-2.

From these data, we can see that the number of chart pulls appear to largely be centered between 10 and 30 per day, with a few days of higher volume, and one with lower volume. What would be helpful for analytic purposes would be to have a set of summary statistics to describe the data. The statistic that is the mathematical center of a data set is the average, or *mean*. It is the foundation for many other statistical concepts as well. To calculate the *mean*, simply add up all

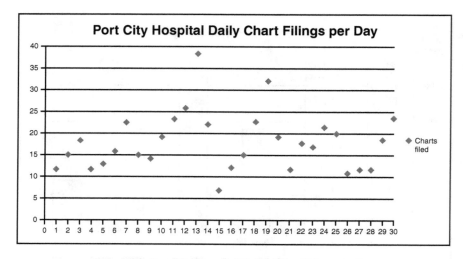

Figure 2-2 Port City Hospital Daily Chart Filings per Day

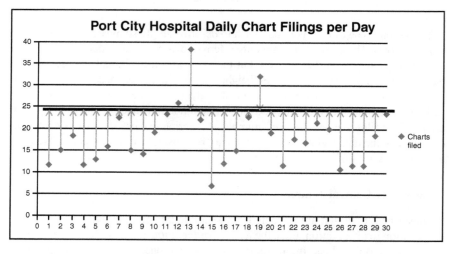

Figure 2-2A Port City Hospital Daily Chart Filings per Day Part 2

the values and divide by *n*, which is the number of observations. We can also find the *median*, which is the center of the distribution of data when all the observations are arranged from lowest to highest. The *mode* is the more frequently reported data value. Given our data from Figure 2-2, Table 2-2 reports these measures of central tendency.

Table 2-2 Port City Hospital Daily Chart Filings per Day

Day	Charts Filed	Day	Charts Filed
1	12	16	12
2	15	17	15
3	18	18	23
4	12	19	32
5	13	20	19
6	16	21	12
7	22	22	18
8	15	23	17
9	14	24	21
10	19	25	20
11	23	26	11
12	26	27	12
13	38	28	12
14	22	29	18
15	7	30	23
Mean	**18**		
Median	**18**		
Mode	**12**		

In this instance, the median and mean are the same value, 18. The mode is 12. Had the mean been higher than the median, it would indicate that there were some high values of the data that were pulling the mean upward. Examine the following range of income values: $13,000, $25,000, $33,000, $42,000, $56,000. The mean of these data is $33,800. The median is $33,000. If, however, we replace the value of $56,000 with $120,000, notice what happens. The median is still $33,000, yet the mean increases to $46,600. This is because the median is not dependent on all other values in the distribution. It is what we call a *robust measure*, or one that is resistant to outlying values. The mean is not robust, as we demonstrated. When examining data distributions, it is sometimes helpful to look at both the mean and the median. Doing so can quickly tell you something about the presence of outlying values and the spread of the data.

Measures of Spread

Although the mean, median, and mode tell us something about the middle or centrality of the data, we may also be interested in how varied and spread out the data are. This is both helpful to understand the range of data values, and also to examine the possibility of outlier values that might be affecting our measures of central tendency. Examine again the data in Table 2-2 and Figure 2-2. We know that the mean of these data is 18 charts filed on average. We also know that there are many days when the number of charts filed exceeds 18 per day and also falls short of 18 per day. The maximum and minimum values tell us this, and are important measures for summarizing our data. Here they are 48 and 7, respectively. Their difference, or 41 ($48-7$) is what is known as the *range*. Examining the range in addition to other measures of central tendency allows a clearer picture of the data distribution (even without a graph!).

There is one final measure of spread that should be considered. If we were to draw a line at the mean in Figure 2-2 we would see that about half of the data points were clustered above and half below (and although this is always true of the median, it need not always be so for the mean) (see Figure 2.2 A). Here we see that some points lie closer to the mean than others, whereas some lie on the mean. Thus, each point of observation lies some distance from the mean, whether positive or negative. What would be interesting is to know how far from the mean are the data *on average*. The final summary measure of spread does this, which is the standard deviation. Simply put, the standard deviation is the average distance of a given data point to its mean. In the chart filing example, we are asking on average how far do the data points diverge from their mean, which is 18? To do this we could start by measuring the distance of each point to the mean, and then simply dividing by n to get the average. But wait. Because the mean is the mathematical average of all the points, the distances when summed will total zero. Dividing zero by anything is a mathematical impossibility. So, to counter this problem, the negative distances need to be eliminated by squaring all of the distances. This eliminates our zero total problem, but also converts all our original distances into *squared* distances, so that when we add them up and divide by n, we have the average total squared distance, also known as the *variance*. In this case, this creates a measure interpreted as the number of charts pulled squared. This creates an interpretive problem in that we no longer have the same units with which we started. To return to our original units requires that we eliminate the squared term by taking the square root, thus providing the standard deviation.

Working with Samples

The preceding calculation provides the standard deviation for a set of data. If those data constitute a complete set of observations, and generalization to some larger population is not being made; for example, from a sample of chart filings to estimate all chart filings, then the standard deviation should be calculated in this way. However, if we are using a sample value, which is known, to say something about a population value, which usually cannot be known, we must make an adjustment. Samples are inherently more variable than populations. We are simply more likely to get data points further away from the "true" population mean in a sample than were we to continue to collect more and more data. Because of this variability, when calculating our standard deviation, we divide by $(n - 1)$.

When dealing with sample data, we also need to be careful when interpreting the mean of the data. Table 2-2 is a sample of data for 1 month of chart filings. If we are only interested in that month, we can treat the data as a population. However, if we want to treat this 1 month as representative of all months, some adjustment is required. The mean of the data in Table 2-2 was 18 chart filings. If we were to resample these data over another time period, what is the likelihood that 18 would again be the mean? If we designate 18 as a sample value representative of the "truth," we are in fact saying that it *is* and *always will be* 18. This is quite unlikely in this instance. However, it is often not possible for us to know the "truth" for all present and future data. Instead we can create an interval that we can say with some level of confidence contains the "true" population mean. The formula for constructing a confidence interval at the 95% level of confidence, our default for most analyses, is:

$$\text{Mean} \pm 1.96 \times \text{standard error}$$

where the standard error = standard deviation / square root (n).

The value of 1.96 is the value that cuts off the upper and lower 2.5% of the standard normal distribution (discussed briefly later in this chapter) and the use of the standard error rather than the standard deviation is to adjust for the fact that we are using a sample (with greater variability) to represent a population. The reporting of confidence intervals should be included with any mean that has been derived from sample data.

LEARNING OBJECTIVE 2: TO BE ABLE TO COMPARE DIFFERENT TYPES OF DATA USING STATISTICAL INFERENCE AND HYPOTHESIS TESTING

Bivariate Analysis

The second primary function of managerial statistics is to be able to compare two or more variables within a set of data. This can mean comparing a variable measured at two points in time, such as the number of births from one year to the next, or in two locations, such as comparing births between hospitals. It can also mean comparing two different types of data, such as the number of emergency department (ED) visits over a time period with the number of lab tests performed during that same period. Each type of analysis again requires knowing what types of data you are comparing. Like descriptive statistics, there are certain types of analyses that you will perform and others we can set aside depending on how the data are measured. Before doing so, however, we first need to review the need for hypothesis development and testing.

Hypothesis Testing

Students may recall from an introductory statistics course, that comparisons of variables are best tested using hypotheses. These are simply statements of association that are first stated and then, using analysis, either supported or refuted. The reason for doing this is that most data are simply representations of phenomena that exist in real life. The problem is that it is usually unrealistic or impossible to measure all phenomena completely. Think about measuring population. We may want to know the actual number of people in the United States, but our ability to measure this is limited. Realistically, we cannot find and count everyone in the United States without missing some people, and the number of people changes daily because of births and deaths, so that by the time we were done measuring, the "real" answer would have already changed. Yet, we also know that for a given point in time there is a "real" measurement; we just are unable to observe it. We *can*, however, estimate within some level of certainty, whether or not the measurement we observe, or the data comparison we make, is likely to be representative of what is "real" at that point in time.

This is why we create hypotheses and then use statistical tests to either support or refute them. Two primary types of hypotheses are used in statistical analysis. The first is the null hypothesis, which is always the hypothesis of no association or difference. The second is the alternative hypothesis, which is most often the converse of the null, but that can be directional, such as two data elements having a positive or negative association. Both are examined here briefly.

Managers in healthcare settings are often assessing data for comparative purposes, and often they use samples of data taken at a point in time. The question managers should be concerned with is not only if there is an observable difference or association in the data, but with what level of confidence can you believe it to be true and not because of chance. Otherwise stated, if the manager collected another sample of data, could the association or difference reverse itself or would the data be reflecting the same pattern? These are the foundational questions behind hypothesis testing. For example, consider a manager who has collected data on the number of safety protocol violations within two units of the hospital. In summarizing these violations, she finds the mean number of violations of unit A to be 21 over a 1-year period, and 27 in unit B over the same period. In real terms, unit B does report more violations than unit A. The question is whether this trend is a "real" trend, or simply a result of chance. Thus, the question we ask is how likely are we to record or see a difference as big as we have when the difference is actually zero in reality.

Often, the stating of hypotheses is unduly confusing. In fact, it is quite simple. The null hypothesis always states that there is no difference or association between the two things being observed (i.e., data variables). For example, we could hypothesize that the mean number of violations in site A is actually no different than the mean number of violations at site B "in reality" if we were to continue to measure over time. The alternative is that there is a real difference between the two things being observed. But here we have an option. We can say that we think, for example, that the mean number of violations at site B is simply different than site A, whether that is higher or lower. When direction doesn't matter, we are conducting a two-tailed hypothesis test. Our second alternative is to say that one will be higher than the other or lower than the other. In this case we might say the alternative hypothesis is that the mean number of violations at site B is higher than the mean number of violations at site A. In this case we are conducting a one-tailed hypothesis test. The difference occurs primarily with respect to interpretation of the tests and is explored later in the chapter. The stated null hypothesis, abbreviated H_0, or that of no difference, for this example would be:

H_0: *There is no difference in the mean number of safety violations between site A and site B over the 1-year period.*

The stated alternative hypothesis, abbreviated H_a, is the converse of this and, assuming a two-tailed test, would be:

H_a: *There is a difference in the mean number of safety violations between site A and site B.over the 1-year period.*

The analysis we perform will allow us to either reject or fail to reject our null hypothesis. The rule here is that we *never* accept a hypothesis. Why? Because we can never be 100% certain what the relationship between two things is "in reality" at a given point in time, for reasons stated earlier in this section. Instead, we use hypothesis testing and statistics to make probabilistic inference into the relationship between two sets of measured data or observations. Interpreting our hypotheses now requires the use of statistics, and also a brief introduction to theoretical probability distributions, otherwise thought of as *why we can be certain we are at least partially certain.*

Probability Distributions

If someone were to ask you what the probability of flipping a normal coin and having it come up heads, you would no doubt say that it is a 50/50 chance, or 50%

of the time. Yet you would also likely agree that it is quite possible that you could flip a coin and heads would come up three times in a row. How can this be? Two reasons. One is that each coin flip is not dependent on the previous one. There are two sides of the coin, so you only have two possible outcomes. Each time you flip, they are equally likely to come up (if the coin is balanced and not a trick coin). The second is that we know if you continue to flip over and over again, the number of heads and the number of tails will start to equal out. In statistical language, we would say the probability of heads grows closer to 0.5 as your n (number of flips) increases. Suffice it to say that flipping a coin has a known probability. Could we observe 37 heads in a row? Sure, but it is highly unlikely.

Most phenomena in the world have a distribution of measurement, whether height, weight, income, hair length, etc. Consider height. There are a range of heights of individuals throughout the world. Some are quite tall, and others are not. If, for example, we see someone who is 8 feet tall, we might think that it is unusual, but not impossible. (Seeing is believing.) But how do we test this statistically?

Here we offer a non-statistical explanation of a statistical occurrence. As we stated before, at a point in time, all phenomena are theoretically measurable. If we are examining a data element that is continuous in nature, such as height, then at a point in time there is also a "true" mean of the observed data—right now there is a "true" mean height of all people in the world. Similarly, if we were to measure all persons, there would also be a "true" standard deviation around that mean. Some measurements will be close to the mean and others further away. We would expect that observations that were further from the mean would be less likely to occur, as with our 8-foot friend. From statistics we know how likely certain data will be to occur in relation to its mean by measuring how far those observations are from the mean in units of standard deviation. The reason for this is that many types of data are distributed normally, or in a fashion in which there is a mean and a symmetrical distribution of values on either side in the shape of a bell curve (Figure 2-3A). For example, if we were to know that the "true" mean of heights in the United States for men is 68 inches, and the "true" standard deviation is 2 inches, someone who is 8 feet tall (96 inches) would be 14 standard deviations above the mean or $(96-68)/2$. And because all data can be examined by how far in standard deviations they are from the mean, we can construct a theoretical normal distribution in which the mean is zero and the area under the curve represents units of standard deviation, called z-values. Why is the mean zero? If the distances under the curve are measures of standard deviation, then how many standard deviations away from the mean is the mean? Zero. Not only does this allow us to assess the probability of occurrence for certain data, it allows us to compare any type of data because the units are the same (standard deviations) (see Figure 2-3, A,B).

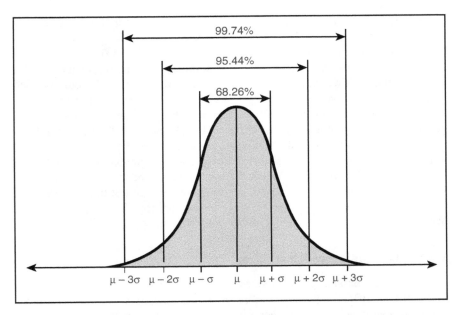

Figure 2-3A Normal Distribution Showing Mean, Standard Deviations, and Percentage of Observations Falling Within the Standard Deviations

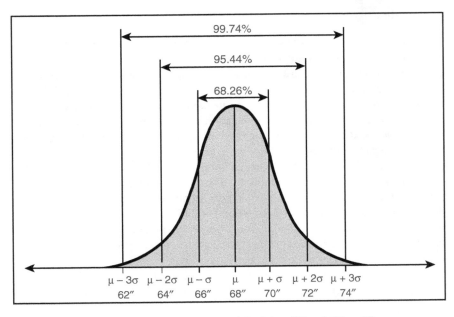

Figure 2-3B Distribution of Height (M = 68″ and SD = 2″)

Further, we know that the areas under standard normal distributions have known probabilities. The 68-95-99.7 rule states that approximately 68% of observations fall within one standard deviation of its mean, approximately 95% of observations fall within two standard deviations of the mean, and approximately 99.7% of observations fall within three standard deviations of the mean. In addition, each z-value under the curve has a known probability of occurrence. There are also other distributions that do not quite follow the symmetrical shape of a z-distribution (standard normal distribution), but nonetheless have known probabilities under them, such as t-distributions and f-distributions to name only two. For our purposes, it is not important to know what these distributions look like, but that they have known probabilities, and so any observations we may make can be tested to see what the likelihood of its occurrence is. All we need to know is what test to run to for what type of data, and then how to interpret the results we get from our computer analysis. We next examine this for a number of data comparisons.

Comparing Continuous Data

There are different analytic techniques for comparing a continuous data variable measured at different points in time or across locations, and two different continuous variables to one another. First, let us examine comparing two different continuously measured variables, lab tests and ED visits.

Correlation

In this instance, we look to statistics to provide a measure of association between two differently measured phenomena. Because they are measured in increments of equal distance, respectively, we can assess how unit changes in one variable are correlated to unit changes in the other. This becomes an algebraic relationship, in which if we label one variable x and the other y, we can express y as being some function of x. Examine Table 2-3, which measures the number of both ED visits and lab tests for a sample period during the month of September. If they were perfectly correlated, these variables would have a one-to-one relationship. In this example, a perfectly positive correlation would mean each additional ED visit would result in the same additional number of lab tests. Similarly, if there was a perfectly negative relationship, for every ED visit, lab tests would consistently decrease by a set amount. To do this we calculate the linear correlation coefficient (r), which will indicate the associative, but not causal relationship between the number of ED visits and the number of lab tests performed per day. The correlation coefficient will also indicate the strength of the linear association between the two variables.

Statistics indicates that a correlation coefficient (r) of $+1.00$ indicates a perfectly positive correlation (an increase in X is always associated with a parallel

Table 2-3 Observational Data for ED Visits and Lab Tests

Date	Ed Visits	Lab Tests	
15-Sep	5	12	
16-Sep	8	12	
17-Sep	9	24	Correlation Coefficient
18-Sep	12	36	$r = .977$
19-Sep	14	48	
20-Sep	2	0	Critical value of $r = .532$
21-Sep	4	0	with $n = 14$
22-Sep	8	12	
23-Sep	7	12	
24-Sep	12	36	
25-Sep	14	48	
26-Sep	6	12	
27-Sep	18	60	
28-Sep	12	36	

increase in Y) and that a negative correlation coefficient of -1.00 indicates a perfectly negative correlation. By definition, correlation coefficients can only range from $+1.00$ to -1.00. For the data in Table 2-3, the correlation coefficient is 0.977, which indicates a strong positive correlation between ED visits and lab tests. Although this seems to be indication of a powerful correlation, the association cannot yet be said to be statistically significant or not one because of random chance.

Here we have collected a sample of data based on 14 days of observation. The question we must ask is whether the observed phenomenon could be owing simply to chance rather than some real association. Stating our hypotheses is helpful in doing this. Here, our null and alternative hypotheses are:

H_o: *There is no relationship between the number of ED visits and the number of lab tests.*

H_a: *There is a relationship between the number of ED visits and the number of lab tests.*

To address our hypotheses, we must now determine a critical value of r to assess the likelihood of the relationship being because of chance. Although some computer programs give the actual probability, or likelihood of the relationship with a

Table 2-4 Critical Values of the Correlation Coefficient r for Various Sample Sizes n

n	r	n	r
5	0.878	18	0.468
6	0.811	19	0.456
7	0.754	20	0.444
8	0.707	22	0.423
9	0.666	24	0.404
10	0.632	26	0.388
11	0.602	28	0.374
12	0.576	30	0.361
13	0.553	40	0.312
14	0.532	50	0.279
15	0.514	60	0.254
16	0.497	80	0.220
17	0.482	100	0.196

p-value, others, such as Excel, do not. Here we present a table of critical r-values, shown in Table 2-4, which gives the critical values of r at various sample sizes (n) at the alpha of 0.05. Given our example, we would use the critical value of r for $n = 14$, which is 0.532. If r-calculated $> r$-critical, we can be 95% confident that the association is not because of random chance. Note that analysis programs such as Excel will compute the correlation coefficient r, but do not provide the critical value of r, or the probability associated with r. Here, r-calculated (0.979) is greater than r-critical (0.532), so we can say that there is a statistically significant positive correlation between ED visits and lab tests. For each additional ED visit (1 unit), we would expect lab test volume to increase by 0.977 units.

T-Tests

A second common analysis is to examine a continuously measured variable at two points in time, or in two locations. For example, say we wish to compare the number of births as Port City Hospital with other U.S. hospitals of similar size. To do so we collect data over 12 months, shown in Table 2-5.

Examining the data we see that for all months, Port City Hospital performs more births than the average hospital of similar size in the United States and that the mean number of births over the period was 37 at Port City and 29 at other hospitals. Our question is whether the data we see here for 1 year represent the "true" relationship between Port City and other similar size hospitals. Because this is only a sample of data from 1 year, we must use statistics to assess this. First, however, we should state our hypotheses.

H_o: *There is no difference between the mean number of births at Port City Hospital and other U.S. hospitals of similar size.*

H_a: *There is a difference between the mean number of births at Port City Hospital and other U.S. hospitals of similar size.*

To test the difference between two means requires the use of a *t*-test. *T*-tests are used to compare means between groups. These groups can be paired, as would be the case with a group who is measured on some variable, for example, blood pressure, undergoes some intervention, for example, an exercise routine, and re-measured. The groups can also be different, as is the case with our comparison of mean births at Port City Hospital with other hospitals. What cannot be compared are means for different variables, such as the mean average length of stay compared with the mean number of births. The means must be measured in similar units for comparison with a *t*-test.

Table 2-5 Comparative Monthly Births

	Port City Hospital	U.S. for Similar Size Hospitals
January	24	22
February	25	21
March	33	26
April	35	27
May	37	31
June	38	25
July	41	36
August	35	27
September	45	39
October	39	35
November	42	34
December	50	23
Mean	*37*	*29*

Most analytic software including Excel can calculate a number of *t*-tests. What is important to note is that the different types of *t*-tests (paired, assuming equal variances, and assuming unequal variances) revolve, as the names suggest, around variation of the data. For our purposes, we will assume that variances are unequal in cases other than paired data. In practice, this difference in variances would be analyzed with an *f*-test, and some programs will provide output for both equal and unequal variances assumed. Because Excel does not do this, assume unequal variances. Rarely will the interpretation differ between the two, but it can. The *t*-test output for our data is shown in Table 2-6.

In Table 2-6 we are given a number of analytic outputs. The first is the mean of the data for both Port City and the United States. We are also given the variance and the number of observations. The hypothesized mean difference is simply the null hypothesis restated. Examining the lower half of the table we are given the *t*-statistic, the probability of *t* for both one-sided and two-tailed tests, and the critical value of *t* that cuts off the upper *or* lower 2.5% of the distribution (one-tailed) and the value of *t* that cuts off the upper *and* lower 2.5% of the distribution (two-tailed). Thus, values of the *t*-statistic that lie beyond the critical value are statistically significant (different) at the 95% level of confidence. The *p*-value gives the exact probability that our means are truly different and that the observed difference is not because of random chance. Here, we would use a two-tailed *p*-value because our hypothesis was not directional. That is, our null stated that the mean number of births was different, but not in which direction (greater than or less than). Doing so would require a one-tailed test, because we would only be interested in values

Table 2-6 Excel Output *t*-Test: Two-Sample Assuming Unequal Variances

	Port City	U.S.
Mean	37	28.8
Variance	56	36.0
Observations	12	12
Hypothesized Mean Difference	0	
df	21	
t Stat	2.9499	
P(T≤*t*) one-tail	0.0038	
t Critical one-tail	1.7207	
P(T≤*t*) two-tail	0.0076	
t Critical two-tail	2.0796	

at one end of the distribution. Here it doesn't matter, so we conduct and interpret the two-tailed test. Interpreting the *t*-statistic we see that:

T Stat (2.95) > *t* Critical two tail (2.07) *or* p(T ≤ *t*)(0.0007) < 0.05

In either case, we would reject the null hypothesis.

Otherwise stated, our hypotheses ask what is the likelihood of seeing a difference in observed means as large as the one we did (8.2, or 37−28.8) if in fact the real difference were zero (the null hypothesis). Examining our *t* Stat relative to the critical values tells us the likelihood is less than 5% of the time. Examining our *p*-value tells us the exact likelihood, or less than 0.7% of the time (0.007). So, if we continue to collect samples of data, the means would likely only be the same in 0.7% of samples.

Comparing Categorical Data

Finally, we may often be interested in analysis of two variables that are measured categorically through either rates or proportions. Examples of these types of data include: What type of insurance does the patient have; what is the gender; and were they satisfied with their visit? Summarizing these involves creating counts and percentages. However, often we wish to compare how two groups of categories compare with one another. We do this using the chi-square statistic (χ^2), which compares the observed differences in proportions with what would be expected if proportions were equal. For example, if we were to examine the satisfied/unsatisfied percentages of 40 men and 40 women on a satisfaction questionnaire, we would expect that if they were equal, 20 would say satisfied and 20 would not in each gender category (or 50% for each). When we observe actual data, however, we often see different results. The basic null and alternative hypotheses hold true here. The question we are asking is what is the chance of seeing a difference of the magnitude observed in the collected data if in fact there is no true difference (all proportions are equal) in the population. The chi-square statistic and its associated probability allow us to test these hypotheses. The simplest form of chi-square analysis is of two variables using a 2 × 2 contingency table, shown in Table 2-7.

Table 2-7 2 × 2 Contingency Table

	Group 1	Group 2	Total
variable 1	a	b	$a + b$
variable 2	c	d	$c + d$
Total	$a + c$	$b + d$	$a + b + c + d$

Table 2-8 Patient Satisfaction Comparison Using Chi Square

	East Campus	West Campus	Total
Satisfied	36	17	53
Not satisfied	30	35	65
Total	66	52	118

Examine the data in Table 2-8 that depict satisfaction responses from a survey at two campuses of a clinic group. The null hypothesis would state that there is, in truth, no actual difference between satisfied and unsatisfied respondents by campus location. The alternative would be that the difference observed is real.

To calculate the chi-square, we use formula 2-1:

$$X^2 = \Sigma \left(\frac{(\text{Observed} - \text{Expected})^2}{\text{Expected}} \right), \text{ where the expected count is}$$

$$\frac{(\text{Row Total} \times \text{Column Total})}{n}$$

This formula yields the results in Table 2-9 and the chi-square statistic of 5.69. Constructing the expected values will be further helpful when using Excel to calculate the chi-square statistic.

This generates a chi-square statistic that must then be examined relative to the distribution of chi-squares for the given degree of freedom. Degrees of freedom are calculated by taking the number of rows minus one multiplied by the number of columns minus one. In this example we have one degree of freedom, or $(2 - 1) \times (2 - 1) = 1$. We now examine Appendix Table 1 to assess where our chi-square statistic falls relative to a given alpha level. We can see that for one

Table 2-9 Chi-Square Calculations for Patient Satisfaction Data

	Observed	Expected	O − E	(O − E)²	(O − E)²/E
	36	29.6	6.40	40.96	1.38
	17	23.4	−6.40	40.96	1.75
	30	36.4	−6.40	40.96	1.13
	35	28.6	6.40	40.96	1.43
Total	118	118	0.00	163.84	**5.69**

degree of freedom, a chi-square statistic of 5.61 falls beyond the alpha of 0.02. This means that we would be likely to see a difference in proportions of this magnitude when in fact they were equal less than 2% of the time. If our cutoff for significance was set at 5%, we would reject the null hypothesis in this instance.

In practice, most computer programs provide the chi-square statistic and corresponding significance when examining two or more categorical variables. When examining any categorical variable with more than two response categories, such as satisfaction levels or agreement scales, the chi-square statistic has a slightly different interpretive meaning. The null hypothesis remains the same in this case. However, we now observe differences not just between two categories (one and two), but between multiple categories (two and three, one and three, three and four, two and four, etc.). The chi-square can only tell us if the differences overall between the categories is significantly different than what we would expect, but does not test the differences between individual categories. Such analysis is beyond the scope of this book.

SUMMARY

Here we have presented a toolkit of basic statistical techniques to help guide the health services manager with basic quantitative analysis. This was not meant to be an exhaustive statistical review, but an applied, user-friendly introduction to statistics commonly used in making many healthcare related decisions. The first step in any analysis is to determine whether one is examining one variable or data point, or comparing more than one variable. When examining one variable at a time, we use descriptive statistics, and depending on whether the variable is continuous or categorical, different analyses are used. Table 2-10 provides a summary of these techniques for both describing and comparing data types.

Performing the right type of analysis on the data at hand can often be confusing for many, which is why we have attempted to segment analysis by the type of data being examined. These analyses will be referred to throughout the remainder of the text.

Table 2-10 Comparative Statistics Summary Table

Descriptive	Continuous		Categorical	
	mean, median, mode, standard deviation, range, variance		*counts, percents, rates and proportions*	
Comparisons	Continuous		Categorical	
	Same variable	Different variable	Same variable	Different variable
Continuous	*t-test*	*correlation*	-	*t-test*
Categorical	-	*t-test*	*chi-square*	*chi-square*

LEARNING OBJECTIVE 3: TO BE ABLE TO PRESENT DATA EFFECTIVELY AND EFFICIENTLY IN VISUAL FORM

An important part of relaying messages gleaned from data is being able to effectively create visual representations of your data and your analyses. If we think about our presentation of data similarly to the way our data were analyzed; that is, descriptions of one point of data or variable at a time, and comparisons of data, we can examine a few simple tools and foundations for effective presentations. This section is by no means an effort to exhaust the functional abilities of graphical computer programs such as Microsoft Excel, but to provide a few basic tenets. Here we present uses of tables, bar/column graphs, pie charts, line graphs, and dual axes graphs.

When creating tables and graphs, it is always helpful to think of them as stand-alone documents. That is, if the table or graph you have created were to get copied or removed from the larger text or presentation it comes from, would it contain enough information for a user to make accurate inferences, know what the data represent, and know where the data are from. Consider, for example, Table 2-11.

This table presents information for a subset of patients at Port City Hospital who were overweight or obese upon admission by age group for 1 year. There are a number of ways to present this information graphically. These data are descriptive, in that we are measuring one thing, the percent of patients who were overweight or obese upon admission, and then segmenting the data by the age of the patient. Ages have been broken into categories for easier presentation, which is often done with continuous data. If we had attempted to count how many patients fell into each age, theoretically ages 1 through 100 plus, we would have over 100 bars on our chart. Therefore, categories help to distill down the data. For data arranged into categories, bar or column charts should be used. They can then depict either the

Table 2-11 Percent of Patients Overweight or Obese by BMI Score

Port City Hospital, 2008			
Age group	Percent	(95% CI)	Sample Size (n)
18–24	36.7	(30.2, 43.3)	93
25–34	48.6	(44.3, 53.0)	289
35–44	56.6	(53.2, 60.1)	519
45–54	65.3	(61.7, 69.0)	488
55–64	68.1	(63.8, 72.3)	353
65 and older	59.7	(55.6, 63.8)	389
BMI ≥ 25 is considered overweight, as BMI ≥ 30 is considered obese.			

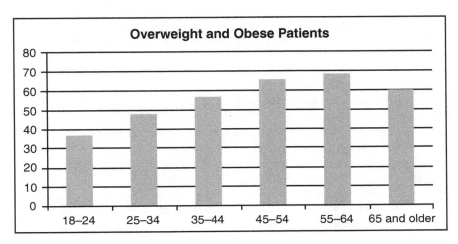

Figure 2-4 Overweight and Obese Patients

number of percent of the data points that fall into each category. Figure 2-4 shows one graphical representation.

Note here that we have bars for each age category and a title that states "Overweight and Obese Patients." Although semi-informative, there are limits to what we know about these data. If this chart were given to you by itself, what other questions might you have about its contents?

Figure 2-5 shows a slightly different view. Here error bars have been added to represent the 95% confidence intervals from column three of Table 2-11.

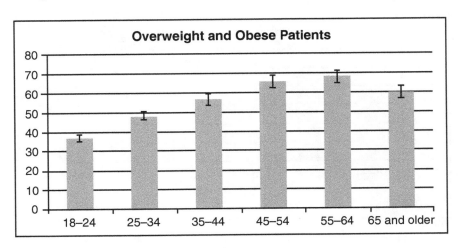

Figure 2-5 Overweight and Obese Patients Part 2

These are important because they denote that the data are taken from a sample of patients and should not be considered as representing the entire patient population. They also show that there is a 95% probability that the "true" population percentile for overweight and obese patients fall between the two ends of each error bar.

Finally, in Figure 2-6 we include the source of the data (Port City Hospital for 2007), labels for the *y*-axis, and a definitional text box for what BMI levels constitute overweight and obese. Figure 2-6 does the best job at becoming a stand-alone graphic, and conveys a detailed level of information.

A second form of categorical presentation is the pie chart. A perennial favorite with students, the pie chart should only be used when the categories constitute parts of a whole. Consider for example Table 2-12 and Figure 2-7. The slices of the graph represent divisions of the entire medical/surgical expenditures for the hospital and are exhaustive. When using pie charting there are a number of formatting considerations. The first is whether or not to include data labels, and then whether to use percents or whole numbers when labels are used. Figure 2-5 provides an example of using percents; however, it may be more appropriate to include the dollar amount each category represents, or perhaps both. The use of the data and their audience should define which is used. A final consideration is whether or not the graph will be printed in color. Colors allow for a clearer distinction between slices, whereas black and white graphs necessitate the use

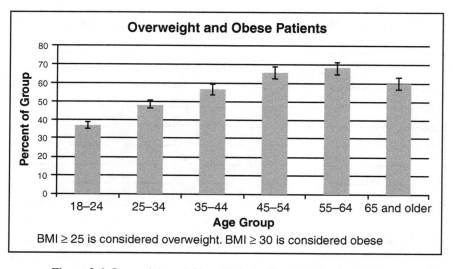

Figure 2-6 Overweight and Obese Patients: Port City Hospital, 2007

Table 2-12 2007 Expenditure Categories

Port City Hospital		
	Med Surg	*ICU*
Supplies	$ 189,654.00	$ 210,157.00
Professional	$ 1,085,623.00	$ 1,527,560.00
Pharmacy	$ 228,290.00	$ 142,152.00
Ancillary	$ 45,620.00	$ 33,158.00
Facilities	$ 624,877.00	$ 218,906.00
Administrative	$ 328,176.00	$ 3,235,148.00
Total	$ 2,502,240.00	$ 5,367,081.00

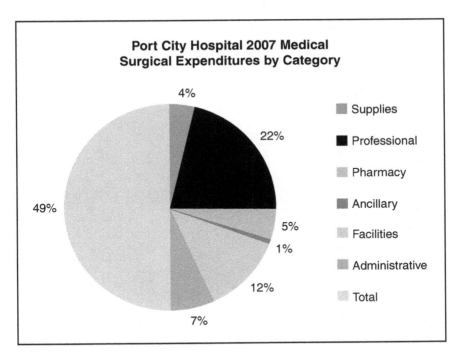

Figure 2-7 Port City Hospital 2007 Medical Surgical Expenditures by Category

of patterns within the slices to differentiate between them. Care should be taken to ensure that no two categories are easily confused because of similar hues or patterns.

A third basic technique for visually displaying information relates to time series data. When observations are measured over time, line graphs should be used to reflect the continuous nature of the data. Line graphs also allow for examination of visual trends over time that may not be readily discernible in table form. Consider Table 2-13, which examines births at Port City Hospital from 2005 through 2008. The data as presented do not lend to the immediate identification of trends by month, collection of months, or year. However, when placed in graphical form, as shown in Figure 2-8, two trends become evident. The first is that the number of births has risen each year. The second is that there a constant trend is reflected throughout the year shown by the peaks and valleys in the data over time. This seems to reflect a seasonal trend in which births spike in May and then decline during summer months, rising again late in the year. By examining these data using a stacked line graph, we can see both trends simultaneously.

The final graphical tool we will explore is the dual axis graph. This type of graph is suitable when two sets of data are to be shown together on one graph,

Table 2-13 Port City Hospital Births, 2005–2008

	2005	2006	2007	2008
Jan	21	25	30	39
Feb	25	30	35	42
Mar	21	31	37	51
Apr	24	34	41	53
May	35	35	42	57
Jun	14	20	30	44
Jul	21	23	27	41
Aug	27	25	31	40
Sep	33	37	45	55
Oct	37	40	50	60
Nov	30	38	42	62
Dec	36	45	48	58

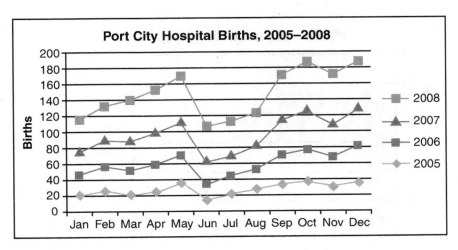

Figure 2-8 Port City Hospital Births, 2005–2008

but the units of measurement of the two variables are different. For example, consider Table 2-14, which shows the number of full time equivalent (FTE) employees and the total expenditures by hospital department. The visual representation allows for the comparison of two data elements, one measured in person equivalents and one in dollars to be viewed simultaneously (Figure 2-9).

Table 2-14 FTE Employees and Total Expenditures by Department

Port City Hospital 2008		
	FTE employees	*Total Expenditures*
Med/Surg	23	$ 5,645,230.00
ED	14	$ 825,180.00
ICU	17	$ 1,236,450.00
Neonatal	12	$ 1,647,264.00
Radiology	6	$ 546,230.00
Lab	6	$ 427,451.00

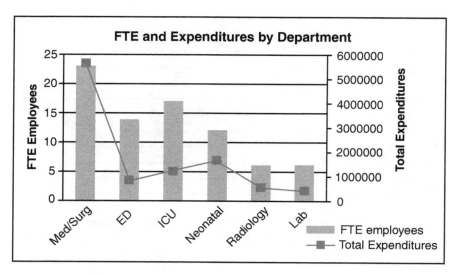

Figure 2-9 FTE and Expenditures by Department

It would be incorrect to place them relative to one vertical axis given that FTEs are measured in the tens (10, 12, 20 etc.), and total expenditures reach into the millions. To accommodate such large numbers for expenditures, the scale of the axis would reach up to the highest data point, here over $5 million, which would in turn mute any differences between the number of FTEs when those differences are so small.

Sound statistics and presentation skills afford the healthcare manager a clear and defensible way to both ask pertinent questions and construct evidence to answer those questions. The job of the competent manager is to know what the right questions are to ask, and then how to construct hypotheses and analyze data in an appropriate way. By following the simple rules presented here, data can be categorized by how they are measured (categorical or continuous) and following from that are a defined set of analysis options for each type. It is further incumbent upon the analyst to present the data in a clear and understandable way, but also to take care to describe fully and cite the data used. These basic analyses will provide the foundation for many of the other managerial competencies described later in this book.

EXERCISES

2-1 Your organization collects data on individual patients shown in Appendix Table 2. Identify whether each variable is measured nominally, ordinally, or as an interval/ratio variable.

2-2 What statistical measures would you use to summarize the variable for age? What about for gender? For convenience satisfaction? How would you present these graphically?

2-3 If you are interested in whether satisfaction scoring differed by the amount the individual paid as a co-pay, how would you state this inquiry as testable hypotheses (the null and alternative)? What statistical test would you run to test this hypothesis?

2-4 Perform the test defined in Table 2-3. State your conclusions.

2-5 Compare gender and having Rx coverage. State your hypotheses. Perform the appropriate statistical test and interpret.

Appendix Table 1 Chi-Square Values by Alpha Level and Degrees of Freedom

Df	0.5	0.1	0.05	0.02	0.01	0.001
1	0.455	2.706	3.841	5.412	6.635	10.827
2	1.386	4.605	5.991	7.824	9.210	13.815
3	2.366	6.251	7.815	9.837	11.345	16.268
4	3.357	7.779	9.488	11.668	13.277	18.465
5	4.351	9.236	11.070	13.388	15.086	20.510

Appendix Table 2 Patient Satisfaction, by Insurer, Same Day of Appointment, Prescription Coverage and Level of Co-pay

Gender	Age	Convenience Satisfaction	Insurer	Same day appointment?	Rx coverage	Co-pay ($)
M	22	5	Select	Y	Y	15
M	24	4	Select	Y	N	15
F	45	5	Select	Y	Y	10
F	38	5	Select	Y	Y	10
F	48	3	Select	Y	N	10
F	50	4	Select	Y	Y	20
M	67	4	Medicare	Y	Y	5
F	23	5	Tri-state	N	Y	10
F	19	5	Tri-state	N	Y	15
M	14	3	Tri-state	Y	Y	20
F	27	5	Reliant	Y	N	15
M	33	3	Reliant	N	N	0
F	39	4	Reliant	N	N	5
F	47	4	Tri-state	N	Y	5
M	42	5	Tri-state	N	N	5
M	31	5	Reliant	N	N	15
M	20	4	Reliant	N	Y	15
F	72	5	Medicare	Y	Y	15

F	44	4	Tri-state	N	N	20
M	45	5	Select	Y	N	20
F	60	3	Reliant	Y	Y	20
M	63	5	Tri-state	Y	Y	5
F	27	5	Tri-state	Y	Y	5
M	68	5	Medicare	N	Y	5
F	33	5	Reliant	N	Y	10
F	38	3	Reliant	N	Y	15
F	55	4	Medicare	N	Y	15
M	51	5	Select	Y	Y	15
F	48	4	Tri-state	Y	Y	20
M	49	5	Tri-state	Y	Y	0
M	55	5	Select	N	Y	5
F	61	4	Reliant	Y	Y	0
F	23	5	Medicare	Y	N	0
M	69	5	Medicare	N	N	20
F	41	4	Tri-state	Y	N	5
F	14	4	Medicare	Y	N	0

Chapter 3

Flow Charting

LEARNING OBJECTIVES

1. To describe and evaluate general systems flow charts.
2. To construct a general systems flow chart.

REAL WORLD SCENARIO

When a patient presents a health insurance card, a walk-in clinic has found it necessary to check whether the insurance is in force, and whether any deductible associated with ambulatory care has been met before it issues a bill. Cash payment is expected at time of service if a patient has not satisfied the health plan's deductible. The clinic is experiencing confusion as to the most efficient process to follow. Last month approximately 8% of the bills involving private health insurance with indemnity coverage and deductibles were in error. The clinic's receptionist and billing clerk need clarification as to who should do what to address this confusion and produce more accurate bills.

LEARNING OBJECTIVE 1: TO DESCRIBE AND EVALUATE GENERAL SYSTEMS FLOW CHARTS

This chapter presents the general rules and conventions associated with general systems flow charting. General systems flow charting is a graphical technique used to create a descriptive picture of an operational system. Once described using general systems flow charting, the system can be analyzed and redesigned as necessary. General systems flow charting is also used to design new systems.

Operations and processes within the healthcare organization are complex. Any operation, such as preparing a meal, sending a letter, admitting a patient to the hospital, or developing a budget is a complex process that requires the systematic interplay of numerous people doing different things in some predetermined order or sequence. Just because a process is complex, however, does not mean it is chaotic. Consider the example of sending a letter:

1. Someone has to write or compose the letter.
2. Someone has to type the letter.
3. Someone has to proofread the letter and sign it.
4. Someone has to save a copy of the letter for the file.
5. Someone has to create an address label.
6. Someone has to put the letter into the envelope.
7. Someone has to affix sufficient postage to the envelope to pay for the mailing.
8. Someone has to take the letter/envelope to an appropriate place to be mailed.
9. Someone has to decide when the copy of the letter can be deleted from the file so that over the long term the files only retain copies of important correspondence.

Sending a letter is a complex (and routine) process in any organization. Because it is a routine or commonly done process, the steps may seem a natural and implicit sequence of events performed by specific people. Duties and responsibilities are usually set by job descriptions and traditions; for example, a secretary or administrative assistant may do some of steps, whereas other staff may have responsibility for other tasks. Efficient systems are orderly. They seek routine. They seek stability. They adhere to precedents. How a process or operation was done yesterday is a very good predictor of how that operation or process will be done tomorrow. When systems and the people who function in them confront uncertainty and ambiguous expectations, they attempt to drive out uncertainty and replace it with explicit (or implicit) direction.

Managers make systems more efficient by establishing explicit expectations. For example, using the process referred to as "division of labor," they decide who in the organization does what tasks and they establish the qualifications needed to perform the tasks. Similarly, using the management process referred to as "coordination," managers establish formal and informal mechanisms so that different parts of systems act in a predetermined, efficient, and effective manner. Organization and system efficiency and effectiveness are not accidental. Efficiency and effectiveness are management concerns, not peripheral byproducts.

To create order and routine and drive out as much uncertainty as possible, managers need a technique able to describe current operations as well as design new or revised complex operations. The technique needs to encompass the macro elements of the system (i.e., goals and objectives) and the micro elements, such as who does what, in what order. General systems flow charting provides the health services manager with a technique able to capture both the micro and macro elements of a system. It is used to describe and analyze the processes used to convert inputs into outcomes at the system and subsystem level.

To use a general systems flow chart requires two conditions. First, the work process should be complex. It should involve at least two or more people engaged in at least two or more steps to accomplish some predetermined objective, such as sending a letter or admitting a patient to a hospital. Second, the work process must have a formal start and stop point. General systems flow charting requires the ability to define when a complex process starts and stops, even if the process or operation is continuous or repetitive. For example, a hospital continuously admits patients. Even though the complex process of admitting patients may be continuous, it can be defined as a process with a formal beginning (e.g., when a specific patient arrives at the door) and end (e.g., when the patient is formally admitted into the hospital).

When these two conditions are met, general systems flow charting provides health services managers the basis to describe complex work processes and then to use the descriptions to analyze, improve, and/or change the complex work process. As implied by the name of the technique, two general properties are included in general systems flow charts—systems and flows. Charts depict and describe a system or sub-system (i.e., inputs, conversion processes and outcomes, and feedback loops) as well as the flow or sequence of inputs and conversion processes and feedback loops.

A general systems flow chart should be developed for any new complex work process in the healthcare organization. After a new system is designed using general systems flow charting, written work procedures can then be developed and work tasks grouped into new or revised job descriptions to support the new system.

General systems flow charting has returned as a foundation methods competency in health services management. The technique was initially developed by industrial engineers and then used by systems analysts when they designed computer-based information systems. For many healthcare organizations, general systems flow charts are new, even though their original popularity was decades ago in production line settings. Today, interest in total quality management (TQM) has again made the technique most relevant and served to introduce the method into healthcare organizations. The technique forces examination of the micro work process used to convert inputs into outcomes. It provides a systematic approach to determine how things are done and change processes to achieve higher levels of efficiency and effectiveness. This is a technique with very broad applications. Although it looks basic, as a technique it is one of the most robust in the health services manager's repertoire.

All techniques have specific rules and convention. For example, mathematical forecasting relies upon the rules of algebra to solve mathematical equations. Although not mathematical, general systems flow charting also has specific rules.

1. Charts flow from top to bottom and from left to right.
2. Decisions included in a chart must be able to be answered as either YES or NO. If possible, the "routine or most common" answer flows downward; the non-routine answer flows horizontally.

3. Lines on charts have arrowheads that indicate flow and sequence.
4. Specific symbols are used. Figure 3-1 includes the commonly used symbols.

Using these symbols and descriptive labels, charts are constructed that describe the operation of a current work process. Managers create charts that describe how the current processes work. In the development of these charts, the manager must ensure that all logical possibilities are included on the chart.

Flow Chart Symbols

Certain prerequisites must be satisfied before the actual general systems flow chart is constructed. The health services managers must know the goal of the system

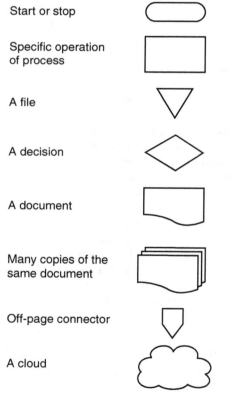

Figure 3-1 Flow Chart Symbols

or work process being analyzed. The goal might be "to prepare and mail a letter." It might also be to "admit a patient into the hospital." Or, it might be to "render appropriate patient care to patients who arrive for service." Whatever the goal, the manager must know the goal and use this "goal" as the central and unifying theme of the general system flow chart. Knowing the goal of the system or work process also provides the ability to use general systems flow charts to improve operations. Improvements can involve increased efficiency and/or increased quality of service. Rarely, if ever, will the manager be asked to merely analyze a system without an agenda for change, such as to fix a problem, increase its efficiency or enhance its quality. Therefore, the agenda for change becomes an important aspect of the goal statement.

The general systems flow chart must describe how the current work operation is done. The creator of the chart must determine what is done, by whom, and in what sequence. Often this information is determined by interview and/or direct observation. Copies of documents created and used in the work process are collected and traced. This type of information is needed before the chart can be constructed. The description of the current system that emerges from these questions and information is expressed in a general systems flow chart.

After the flow chart is developed and verified, the manager uses the general systems flow chart to design improvements to "fix" the system. Often, redesign will involve the workers directly affected by any change. Often, redesign will involve some actual trials before the redesign is finalized.

LEARNING OBJECTIVE 2: TO CONSTRUCT A GENERAL SYSTEMS FLOW CHART

Creating general systems flow charts usually takes a few tries before they are completed correctly. The process of constructing and drawing the chart often identifies "new questions" or "issues" that lead to beginning again with a clean sheet of paper and collecting more data. After the chart has been prepared and verified (verbally checked to ensure that all pathways and options lead to a logical "stop" point), the manager can use the chart to "try" some new ways to accomplish system goals. Perhaps, these new ways might involve simplifying procedures or the process. Often, systems seem to "grow" needless steps that can be eliminated. In other instances, many steps can be repackaged into more efficient work packages. In still other instances, individual steps can be reordered and/or new steps added so that system outcomes better correspond with system goals. The primary point being that these "new ideas" for improvements need to be developed as changes to the original systems flow chart and "field tested" in the general system flow chart to insure that desired outcomes are realized.

The first time a chart is drawn is never the last. Novices usually have many editions before the chart meets requirements. Experienced managers usually are more efficient—experience provides sharper senses to detect flow and sequence in a system. Do not underestimate the difficulty associated with using this simple technique. The only way to create a general systems flow chart is by trial and error. Create a version and then test it to determine whether it actually reflects how the process is done. Be prepared for many drafts before the process is completed.

The first task, sometimes referred to as a task list, is to specify in order the individual steps and sequencing in the overall process. Once the task list is established, adding decisions, files, documents, and other aspects of the process creates the general systems flow chart. Sometimes, for purposes of simplicity, charts are prepared in levels. Any chart must incorporate sufficient detail to satisfy its analytical role. It is sometimes very helpful to organize charts into levels. Level I could be a simple summary chart that depicts the system at a macro level, which is then backed up, by numerous charts (Level II) that depict individual steps in the master process depicted on the Level I chart.

Consider the example in Figure 3-2. Examine this chart for flow and sequence. Determine whether the chart is a complete process.

Flow Chart: To Complete an Acceptable Term Paper

As can be seen from this example, more detail could have been added by expanding the number of steps in this chart. The example could be considered a Level I or macro chart with other more detailed charts (Level II) to cover each individual work process such as collect data, write first draft, etc.

This chapter has established general rules and conventions associated with general systems flow charting. Developing the skill to flow chart requires practice as well as patience. Although a basic method, it is very robust in identifying the operation of current work processes and options to enhance the efficiency and quality of work processes. Be aware that contemporary attempts to improve service quality, such as total quality management (TQM) and continuous quality improvement (CQI) rely upon general systems flow charting as a basis for system and process analysis.

Unlike other management methods that rely upon mathematics, general systems flow charting does not involve numbers and equations. In this sense it is not a quantitative method. It does, however, provide the manager a form of symbolic logic to use to describe and improve operations and design new systems. As such, general systems flow charting is a systematic method that should be incorporated into the repertoire of any health services manager.

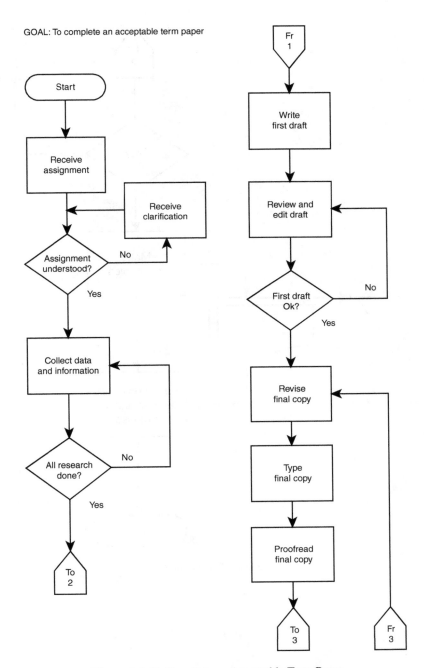

Figure 3-2 To Complete an Acceptable Term Paper

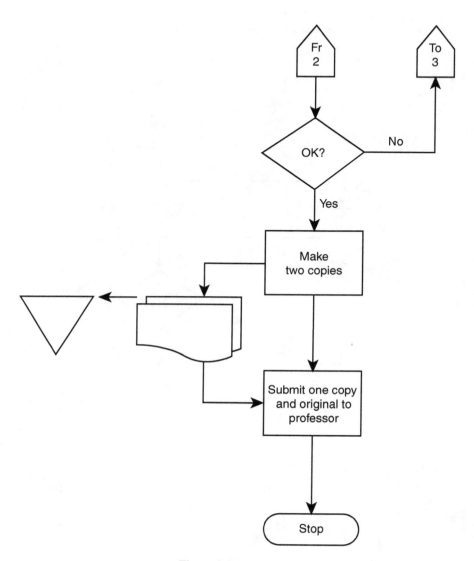

Figure 3-2 *continued.*

EXERCISES

3-1 Develop a general systems flow chart that describes the process of filling a car with gasoline. After "start" have as the first process "Arrive at Gas Station." Immediately before "stop" have as the last process "Leave Gas Station."

3-2 Using a general systems flow chart design a system for arrivals at an emergency room of a hospital.

3-3 Using the following narrative, create a general system flow chart. When a patient arrives at the clinic the patient first sees the receptionist, who checks to see if the patient was seen before. If so, the receptionist pulls the medical record from the file. If the patient is new, the receptionist has the patient complete the necessary forms and creates a medical record. Patients are seen by the physician in the order they arrive. If one of the two examination rooms is empty, the nurse escorts the patient to the examination room and records the complaint. The nurse performs routine tests. The nurse writes the complaint and findings on a medical examination form, a form that will be subsequently filed with the patient's medical record. The physician examines the patient and orders medical tests, if necessary. A diagnosis and treatment plan is presented to the patient by the physician; a written copy of this plan and any other appropriate instructions. [Notes are written on the medical examination form.] When the physician releases the patient, the patient returns to the receptionist, who prepares a bill. If the patient has health insurance, the bill is sent to the health insurance carrier. The patient leaves after either paying the bill (by cash, check, or credit card) or signing the forms to authorize payment by his or her health insurance company. If the health insurance company refuses to pay or partially pays the bill, the receptionist bills the patient by mail. Any patient with an unpaid bill or bad credit history is refused subsequent treatment until the old bill is paid.

3-4 Every pharmaceutical listed on the hospital's formulary has a minimum reorder level. When the inventory level of the specific drug reaches this minimum reorder level, an order is issued to replenish the available supply maintained in the pharmacy. This is done to ensure that the pharmacy always has available inventory to meet the medical needs of patients. The system requires that the chief pharmacist authorize all orders. Using the following narrative, create a general systems flow chart. At 6 AM each day the pharmacy information system reports the existing inventory level for each item listed on the hospital's formulary. It produces three lists. List A includes those drugs that will need to be reordered today. List B includes those drugs that will need to be reordered in 2 to 21 days. List C includes drugs that will need to be reordered in more than 21 days. The chief pharmacist must review list A, authorize the purchase, and then send list A to the director of materials management, who must order the drug. When drugs are received by central supply, the receipt for the order (if documented), and the order are sent to the pharmacy for storage in inventory. Once you have completed the flow chart of the existing system, suggest three improvements to enhance the pharmacy inventory system. Aside from lists A, B, and C, what other reports should the pharmacy inventory control system produce? Should special provisions exist for ordering and handling narcotics? Where would you expect the existing system to breakdown?

Chapter 4

Time Value of Money

LEARNING OBJECTIVES

1. To understand the concept of the time value of money.
2. To be able to compute the future or present value of money (i.e., compounding and discounting).

REAL WORLD SCENARIO

Eugene Righter is manager of strategy for St. Clement's, Mercy Medical Center in a Midwestern city. He is presented with an offer of $100,000 to purchase a new piece of laboratory equipment that the medical center has begun developing. The prospective purchaser of this equipment has offered him an option of receiving the $100,000 for the rights to the equipment immediately or in 12 months. Righter is planning to sell the rights anyway, and there is no prospect of generating any revenue from the use of the equipment in the coming 12 months. Should he accept the money now or in 12 months? This is an easy choice: Righter elects to receive the $100,000 now, rather than waiting for 1 year. But what were the reasons behind his decision?

There are at least two factors that influenced the decision:

1. Assuming that some level of inflation will occur within the next 12 months, $100,000 can buy *more* today than in 12 months.
2. There is always an option of investing the $100,000 today or during the next year, an option that may result in greater financial return or gain in 12 months than accepting $100,000 in 12 months. At a minimum, the $100,000 could be used to purchase a certificate of deposit or a government note of minimum risk, where it would earn interest for the period of the investment.

LEARNING OBJECTIVE 1: TO UNDERSTAND THE CONCEPT OF THE TIME VALUE OF MONEY

This simple example illustrates one of the fundamental concepts of management: There is a time value associated with money. All other things being equal, money that you have today is worth more than the same amount of money received in the future. This concept, known as the *time value of money*, comes from the field of finance.

Issues related to the time value of money become more critical as the period of time in question increases. As many accounting issues pertain to issues with relatively short time horizons; e.g., less than 12 months, managers may not consider the time value of money in analyzing strategic decisions. Over longer periods of time, however (and occasionally shorter as well), the relationship between time and the value of money is a critical management consideration. Given the fact that most investments or project opportunities have "lives" extending over time horizons greater than 12 months, the importance of the time value of money is magnified. Effective managers take a financial perspective of projects, including considerations of the time value of money, not simply an accounting perspective (such as short-term profit or loss), although both are important.

The preceding example is simple; however, most decisions faced by managers are not as straightforward. For example, suppose the manager is offered the same $100,000 now for the equipment rights or $110,000 in 12 months. Should the manager sell the rights now, or sign an agreement to sell at the later time? Is it more beneficial financially to have the $100,000 in hand now, or is it more advantageous to wait for a year and receive a larger sum of money?

Responding to opportunities such as this requires competency in the management skill of calculating what is known as the present value of money received at a later time. This competency enables managers to assess opportunities on an "apples to apples" perspective financially; in other words, it takes into account the time value of money. The overall objective of this chapter is to introduce the key management methods associated with the time value of money. It must be added that, although financial factors should never be the only criterion used in making management decisions, particularly in health care, it is also true that such factors often take precedence in decision making.

LEARNING OBJECTIVE 2: TO BE ABLE TO COMPUTE THE FUTURE OR PRESENT VALUE OF MONEY (I.E., COMPOUNDING AND DISCOUNTING)

The fundamental concepts underlying the idea that the value of money changes in relation to time are known as compounding and discounting. *Compounding* refers to the idea that, if money is invested (e.g., put in the bank or used to buy a bond with fixed returns in the future), this amount of money grows or compounds in the future. Compounding refers to the process of going from today's value of money, known as the present value, to some future value of money.

It is useful to think of discounting as the inverse of compounding. *Discounting* is a way of looking at some future amount of money, known as the future value, and calculating its value today (i.e., calculating its present value). The following sections present the ideas of compounding and discounting and give several examples of how to compute future and present value. Additional examples of how to apply the ideas and tools introduced in this chapter are found later in the book, notably in Chapter 13.

Calculating the Future Value of Money: Compounding

The simplest example of money growing over time (compounding) is a savings account at a bank. Individuals choose to deposit money in the bank for a variety of reasons, including the knowledge that money invested in the bank grows because interest is earned on the money. For example, if an initial deposit of $100 is made in a bank that promises to pay 2% interest annually, at the end of 12 months a total of $102 is available. The original deposit has grown or compounded from $100 to $102. The additional $2 is the interest earned on the deposit.

If the money is left in the bank for another year, assuming no change in the interest rate, at the end of year 2 a total of $104.04 is available in the account. The original $100 has grown or compounded by $4.04 as a result of interest earnings on the account. Thus, using conventional terminology, the future value of $100 invested for 2 years at an interest rate of 2% compounded annually is $104.04. The increase in the account in the second year is $2.04, not $2.00, as was earned in year 1. This is because the amount in the account at the end of year 1 (i.e., the amount that is compounded for an additional [second] year) was $102 (the original $100 deposit + $2 of interest earned to that point in time). Thus, during year 2, 2% was earned on $102, not $100.

In situations involving compounding or discounting, it is helpful to create a "picture" or timeline of the investment scenario. A timeline is used to indicate the present and future value of money, the applicable interest rate, and the length of time involved. In fact, always beginning a time value of money analysis with a timeline may be a prerequisite for accurate calculations.

For example, Figure 4-1 depicts the situation just described. Note that time period "0" refers to the present time (i.e., now), and that the future value refers to the size of account at the end of the time period indicated. The compounding (interest) rate is shown on the timeline for the appropriate time periods. Creating a timeline is a simple, yet helpful tool to organize the "facts" of the investment opportunity and to help ensure that mangers have all the information required for decision making.

In general terms, compounding is represented by the following equation:

$$\text{Future Value} = \text{Present Value} + \text{Interest Earned (I)}$$

where

$$\text{Interest Earned} = \text{Present Value} * \text{Interest Rate } (i)$$

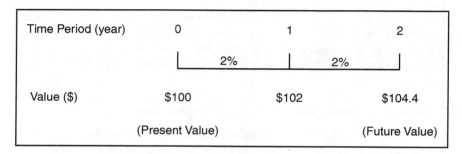

Figure 4-1 Timeline Showing Present Value (PV) and Future Value (FV) of $100 Invested for 2 Years at a 2% Annual Rate

Stated another way:

$$FV = PV + I$$

which is the same as:

$$FV = PV + (PV*i)$$

Simplifying:

$$FV = PV(1 + i) \qquad \text{Equation 4-1}$$

Using Equation 4-1 for the preceding example described, where the present value is the amount of the original deposit (i.e., $100) and the interest rate is 2%, the future value at the end of year 1 is calculated as:

$$
\begin{aligned}
FV_{\text{year 1}} &= \$100(1 + 0.02) \\
&= \$100(1.02) \\
&= \$102
\end{aligned}
$$

In the second year, another year's interest is earned. To reflect this second year of interest, using Equation 4-1:

$$
\begin{aligned}
FV_{\text{year 2}} &= PV(1 + i)(1 + i) \qquad \text{Equation 4-1} \\
&= PV(1 + i)^2
\end{aligned}
$$

This is the same as:

$$FV_{\text{year 2}} = FV_{\text{year 1}}(1 + i)$$

Each term $(1 + i)$, known as the compounding factor, indicates an additional period during which interest is being earned. In this example, it is said that interest is compounded for two periods. Substituting numbers in the equation, the future value at the end of year 2 is calculated to be:

$$\text{FV}_{\text{year 2}} = \$100(1 + 0.02)(1 + 0.02)$$
$$= \$100(1 + 0.02)^2$$
$$= \$100(1.02)^2$$
$$= \$100(1.0404)$$
$$= \$104.04$$

Equation 4-2 is a general equation for compounding that takes into account the number of compounding periods (n):

The General Compounding Formula

$$\text{FV}_n = \text{PV}(1 + i)^n \qquad\qquad \text{Equation 4-2}$$

where FV_n = future value in time period n
  PV = present value
  i = stated interest rate
  n = number of time periods

For example, if the original $100 investment remains in the bank and is compounded annually for a period of 5 years, the future value calculation is:

$$\text{FV}_{\text{year 5}} = \$100(1.02)(1.02)(1.02)(1.02)(1.02)$$
$$= \$100(1.02)^5$$
$$= \$100(1.1041)$$
$$= \$110.41$$

Equation 4-2 can be used without modification in any compounding problem as long as there are no changes in the interest rate or the compounding period. (Examples in which these factors do change are considered later.) Any standard calculator with an exponent key can be used to calculate future value easily. A business/financial calculator has special keys, and spreadsheet software, such as Microsoft Excel, contain functions to simplify the calculation.

Compounding More Frequently Than Annually

In the simplest cases, as shown in the preceding, the value of money compounds once a year. In many cases, however, compounding occurs more frequently than annually. For example, interest on a savings account may be compounded semiannually (i.e., twice a year). In this case, the number of compounding periods doubles, but the interest rate at which the money grows is divided by two to account

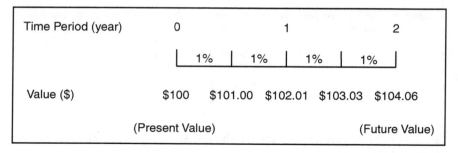

Figure 4-2 Timeline Showing Present Value (PV) and Future Value (FV) of $100 Invested for 2 Years at a 2% Annual Rate, Compounded Semiannually

for the two periods in each year. The timeline in Figure 4-2 shows a situation in which the $100 in the earlier example is placed into an account that compounds interest semiannually.

The $100 deposit will grow to $102.01 in 1 year when the 2% interest compounds semiannually. Using Equation 4-2, this calculation is:

$$Fv_n = PV(1 + i)^n$$
$$FV_{year\ 1} = \$100(1.01)^2$$
$$= \$100(1.0201)$$
$$= \$102.01$$

Note that the number of compounding periods (n) has increased to 2, and the interest rate is now 1% for each compounding period. At the end of year 2, the account will be $104.06. This simple example demonstrates one important characteristic of the time value of money: As the frequency of compounding increases, the future value increases as well. For example, if the frequency of compounding is quarterly, the initial deposit of $100 will grow to $104.07, and for monthly compounding it will grow to $104.08. In this example, the difference in the future value of the account under varying compounding frequencies is obviously quite small; however, the differences will become more substantial as the size of the account increases.

Using Effective Annual Rates to Assess Opportunities

It is often important for a manager to compare different investment opportunities involving compounding, and these opportunities may not have the same compounding periods. In the examples described in the preceding, the stated annual interest rate is 2% (also known as the nominal annual interest rate), but because the compounding frequencies differ, the future values of the investments differ. To facilitate a meaningful comparison among investment opportunities, it is important that adjustments be made to account for the differing compounding periods. This adjustment is made by calculating what is known as the effective annual rate (EAR).

The EAR is the compounding rate that would have increased the initial investment to the higher future value (i.e., the amount calculated for the scenario with more frequent compounding), assuming annual compounding. In the example with semiannual compounding, the effective annual rate is the rate that would have increased the initial $100 deposit to $102.01 after 1 year, assuming annual compounding. This EAR is calculated as follows:

$$\$100(1 + i) = \$102.01$$
$$(1 + i) = (\$102.01/\$100)$$
$$i = (\$102.01/\$100) - 1$$
$$= (1.0201 - 1.000)$$
$$= .0201$$
$$= 2.01\%$$

The EAR of 2.01% is greater than the stated or nominal rate of 2%. Therefore, the opportunity with semiannual compounding is more attractive.

When compounding occurs annually, the EAR is equal to the nominal or stated rate. A manager evaluating the impact of different compounding periods should compare the EARs and draw conclusions about the relative attractiveness of the opportunities. When assessing opportunities, assuming comparable risk levels, the same stated interest rates, and the same present value, those opportunities with more frequent compounding have higher future values.

Equation 4-3 is the general equation for the EAR:

$$EAR = [1 + (i/m)]^m - 1.0 \qquad \text{Equation 4-3}$$

where i = stated or nominal interest rate
m = number of compounding periods per year

Calculating the Present Value of Money: Discounting

Earlier in the chapter, a manager was presented with an opportunity to receive $100,000 now or $110,000 in 12 months. This is a typical financial management decision. The manager's choice is based on determining the present value of the amount of money to be received in the future, in this case $110,000. That is the same as asking, How much is that future sum of money worth today? This is essentially the reverse of the compounding question discussed in the first part of this chapter. Recall that Equation 4-2 states that:

$$FV_n = PV(1 + i)^n$$

where FV_n = future value in time period n
      PV = present value
       n = number of time periods
       i = interest rate (discount rate)

This new problem requires solving for the present value, the equation for which is shown as $6 - 4$ (the general discounting formula):

$$PV = FV_n/(1 + i)^n \qquad\qquad \text{Equation 4-4}$$

where PV = present value
     FV_n = future value in time period n
      n = number of time periods
      i = interest rate (discount rate)

Looking at this equation it should be apparent that, as it stands, there is not enough information to solve the problem—there is no interest rate (i) provided. Therefore, an interest rate must be assumed. The question is how to determine an appropriate rate. One way to determine such a rate is based on the concept of opportunity cost.

A manager typically has multiple options for investing money. For example, several certificates of deposit or bank savings options may be available, each paying a specified rate of return. Suppose the manager is considering two separate savings options. Option A pays 2.5% annually and option B pays 1.75% interest on savings. If the manager selects option B for investment, he or she is therefore foregoing the return available with option A. The rate of return on the option(s) *not* selected is known as an opportunity cost. So, in this example, selection of option A carries with it an opportunity cost of 2.5%.

Of course, not all investment opportunities are the same. For example, the manager could decide to take a very financially conservative approach and deposit money in a bank savings account. The financial return from this strategy is likely to be relatively modest, but the level of risk associated with this investment strategy is quite low. Alternatively, the manager might choose to invest available funds in the bonds of a highly speculative new company. Under this scenario it is likely that the potential financial return will be higher than the bank deposit, but this investment strategy carries substantially more financial risk.

Note that in rational financial markets, there is a direct relationship between risk and potential reward; that is, as the level of riskiness increases, so too does the level of potential reward.

The key to selecting an appropriate interest (or discount) rate to use in an analysis is to use the interest rate available on an alternative investment of similar type, level of risk, and time horizon. In other words, the manager should identify an investment opportunity, with a stated interest rate that is similar to the project being considered and use that stated rate to compute the present value.

So, for example, following thorough research, the manager concludes that investments of similar type, risk, and time horizon pay a 3% return annually; this is the discount rate that should be used. A timeline for this project is shown in Figure 4-3.

Using Equation 4-4, the present value of the proposed investment is computed to be $106,796. This means that all other things being equal, the manager should be willing to invest no more than $106,796 in this project. If the manager can accept this opportunity at a cost of less than $106,796, it will yield a better financial return than the investment alternative; however, if the cost of this opportunity exceeds this amount, then the manager should decline this opportunity and pursue the alternative. That is, the manager—as a prudent investor—should be willing to pay no more than $106,796 for this opportunity.

Just as was the case with the compounding formula (Equation 4-2), a manager can use the discounting formula (Equation 4-4) to calculate crucial variables in addition to the present value. The formula can be used to calculate either the number of time periods required to generate a specified future value given a known present value and interest rate, or the discount rate given a known present value and number of periods.

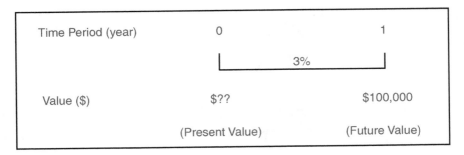

Figure 4-3 Timeline Showing Format for Discounting

CONCLUSION

All management decisions involving the time value of money require the use of the tools of compounding and discounting. Competency in these two skills enables the manager to evaluate a wide variety of situations. Often, the greatest challenges for managers involve identifying the unknown variable in the equation (i.e., deciding what needs to be determined or calculated), and determining the appropriate discount rate. Regardless of the situation being analyzed, however, the simplest tool and most important starting point for analysis is a timeline that indicates the information available and assists in identifying what variable or factor is missing. Therefore, the first step in assessing the time value of money always should be to draw such a timeline.

EXERCISES

4-1 You decide to invest $100,000 in a program that is guaranteed to grow by 2.5% for each of the next 5 years. At the end of the 5 years, how much is your investment worth?

4-2 What is the effective annual rate of an investment that pays 6% for 5 years, compounded semiannually?

4-3 What is the present value of a single cash flow of $25,000 received at the end of 10 years, if we assume a discount rate of 5% annually? With a discount rate of 7%?

4-4 Suppose you deposit $100 in a savings account that compounds annually at 2%. After 1 year at this rate, the bank changes its rate of compounding to 1.5% annually. Assuming the compounding rate does not change for 4 additional years, how much will your account be worth at the end of the 5-year period?

Forecasting Competencies

Chapter 5

The Art and Science
of Forecasting

LEARNING OBJECTIVES

1. To describe the concept of forecasting as a managerial tool.
2. To describe the difference between analytic and non-analytic forecasting.
3. To understand the assumptions of analytic forecasting.
4. To describe the limitations of forecasting and the challenges forecasting presents to the health services manager.

REAL WORLD SCENARIO

Molly Adel is the director of University Health Services for Northern College, a large liberal arts college in the northeast. Northern College Health Services serves undergraduate and graduate students who live both on and off campus with a broad range of primary care services. In recent years, visit volume has been increasing, both during the academic year and the summer months. At times, the staffing and supply resources of the College's Health Services have become strained. Molly has decided that it would be best to attempt to forecast upcoming visits to Health Services to better anticipate resource demands. She would like to understand the type and precision of each type of forecasting available to her. As director, she hears anecdotal stories of increased workloads from staff over the past 6 months. She believes there has been an increase in visits, but she would like to quantify these claims and attempt to understand if her own expert intuition of volume is a good substitute for a more analytic forecast.

LEARNING OBJECTIVE 1: TO DESCRIBE THE CONCEPT OF FORECASTING AS A MANAGERIAL TOOL

A forecast is an attempt to predict the future. Such attempts, however, are usually guesses of some form or another, as no one is able to see into the future or predict it with absolute certainty. Managers are not clairvoyant. They do not employ crystal balls or use fortune tellers as consultants. Yet managers must anticipate the future to prepare for it. Budgets are based upon forecasts. The number and type of employees are based upon present as well as future demands for service. Hiring and reductions in staff are based upon forecasts of the future.

Any forecast is, at best, an imprecise estimate. Few forecasts will be completely accurate, and so most contain some degree of inherent error. The challenge faced by managers and analysts is to minimize this error; or otherwise stated, managers must attempt to minimize the difference between what is predicted and what actually happens.

For example, if F = the forecast made yesterday of today's temperature and TEMP = Today's actual temperature, the only way F can equal TEMP (F = TEMP) is if:

1. The Forecast was absolutely correct, *or*
2. The formula is revised to be F = *TEMP* + *E*, where *E* is the positive or negative error of the forecast.

If today's temperature was forecasted to be 65 degrees and the actual temperature is 65 degrees, then the error in the forecast would be zero. However, if the forecast for today's temperature was 80 degrees, given the formula relationship, F = *TEMP* + *E*, the (*E*) error would be: *E* = 80 − 65 or 15 degrees.

Managers are very interested in methods that can minimize the error that is included in all forecasts. The challenge with forecasting is to strive for accuracy and come up with a "best" forecast, or one that employs the least amount of error. However, not all error is created equally. Error can be thought of as both systematic error—error that can be controlled for by the appropriateness and precision of the forecasting technique being used, and also random error—or error that is inherent in every forecast.

In our real world example, if Molly Adel did not account for the seasonal trends in visit volume to Northern College's Health Services, she would be allowing systematic error to bias her forecasting estimates. At the same time, even if Molly did account for this variation, it is still possible that she could see a spike in visit volume over the summer months, for example, which could be entirely owing to random chance. This would be an example of random error, and there would be no way to predict its occurrence. The goal of all managers is to control for systematic error while being aware that random error is unpredictable and always possible.

LEARNING OBJECTIVE 2: TO DESCRIBE THE DIFFERENCE BETWEEN ANALYTIC AND NONANALYTIC FORECASTING

As the chapter title implies, forecasting is both an art and a science. To that end, there are two branches of forecasting: analytic, or statistical forecasting, and nonanalytic forecasting, often called judgmental, genius, or expert forecasting. Both have their merits and limitations.

Nonanalytic Forecasting

Judgment forecasting does not strictly imply making decisions based on intuition, although this can be the case. Most forms of this type of forecasting are both less accurate than analytic forecasting, and can be very labor intensive depending on the forecasting need.

For example, the Delphi method is a systematic method to collect opinions—usually from experts—and use these opinions in multiple round-robin cycles in an effort to arrive at a forecast that captures the essence of all the individuals (e.g., experts) used in the forecasting exercise. This type of effort may be good for forecasting a phenomenon that is relatively new, or for which there are little existing data, but it is not something one would use to predict the annual inventory for a services organization, for example.

Other examples of judgment or genius forecasting can be found in multiple forms—usually in newspapers or cable television when noted "experts" forecast the outcome of a certain situation, such as what stock performance will be, who will be wearing what next season, or what the new year will bring.

This chapter is not devoted to this type of forecasting. Except for the Delphi method, all forms of judgment forecasting are based upon individual opinion. Obviously, sometimes the individual will be right and other times wrong. It is important to remember that the challenge in forecasting is to minimize the error inherent in all forecasts. Judgment forecasting is often used to forecast far-off events that defy other approaches. Generally, the error inherent in judgment forecasting is considered large but unavoidable, although some have attempted to adjust for some of the inherent biases. (Harvey, N. "Improving judgmental forecasts," in *Principles of Forecasting: A Handbook for Researchers and Practitioners*, J. Scott Armstrong (ed.), Kluwer Academic Publishers, 2001, 59–80.)

For example, consider an assignment to forecast the year when a cure will be available for HIV. The only reasonable and logical approach would be to identify either one or multiple experts and ask their opinion(s) on this question. The hypothesis is that the error in their forecasts will be less than the error in other forecasts because they are experts and have greater knowledge of this area than others. Before leaving judgment forecasting, it is important to note that sometimes the forecasting problem requires the use of judgment forecasting, such as with the example involving HIV. Judgment forecasting is still forecasting, even though it can be highly judgmental and not based upon mathematical models.

LEARNING OBJECTIVE 3: TO UNDERSTAND THE ASSUMPTIONS OF ANALYTIC FORECASTING

In contrast to nonanalytic forms of forecasting, analytic forecasting attempts to be more systematic and precise. This usually entails a mathematical approach to analyzing data to predict future outcomes and trends. Most forecasting problems faced by the health services manager can be accomplished using some form of analytic forecasting. Analytic forecasting methods are based on one of two assumptions. One is that the past is a reliable predictor of the future; and second is that the future can be predicted based on knowable cause-and-effect relationships. Each is examined in turn.

ASSUMPTION A: THE PAST CAN PREDICT THE FUTURE

This assumption is founded on the idea that future events are related to what has occurred in the past. Under this assumption analytic approaches are used to examine past and present events and extend or extrapolate the values of these past events forward. In using analytic approaches based upon this assumption, managers count on the past being a valid and reliable predictor of the future.

This assumption needs to be thoroughly considered by health services managers who use analytic forecasting approaches. For example, if the assignment is to forecast the number of patient days a hospital will generate (or produce) in the following month, basing the forecast on past patient-day production or generation seems appropriate because the past may be a reasonable predictor of the future. Examine the data in Figure 5-1. By a quick visual scan, if asked to predict the next month's visits, most would place the forecast near 100. This, however, would be a visual judgment forecast. Instead there are methods to mathematically use past data to predict the future within some range of certainty. One question that first must be answered is, How far back should past data be included in making the forecast? Another is, How far into the future can and should one forecast given the data at hand? What if, for example, you were asked to forecast hospital patient days for the next 10 years? Ten years is a very long time in the future, and many unknown variables could affect the accuracy of such a distanced forecast. Given the ambiguity associated with such a long time interval, most health services managers would be very reluctant to base a 10-year forecast solely upon past data.

Chapter 6 will explore forecasting methods that are based on this assumption. They are:

1. Extrapolations Using Averages
2. Moving Averages as Forecasts
3. Exponential Smoothing in Forecasting

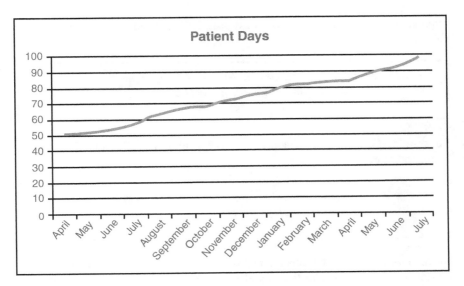

Figure 5-1 Patient Days

ASSUMPTION B: THE FUTURE CAN BE PREDICTED BASED UPON CAUSE AND EFFECT

Many forecasting approaches are based upon cause and effect and are known as *causal models*. The models used in this category of forecasting attempt to capture the primary factors that are believed to cause (therefore the name causal) or influence the future. For example, consider a forecast of the number of patient days to be generated by a hospital: Patient days can be considered the "effect." Using the number of patient days forecasted (PD_f), a conceptual and analytic cause and effect model can be constructed. Based on the knowledge that patient days are a function of both admission and average length of stay (ALOS) we get:

$$PD_f = \text{ALOS} \times \textit{admissions} \qquad \text{Equation 5-1}$$

where ALOS is the average length of stay for patients in the hospital (in days) and admissions is the number of patients to be admitted into the hospital *next* year. This requires that we project admissions next year. To do this, examine the admissions calculation formula, which is:

> *Admissions = Hospital Admission Rate per 1,000 people ×*
> *the Number of People in the Hospital*
> *Service Area*   Equation 5-2

Substituting Equation 5-2 for admissions in Equation 5-1, allows us to develop a cause and effect forecast model:

> PD_f *= ALOS × (Hospital Admission Rate per 1,000 people ×*
> *the Number of People in the Hospital's*
> *Service Area)*   Equation 5-3

In this model, PD_f is the dependent variable. (Its value is dependent upon the causal factors included in the model.) It will take on values based upon the mathematical interaction of the independent variables. It is the model's "effect." The ALOS, hospital admission rate per 1000 people, and the number of people in the hospital service area are all independent variables, or "causes." These are considered independent because their individual values are not affected by the value of the dependent variable. In other words, the forecasted number of patient days will not affect ALOS. (In contrast, however, the value of ALOS will affect the forecasted number of patient days.) Here let us estimate the hospital patient days using an estimated hospital admission rate of 118 patients per thousand population, a base population of 250,000, and an ALOS of 5 days. Doing so, calculate:

$$PD_f = \text{ALOS} \times \text{(Hospital Admission Rate per 1000 people} \times$$
the Number of People in the Hospital's Service Area
per 1,000 people)   Equation 5-3
$$= 5.0 \times (118 \times 250)$$
$$= 5.0 \times 29{,}500$$
$$= 147{,}500 \text{ patient days}$$

In this example, the hospital admission rate per 1000 was estimated based upon known characteristics of the population. The number of people in the hospital's service area was also estimated using known census data and knowledge of patient origin. Here, each independent variable in the model could be quantified and used to solve for the number of patient days. Usually the dependent variable is to the left of the equal sign in any equation and the independent variables are to the right of the equal sign. This is sometimes also called *equational modeling*, and is the foundation for regression modeling, which is covered in Chapter 7.

Sensitivity Analysis

As in the previous example, the cause-and-effect forecast often must be based on estimates of some kind. In this example, estimates of population in the hospital's service area were calculated. However, these estimates may be off. To address this, you may wish to conduct the analysis using more than one estimate of future population. This is called a *sensitivity analysis*. Sensitivity analysis provides the manager with the ability to examine the cause-and-effect relationship while determining the impact a change in one or more independent variables will have upon the dependent variable.

Using the previous model involving hospital patient days and an estimated hospital admission rate of 118 patients per thousand population, with a base population of 250,000 and an ALOS of 5 days, we projected 147,500 patient days. However, if we estimate the population to be 10% less than the previous estimate $(250000 + (250000 \times 0.1) = 225000)$, that our ALOS also decreased by 10% to 4.5 days, and that our admission rate will decrease 10% to 106.2 admissions per thousand, then our new forecast would be:

$$= 4.5 \times (106.2 \times 225)$$
$$= 4.5 \times 23,895$$
$$= 107,527.5 \text{ patient days}$$

This represents a 27% decrease in the forecasted number of patient days from the original estimate.

Sensitivity analysis examines multiple "what if" questions to determine which variable in the model has the most power to change the overall answer or forecast. It is also used to determine the overall effect of changes in specific variables. For example, in the previous example, the value of each variable was adjusted downward by 10%. The overall effect of those adjustments was a 27% decrease in the forecasted number of patient days. In reality, any or all of the variables could be adjusted, something that healthcare managers must take care to do thoughtfully.

Using Epidemiology in Forecasting:

Epidemiology produces many rates that can be incorporated into various types of forecasting methods. Epidemiologic information is critical whenever the manager or policy analyst is required to forecast the need for health and medical care. Epidemiology is usually considered the science that describes and analyzes the need for health and medical care. It is usually defined as the distribution and determinants of health related events (HREs) in human populations. If managers or policy analysts know who has disease, injuries, pregnancies, etc. and the risk factors associated with these, they can accurately design service systems to either treat HREs or prevent them through risk reduction.

Forecasting with use rates appears simple, but requires a high degree of caution because of changes in the population over time, especially with respect to age and socioeconomic status. Rates include:

- Birth rate
- Fertility
- Mortality rate
  - Crude death rate
  - Cause of specific mortality rate
  - Infant death rate and other age-specific rate
- Morbidity rate
  - Incidence rate
  - Prevalence rate

Examples of the application of several of these rates are found in Chapter 15 in the context of strategic planning. At this point it is important to realize that whenever epidemiologic rates are used to forecast, care must be taken to adjust the rates so that approximate equality is achieved in demographic variables involving age, gender, race, income, and other factors thought to have a significant influence on death and disease. For example, if the national crude annual death rate was 8.7 deaths per 1000 people, this rate could not be applied to a specific community or market area until it was adjusted or modified based upon demographic variables. The demographic variables used to calculate the national rate must be matched with the demographic variables in the population being forecasted. If the average age in the nation is 35 and the average age in a specific community is 28, using the national average of 8.7 deaths per 1000 people would grossly overestimate the number of anticipated deaths because of the age discrepancy between the national rate and the demographic composition of the specific community. Rates must be age adjusted.

Adjusting rates to match demographic variables is a challenge when use rates are used in forecasting. National use rates also include utilization rates of health and medical services. Examples include:

- Hospital discharges per 100 or 1000 people
- Average length of stay
- Rate of hospital occupancy
- Average daily census of hospitals
- Average number of visits to a physician's office per year per person

Again, whenever rates are used, the demographic characteristics represented in the national rate must be matched with the equivalent demographic characteristic in the population being forecasted. It is also important to consider that use rates themselves change over time, they are not static.

LEARNING OBJECTIVE 4: TO DESCRIBE THE LIMITATIONS OF FORECASTING AND THE CHALLENGES FORECASTING PRESENTS TO THE HEALTH SERVICES MANAGER

Forecasting is an attempt to predict the future, the unknowable. In this sense it is much akin to guessing. And like guessing, there are levels of reasoning about any prediction. Data and information about the past and about known relationships among variables can help inform reasoning, and forecasting can be approached systematically and thoughtfully. In this sense forecasting is scientific; it is governed by rules and conventions. Being proficient at forecasting requires a sound understanding of these rules and conventions and how to use them. Developing a forecast that minimizes systematic error requires a high level of proficiency and judgment as well as common sense. Thus, forecasting is also an art form. Science is unable to provide health services managers with explicit rules to govern these judgmental aspects of forecasting. Experience and organizational convention, however, help to develop the ability of the manager to use forecasting as an art.

Just doing the math correctly does not always make for a good forecast. Inputting data and using software programs to engage forecasting functions are important and convenient steps to analysis. However, it is the preparation of the forecasts, the assumptions made about the estimates, and the collection of the data that distinguish the accuracy of these methods. It is the responsibility of the manager to minimize errors in forecasting. The primary test of any forecast is whether it has minimized the systematic error. Often, managers forecast using multiple techniques to determine which forecast provides the least error using historical data. Each and every forecast should teach the manager something. Expert forecasters use multiple methods and continue to ask themselves what each method has taught them about the overall forecast as well as the phenomenon under study.

The number one rule of forecasting is to *always plot the data on a graph*. If the assignment is to forecast the number of inpatient admissions or clinic visits, plot any and all historical data. Plot the variables that might influence them. This will illustrate any association that might exist and can assist the manager is developing the appropriate forecast.

Examine Figure 5-2. Here the manager has plotted the data and then used three different techniques to forecast into the future. Each utilized a different technique, covered in the following chapters, based upon the foundation of the past predicting

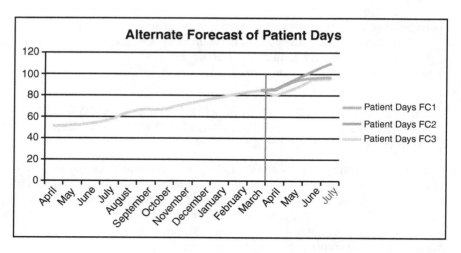

Figure 5-2 Alternate Forecast of Patient Days

the future to arrive at a forecasted number of patient days. The reason for doing this is to attempt to minimize the systematic error. To do this, they would *forecast the past*, or use known historical data as a basis to examine how accurately each method compared with what actually occurred. Similar answers using different methods should add some confidence. Very different answers using different methods should suggest the existence of method bias—one or both methods are biasing the forecast based upon some inherent assumption and should force the manager to proceed with caution. When faced with the need for a forecast, use as many methods as possible.

Analytic forecasting does involve mathematics. If forecasting were just math, however, then mathematicians and actuaries—not managers—would prepare forecasts. Forecasting requires that managers know their data. A classic example in which this is relevant to health services managers involves the use of months in forecasting. Sometimes it is important of realize that months have a different number of days. For example, February usually has 28 days; March has 31 days. Also be aware that different months have different numbers of weekdays as well as Saturdays and Sundays. Sometimes the different numbers of days by month and the ratio of weekdays to weekend days can have a strong impact on what is being forecasted. For example, July 2008 had 31 days, of which 23 were weekdays and 8 were weekend days. In contrast, March 2008 had 31 days, of which 21 were weekdays and 10 were weekend days. These types of minor changes in the number and type of days per month can create artificial variation in data that can be minimized. Managers are responsible for knowing their data and making adjustments as needed.

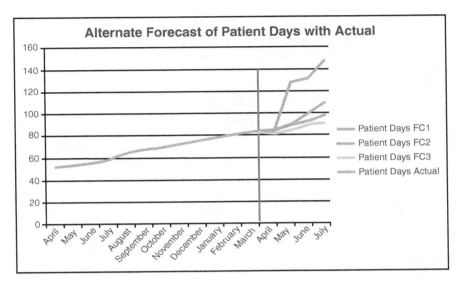

Figure 5-3 Alternate Forecast of Patient Days with Actual

Forecasting also requires knowledge of the phenomena being forecasted. This includes knowing how one variable drives another. Any form of forecasting is a reasoned judgment made by a manager after a series of thoughtful considerations. Examine Figure 5-3, which presents a possible scenario for what could actually occur with respect to future patient days. In this example, none of the three forecasts accurately predicted what was to occur. There could be many reasons for this. One could be that the spike in volume was simply owing to random chance. This is random error, and no amount of analytic consideration will help adjust for it. However, it is more likely that the jump in patient days results from some form of cause and effect. Perhaps a large organization relocated a major office with many employees to the area, or perhaps another competing facility ceased or downsized operations. Managers must know their data but also be aware of its context, which is the nature of the work of the organization and the external environment. Managers should be able to choose the appropriate variables to use in cause-and-effect models.

There are also other limitations to forecasting techniques. As stated, managers need to be careful not to extrapolate their forecasts too far into the future. Doing so may overestimate the ability of past trends to continue. The stock market decline of 1989, often termed "Black Monday," is a good example of how economic conditions that were seemingly powerful and upward trending reversed themselves quickly. In this example, future predictions based on near term historic data would have proved inaccurate. However, those that looked at the underlying trend beyond the cyclical ups and downs of the market would have served investors more responsibly.

In the final analysis, managers are responsible for their forecasts. The future, not the manipulation of formulae, will indicate whether the forecast was accurate. When asked to prepare a forecast, managers are expected to use recognized methods and generate forecasts that are logical and reasonable given the state of existing knowledge and data. If, in the future, it is found that the forecast was highly inaccurate but reasonable, given the available information possessed at the time the forecast was prepared, most organizations will understand the high degree of inaccuracy. If, however, in the future, a forecast was found to be highly inaccurate because the manager failed to consider certain information, or methods, then it may be appropriate to question the competence of the manager.

The following questions should be considered when forecasting:

1. What (variable) is being forecasted?
2. What answers are needed from the forecast?
3. What variable(s) is/are associated with the variable being forecasted?
4. What information is available or will be needed to be made available on these variables?
5. What is known about the relationships regarding the phenomena being forecasted?
6. To what degree are the variables associated (i.e., correlated)?
7. How far into the future does the forecast need to go?

SUMMARY

This chapter provides an introduction to forecasting and how it is used in health services administration. Forecasting is one of the primary tools used by managers to plan for how organizations will position themselves and operate in the near and long term. It can be used to predict volume of services, supply of inventories, and salary expense, make revenue projections, and much more.

Forecasting is also both an art and a science. There are many different methodologies that can be employed to forecast. The two primary types of forecasting are analytic and nonanalytic. Nonanalytic forecasting consists of judgment, genius, or expert forecasting. This method relies on personal knowledge and individual experience to predict the future. Although intuitive in nature, this method is also less analytic and more susceptible to systematic error. Analytic forecasting can include a number of mathematically based techniques that rest on one of two assumptions: The past predicts the future, and cause-and-effect relationships between operational and environmental variables. Predicting the future from the past is a method that is most often used in forecasting, and requires examining visual and mathematical trends in the data to extrapolate into the future. Although these are explained in the next two chapters, this requires putting values or weights on the data, both in terms of how much to value the past relative to the future, and also how to consider the relationship, or correlation between two or more variables.

Managers are also encouraged to use multiple techniques on historical data to examine which technique is more accurate at predicting what actually occurred. This is a process of minimizing the systematic error of the forecasting model. Utilizing sensitivity analysis and confidence intervals can help to create an understanding of the potential impact of the assumptions made and to place limits around your predictions. Managers also need to be cautioned, in that all forecasts have their limitations. The amount of historical data to consider, the length of time into the future one predicts, and unforeseen events can all affect the accuracy of any forecast. At best, forecasting is a gamble, a guess. However, by using proven analytic methods and sound reasoning, a good health services manager can provide a thoughtful forecast within a scope of confidence. What is important is that any forecast be done comprehensively and transparently.

EXERCISES

5-1 Indicate the different ways an individual could forecast his or her weight 10 years from now. Do these methods change based upon whether the individual is 5, 14, 24, or 45 years old? If so, why?

5-2 Using the assumption of the past predicts the future write an equation for the weight forecast. Do the same for the assumption of cause and effect. How does the concept of error play into each?

5-3 Provide examples from the field of health services management of phenomena that are probably best forecasted using genius forecasting. Why?

5-4 Determine the number of weekdays and weekend days in this month? Compare this with the equivalent numbers for next year and last year. What phenomenon forecasted by the health services manager might be influenced by variation in the number and types of days in a month? Be specific and cite examples.

5-5 Calculate the expected number of infants needing neonatal intensive care in a hospital if the historic rate is 5 per 1000 births, and you expect 575 births this year.

5-6 If the annual death rate from smoking is 154 deaths per 100,000 persons, and the annual death rate from firearms is 13.5 deaths per 100,000 persons, how many deaths from these causes would you expect in a community of 1 million people?

Chapter 6

Trend Forecasting Techniques

LEARNING OBJECTIVES

1. To examine the role of time intervals in forecasting models.
2. To examine guidelines for length of future forecasts.
3. To understand forecasting based on average change, average percent change, and confidence intervals.
4. To understand weighted forecasting models by using moving averages.
5. To understand weighted forecasting models by using exponential smoothing.
6. To be able to select between forecasting models based upon the calculated mean absolute deviation (MAD).

REAL WORLD SCENARIO

Molly Adel has determined that a mathematically derived forecasting model is preferable for her management needs. She is primarily interested in staffing and resource needs for the coming 12 months and has collected visit volume to Northern College Health Services by month for the past 60 months, shown in Appendix 6-A. After discussions with the admissions office, they do not predict any stark increases in applications or enrollment to the college; however, this is only a short-range projection, as the cost of other schools' tuition, the availability of financial aid, and any necessary tuition increases will affect enrollment to the college, and thus demand for health services resources. She is also uncertain how useful data from 5 years ago are to projecting volume into the future as the student population has grown and services have changed in that time. Ms. Adel wants to be sure that her forecast is accurate enough to project resource needs into the future, but also flexible enough to anticipate changes in the external environment.

The methods that are described in this chapter are based upon the assumption that the past (and present) can predict the future. Some refer to these models and techniques as naive models in the sense that they only recognize and incorporate the past (and current) state into a forecast. They are naive as to the potential for small or major changes in the contexts that gave rise to the forecasts. In our real world example this might include a dramatic and unexpected enrollment into the college that results in an influx of students seeking care.

Being naive does not make these models inappropriate to use in forecasting. Usually, naive models are used when detailed information on the near past is available and the need is to forecast the near future. For these purposes they can be quite effective. Caution, however, must be taken when extending these forecasts too far into the future, or relying too heavily on past data. Careful consideration should also be given to any trends within historical data, such as seasonality factors, and adjustments made when forecasting ahead.

LEARNING OBJECTIVE 1: EXAMINE THE IMPORTANCE OF TIME INTERVALS IN FORECASTING

Time intervals define forecasts. It is essential that forecasts be prepared in the same time interval as the historical data. For example, if the historical data are expressed in weeks, the forecast should be expressed in weeks. If the historical data are expressed in years, the forecast should be expressed in years and not in months, weeks, or days. In contrast, if the historical data are expressed in days, it is acceptable to express a forecast in a larger time interval such as weeks, months, or years.

Assessing trends within time intervals is also essential. The primary goal of any forecast is to minimize the systematic error associated with the forecast. Some of this excess error can be minimized by critically examining the historical data and determining whether the time intervals are useful for future prediction. For example, if Ms. Adel would like to forecast the number of visits to the Urgent Care Clinic at Northern College Health Services for the month of September, she must determine if the number of visits that occurred in June, July, and August should be used in the forecast. Given that the student population in these summer months is very different than the student population in September, when many more students are back on campus, it may not be prudent to include only these months in her forecast.

In this example, previous Septembers are likely to have greater predictive power when forecasting the next September. In other words, June, July, and August are not equal to September in the sense that the phenomenon being forecasted (e.g., clinic visits) is fundamentally different in these summer months than in September, October, or November, when the campus is fully populated. Thus, the forecast is dependent upon a seasonal trend.

Using equal time intervals can also refer to the length of the time interval. Some months have a different number of weekdays and weekend days, and unequal number of days. In some situations, failure to recognize this may artificially distort the forecast.

Further, a day may not be a day. The number of clinic visits may (naturally) vary by day of the week. For example, the Urgent Care Clinic may be closed Saturdays and Sundays, or have shorter hours on weekend days than on a weekday. Utilization may be higher on certain days of the week, especially those days after a day the clinic was closed, such as a Monday. Although any forecast will have some degree of time interval distance, the challenge is to minimize the excess error in the forecast and achieve time intervals that are as equal as possible.

LEARNING OBJECTIVE 2: EXAMINE GUIDELINES FOR LENGTH OF FUTURE FORECAST

The first guiding principle of forecasting is to always plot the data. Doing so with the historical data provided by Ms. Adel would quickly reveal the seasonal downtrend that occurs during the months of June, July, and August.

Visually examining the data can show linear trends in the data, be they positive or negative. It can also provide clues to underlying trends and historical spikes or declines in the trend that can provide signal points to managers for investigation when possible. Perhaps the change was a one-time shock that could not be anticipated, or perhaps it is an event that reoccurs systematically over time, such as the review of reimbursement

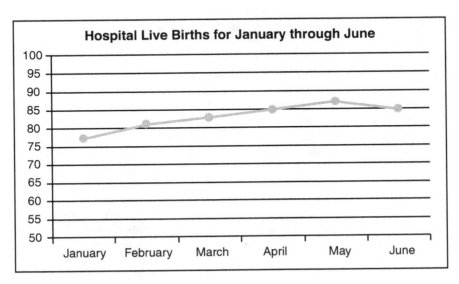

Figure 6-1 Hospital Live Births for January through June Graph

policy, legislative review, or administrative policy. When plotting the data, the x-axis is used to plot time and the y-axis is used to plot the variable of interest.

Second, the length of the forecast should generally not exceed one third the length of the historical data. If 24 months of historical data are being used, then the forecast should be no longer than 8 months, or one third of 24. If 6 weeks of historical data exist, the forecast should be no longer than 2 weeks into the future. This is a convention provided as a guide, not as a rule. It is important that the length of the forecast be appropriate given the historical data. Forecasting the next 5 to 10 years based upon 2 or 3 months of past data, regardless of the approach used, would be inappropriate.

Another guiding principle of forecasting is to be conservative. Being conservative requires an understanding of what is being forecasted, and how important the estimate is to the organization. It is important to know whether it is worse to be 10% or 20% high or 10% or 20% low with a forecast. For example, it is better to provide a high forecast for a hospital's need for blood as a stock out condition is medically unacceptable and compromises the health of patients. Conversely, it is better to provide a low forecast for the number of hospital inpatient days because that forecast is used to establish budgets and it is usually easier to add temporary staff than reduce core staff. Forecasts should be sensitive to the positive and negative implications associated with being high or low from the actual. Some forecasting techniques permit the calculation of the standard deviation and thus confidence interval associated with the forecast. As stated in Chapter 2, 1.96 standard deviations above and below the forecasted mean provides a 95% confidence interval of where the actual future value will fall. In some instances, setting the forecast to 1.96 standard deviations above the mean will provide a conservative forecast. Other times, setting the forecast to 1.96 standard deviations below the forecasted mean may be more conservative. Sometimes calling the forecast at the 50% level (forecasted mean) also is the conservative approach. In this chapter we will give examples of each. Again, knowing the implications of being high or low with a forecast is essential to an accurate and effective forecast.

A final guiding principle is that forecasts should be transparent. This means that all assumptions as well as calculations used in any forecasting technique should be clearly stated and replicable. If a manager provides a forecast that weights the data based more on current observations than historical ones, this, as well as the degree of weighting applied should be provided with the forecast. This is especially important when forecasting methods are reviewed by others, be they higher level managers or boards of directors, who will want to be able to make comments and/or approvals based on the methods used. Being transparent allows the manager to both solicit helpful input on forecasting techniques, but also ensures that if some unanticipated event should occur, the assumptions and process used to forecast were open and understood.

LEARNING OBJECTIVE 3: TO UNDERSTAND FORECASTING BASED ON AVERAGE CHANGE, AVERAGE PERCENT CHANGE, AND CONFIDENCE INTERVALS

Time series techniques identify a historical trend and base the forecast upon extending this trend into the future. At least three approaches can be used to do this: (1) Extrapolation based upon Average Change, (2) Extrapolation based upon a Confidence Interval, and (3) Extrapolation based upon Average Percent Change. For this section examine the data in Table 6-1.

Before using any mathematical technique, the data must be plotted. Examining Figure 6-1, the data plot or cloud of data suggests a linear relationship with a mostly positive slope. However, visits do drop somewhat in June. One method to extend or extrapolate this historical trend to forecast the number of births for July would be to use a ruler to draw a straight line that "best fit" the historical data plot. This would entail attempting to draw a line that is centered among the data points. Doing so, however, is prone to error unless the line is mathematically derived, which we explore in Chapter 7. The methods described here, however, provide more systematic methods for forecasting these data.

If the data plot looks random, or like a circular cloud of data without any evident linear relationship, one should decompose the time series data. This means examining groupings of the data in pieces and then regrouping it. For example, multiple years of Januarys, multiple years of Februarys, and so forth can be examined to see if this method of plotting the data presents a different image of the data. Also try composing the data by adding months together to create quarters (3-month periods), or group data by days, weeks, months, or

Table 6-1 Hospital Live Births for January through June

Month	Number of births
January	77
February	81
March	83
April	85
May	87
June	85
Total	498
Average	83

any other relevant time period to the organization or external environment. As manager you must attempt to construct the data in a manner that will best lend itself to forecasting.

Extrapolation Based upon Average Change

This approach to forecasting requires examining the month-to-month change that occurs in the data. Table 6-2 includes the month-to-month changes in the data and then computes the average of these changes. Note that month-to-month change is calculated in whole terms, and not the absolute value of the change. Once the average of the month-to-month change has been derived, a forecast of births for June can be prepared. The basis for this forecast is the mean or average level of births experienced over the history of the available data. This approach insures that no single value artificially distorts the forecast.

Using average change also requires that the midpoint of the data be identified. For this example, the midpoint of the data is 3.5, or the data point between the third and fourth data points. To determine the midpoint, a series of steps and a simple formula are used. For an odd number of data points, the midpoint is the number of data points (n) divided by 2 $(n / 2)$. For an even number of data points, the formula becomes $(n + 1)/2$.

For this example, the midpoint of the data distribution is $(6 + 1)/2 = 3.5$. If the example had seven months of data, the midpoint would be $7 + 1$ or 8 divided by $2 = 4$.

Table 6-2 Month to Month Change in Hospital Live Births January through June

Month	Number of births	Change from previous month
January	77	
February	81	4
March	83	2
April	85	2
May	87	2
June	85	−2
Total	498	8
Ave	83	1.6
Md. Pt.		3.5
Forecast for July = 83 + (3.5 × 1.6) =		**88.6**

Extrapolation based on average change uses the following equation:

> Forecast month (FM) = Average of the data +
>   (Midpoint × Average Change)   Equation 6-1

For this example, the average of the data = 83 births per month, the midpoint = 3.5, and the average change = 1.6 births.

Therefore our formula becomes:

$$FM = 83 + (3.5 \times 1.6)$$
$$= 83 + 5.6$$
$$= 88.6$$

Extrapolation Based upon Using Average Percent Change

Extrapolation based on average percent change builds upon that based on average change by calculating the percent change in births from month to month. Table 6-3 revises the data to include the percent change in births from month to month. A common mistake in calculating the percentage change is juxtaposing the numerator and denominator. A rule of thumb when dealing with time series data is to remember to take the change between time periods (future − past/past). We can also take the

Table 6-3 Percent Change in Hospital Live Births January through June

Month	Number of births	Change from previous month	% Change
Jan	77	—	—
Feb	81	4	5.19%
Mar	83	2	2.47%
Apr	85	2	2.41%
May	87	2	2.35%
Jun	85	−2	−2.30%
Sum	498	8	10.13%
Ave	83	1.6	**2.03%**
Forecast for July = 85 + (85 × .0203) =			**86.73**

change from month to month first (future − past) and then divide that by the most recent past time period.

Having determined that the average percent change per month is 2.03%, we use the formula of:

$$FM = \text{Most Recent Month} + (\text{Average Percent Change} \times \text{Most Recent Month}) \qquad \text{Equation 6-2}$$

July forecast = June value + (2.03% of June value)
                = 85 + (85 × 0.0203)
                = 85 + 1.726
                = 86.73 or 87 births rounded into real terms,
                  as there is no such thing as 0.73 of a birth.

Extrapolation Based on a Confidence Interval

As the name implies, this method uses a confidence interval to forecast. It is important to remember that 1.96 standard deviations above and below the mean represents a 95% confidence interval. Revisit Chapter 2 for a more detailed discussion. A forecast based upon this method can be 95% confident that the actual number of future births will be included in this interval. The benefit to constructing a confidence interval forecast is that you can be more confident in your ability to accurately forecast the future period within a range. The caution is that as your confidence level increases, the accuracy with which you can predict lessens. This is the fundamental nature of confidence intervals in that as confidence increases, so does the size of the interval. It is possible to construct a 100% confidence interval, which is simply the entire range of possible values. As the interval narrows, the level of confidence drops.

Using confidence intervals as forecasts becomes helpful to the manager in a number of ways. One is when precision is not the primary motivation for forecasting. If, for example, the manager wishes to forecast visit volume for staffing purposes, knowing that at each level of staffing (e.g., adding one additional staffing unit) allows for moderate flexibility in volume to be handled. Thus a team of one physician's assistant, one nurse, and one physician can see between 1 and 20 visits, but adding another physician's assistant increases that volume to 35. If the manager forecasts using a confidence interval for the coming month and finds the interval to be 21 to 34 visits, she can accurately construct an adequate staffing plan. Another value confidence intervals provide is when they are analyzed within the context of the other forms of forecasting, which is explored later in the chapter.

To use confidence interval forecasting as an approach, the standard deviation and/or standard error is used. If the historical data represent the population of all data and not a sample, the standard deviation can be used. If, however, the historical data are

Table 6-4 Extrapolation Based on a 95% Confidence Interval

Month	Number of births		
Jan	77	**Ave**	83
Feb	81	**Std. Dev.**	3.27
Mar	83	**95% C.I.**	
Apr	85	*Upper = 83 + (1.96 × 3.27)*	
May	87	**89.41**	
Jun	85	*Lower = 83 − (1.96 × 3.27)*	
Sum	**498**	**76.59**	

Forecast for July = (89 − 77) rounded with 95% level of confidence

only a sample of data, the standard error is used, which is simply the standard deviation divided by the square root of n. An example of a sample of historical data would be in attempting to develop a forecast of future births for all hospitals on a state based on only a sample of data from select hospitals. If the forecast is for just one hospital using that hospital's data, the standard deviation will suffice. A more complete description of calculating the standard deviation as well as standard error appears in Chapter 2.

Table 6-4 shows the calculation for extrapolation based on a 95% confidence interval. For example, note that one standard deviation = 3.27 births and that 1.96 standard deviations (the 95% Confidence Interval) = 1.96 × 3.27 = 6.41 births. For the example, the 95% confidence interval is the mean ± 1.96 standard deviations or 83 ± 6.41 or 83 + 6.41 = 89.41 births and 83 − 6.41 = 76.59 births. This provides a forecasted number of births for July based on a 95% level of confidence between 89.41 and 76.59 births or 89 and 77 births rounded into whole terms. The standard error could also be used if data were assumed to be from a sample.

Comparing Extrapolation Techniques

At this point it is important to compare the different forecasting methods for July births given the available data and using the different approaches (Table 6-5).

Although each technique yields a different estimate, collectively the techniques provide sufficient information to venture a forecast. Choosing a technique is not an attempt to determine which provides the correct forecast for the next time frame. Each technique or method provides a "right" answer. These forecasts provide the manager with comparisons and options to select a forecast.

Table 6-5 Comparison of Extrapolation Techniques

Technique	July Forecast
Extrapolation based upon Average Change	87
Extrapolation based upon Average Percent Change	89
Extrapolation based upon 95% Confidence Interval	77–89

Forecasting requires judgment, not just the ability to solve mathematical formula. That is, forecasting is an art as well as a science.

In retrospect, each of these basic methods is based upon different properties of the data used in the forecast. Each assumes a certain degree of linearity in the data and an inherent relationship between time (as the independent variable) and births (as the dependent variable) that has a positive or negative slope. For example, the level of births forecasted for July, in one instance 89, is higher than the actual number of births recorded for June (i.e., 85).

Although helpful in forecasting, these three techniques may be too simple for most applications. These techniques mask variability in the data. In the example used, some of this natural variability is based upon a different number of days per month. These methods also distill the data using the average or average percent change calculations. Except for the confidence interval approach, each method assumes that the forecast will be based on the theoretical line that best represents the past data. Therefore these methods are offered as a starting point for forecasting, not as definitive methods that can be relied upon exclusively to provide a relevant forecast.

LEARNING OBJECTIVE 4: TO UNDERSTAND FORECASTING BASED ON A MOVING AVERAGE

Because historical data often vary, sometimes considerably, it is often helpful to utilize a technique that does not tend to mask the inherent variability of the data, as do the methods described thus far. Moving averages correct for this and provide a method to examine the variability in data and use this pattern of variability in constructing a forecast.

To demonstrate moving averages the data in Table 6-1 have been revised by adding more historical data (July to December) and changing one of the original historical data points (March from 83 to 63). These data are restated in Table 6-6.

Table 6-6 Hospital Live Births for January through June

Month	Number of births
July	68
August	79
September	81
October	55
November	71
December	60
January	77
February	81
March	63
April	85
May	87
June	85
Total	478
Average	79.67

Figure 6-2 is the plot of the data included in Table 6-6. Note that the scale used in this historical data plot has been selected to magnify the variability of the historical data.

Using a moving (time period to time period) average to forecast is a method that first examines the variability in the historical data and then provides the ability to mathematically "smooth or soften" the historical variability in search of a master or underlying trend. The first operation is to choose some time period over which to calculate the moving average. This we will term our n-time period. Here, n can represent a number of time periods, such as a 2-month ($n = 2$), 3-month ($n = 3$), 4-month ($n = 4$), or any n we choose given the availability of historical data. The steps to developing a moving average forecast are:

1. Select an n (n must be greater than 1). Because 12 months of historical data are included in Table 6-6, n could be 2, 3, 4, 5, or 6. To begin, $n = 2$ has been selected.
2. Calculate the n-period moving average. To do this, start with the oldest data and work forward. For example, the forecast for September, using a 2-month moving average, is (July + August)/2. The forecast for October, using a 2-month moving average, is (August + September)/2.

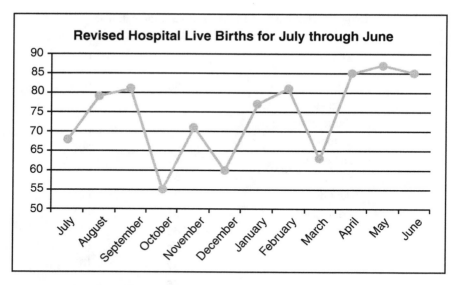

Figure 6-2 Revised Hospital Live Births for July through June

To calculate the *n*-period moving average, take the number (*n*) of months preceding the month to be forecast, add them, and then divide by *n*. The 2-month (*n* = 2) or two-period moving average for July is (87 (May) + 85 (June))/2 = 86.

The 4-month (*n* = 4) moving average for July is (63 (March) + 85 (April) + 87 (May) + 85 (June))/4 = 80. The 6-month moving average for July is calculated as:

$$\text{July moving average} = \frac{(\text{Jan.} + \text{Feb.} + \text{Mar.} + \text{Apr.} + \text{May} + \text{Jun.})}{6}$$

$$= \frac{(77 + 81 + 63 + 85 + 87 + 85)}{6}$$

$$= \frac{478}{6}$$

$$= 79.6 \text{ or } 80$$

Table 6-7 shows moving average calculations for each value of *n*.

The next operation involves selecting the "best" *n* to use in the moving average forecasting model. To do this, we need to determine how effective our forecasting methods are. Although we cannot know what the future will actually be, we do have historical data. Moving averages allow us to go back and forecast what has already occurred using historical data. Table 6-7 shows the *n* = 2, 3, 4, 5, and 6 moving averages for the historical data. Now that we have both the actual historical data and a forecast based on some *n*-months, we can examine the

Table 6-7 Birth Data with Moving Average Calculations for $n = 2, 3, 4, 5,$ and 6

Month	Number of births	$n = 2$	$n = 3$	$n = 4$	$n = 5$	$n = 6$
July	68					
August	79					
September	81	73.50				
October	55	80.00	76.00			
November	71	68.00	71.67	70.75		
December	60	63.00	69.00	71.50	70.80	
January	77	65.50	62.00	66.75	69.20	69.00
February	81	68.50	69.33	65.75	68.80	70.50
March	63	79.00	72.67	72.25	68.80	70.83
April	85	72.00	73.67	70.25	70.40	67.83
May	87	74.00	76.33	76.50	73.20	72.83
June	85	86.00	78.33	79.00	78.60	75.50
Total	892					

accuracy of those forecasts by calculating the forecast error (FE). If F = forecasted number of births for a month and A = actual number of births for the month, then FE = (A − F).

Table 6-8 compares moving averages for the data included on Table 6-7 with the added FE values. Because we are simply interested in how accurate our forecasting method was, our forecast error is taken in absolute terms, or by taking the absolute value of the FE. Doing so shows how far off each forecast for that month is, either positive or negative, in total. The FE gives us a month-by-month picture of variation in the data, and also allows us to calculate both the total, or absolute deviation, and the average, or mean absolute deviation.

The absolute deviation (AD) is calculated by summing the FE columns. The mean absolute deviation (MAD) is calculated by dividing the AD by the number of FE calculations, or by taking the average of the FE column. The "best" interval n is selected based upon the minimum MAD value, which is simply the overall forecast that predicted the historical data with the minimum amount of error. Table 6-9 summarizes the MAD values for each n.

Based upon the example and the calculation of the MAD, $n = 4$ (4-month moving average) should be selected as the best method to use. When $n = 4$, MAD was at

Table 6-8 Moving Averages Forecast Including Forecast Error (FE), and Mean Absolute Deviation (MAD)

Month	Number of births	n = 2		n = 3		n = 4		n = 5		n = 6	
		Mov Ave	Fe	Mov Ave	Fe	Mov Ave	Fe	Mov Ave	Fe	Mov Ave	Fe
July	68										
August	79										
September	81	73.50	7.50								
October	55	80.00	25.00	76.00	21.00						
November	71	68.00	3.00	71.67	0.67	70.75	0.25				
December	60	63.00	3.00	69.00	9.00	71.50	11.50	70.80	10.80		
January	77	65.50	11.50	62.00	15.00	66.75	10.25	69.20	7.80	69.00	8.00
February	81	68.50	12.50	69.33	11.67	65.75	15.25	68.80	12.20	70.50	10.50
March	63	79.00	16.00	72.67	9.67	72.25	9.25	68.80	5.80	70.83	7.83
April	85	72.00	13.00	73.67	11.33	70.25	14.75	70.40	14.60	67.83	17.17
May	87	74.00	13.00	76.33	10.67	76.50	10.50	73.20	13.80	72.83	14.17
June	85	86.00	1.00	78.33	6.67	79.00	6.00	78.60	6.40	75.50	9.50
AD			105.50		95.67		77.75		71.40		67.17
MAD			*10.55*		*10.63*		*9.72*		*10.20*		*11.19*

Table 6-9 Moving Averages Mean Absolute Deviation
(MAD) Comparison

$n = 2$	10.55
$n = 3$	10.63
$n = 4$	*9.72*
$n = 5$	10.20
$n = 6$	11.19

the minimum of 9.72. This indicates that the 4-month moving average, in contrast to the 2-, 3-, 5-, or 6-month moving averages, best minimizes the variation in the historical data and is the recommended moving average to use for forecasting. To forecast the month of July, the previous 4 months of values would be averaged (those for March, April, May, and June).

Once a specific month is forecasted (e.g., July = 80), insert it in the "actual" column on the worksheet and continue to calculate the moving average as shown in Table 6-10. Note, however, that the forecast becomes dampened as it moves forward. This means the forecast is likely to be further from the actual (i.e., observed) value as it extended further into the future.

Once the forecast is extended beyond the selected n, in this case 4, the entire forecast is based upon calculated, not observed values. Therefore, a general convention when using moving averages is that forecasts must include at least one actual data point. For example, with an $n = 4$, we would project only three periods into the future.

Moving averages provide the ability to recognize the variability in time series data and use the pattern of variability to construct an appropriate forecast. Unlike previous methods, moving averages also provide the ability to extend the forecast many time intervals into the future, depending on the number of historical months used in averaging.

A Note on Time Periods

Before covering additional techniques, it is appropriate to clarify some terms regarding time periods. As has been demonstrated in the examples, all extrapolation models rely upon the past to forecast into the future. They are all naive models. In this type of calculation, the present is a point or moment in time (e.g., 12:00 PM on December 31, 2009), not a period of time such as day, week, month, or year. In

Table 6-10 Forecast Using $n = 4$ Moving Average

Month	Births	Moving Average for $n = 4$
July	68	
August	79	
September	81	
October	55	
November	71	70.75
December	60	71.50
January	77	66.75
February	81	65.75
March	63	72.25
April	85	70.25
May	87	76.50
June	85	79.00
July	**80.00**	**80.00**
August	**84.25**	**84.25**
September	**84.06**	**84.06**
October	**83.33**	**83.33**
November*	**82.91**	**82.91**

*Forecast is based on all forecasted values

contrast, the future and the past are time periods. To describe the time intervals in forecasts, consider the following scale:

$$t_{-n}\ldots\ldots t_{-5}, t_{-4}, t_{-3}, t_{-2}, t_{-1}, t_0, t_1, t_2, t_3, t_4, t_5\ldots t_n$$

where

$t_0 =$ the present as a point in time
$t_{-n} =$ the oldest time period in the historical data
$t_n =$ the furthest time period in the future (away from the present) in the forecast

Many forecasting models utilize this type of time interval notation. It provides the ability to acknowledge the difference between the present—a point in time—and the past and future—intervals of time

LEARNING OBJECTIVE 5: UNDERSTANDING WEIGHTED FORECASTING MODELS USING EXPONENTIAL SMOOTHING

Examination of the data in Table 6-6 shows that the numbers of births start at 68 births in July and end with 85 births in June. The data suggest that the future will more likely involve numbers toward the higher levels (i.e., 90), than lower numbers (i.e., 68). In other words, it seems appropriate to base a forecast more on the most recent data than on the older data if some type of linear trend is believed to exist. Exponential smoothing provides a technique to take these types of considerations into account. To smooth, and thereby minimize the effect of this fluctuation in the forecast the initial step is to select a smoothing constant (SC). The SC is a weighting factor that influences the degree the forecasted value (F) and the observed value (O) for a past period have relative to one another in calculating the forecast for a future period. The SC must be between 0 and 1.00.

Exponential smoothing uses the following general formula:

$$F = (SC \times O) + ((1 - SC) \times F_{t-1})$$

Where

$$
\begin{aligned}
SC &= \text{ smoothing constant (a number between 1 and 0)} \\
F &= \text{ forecast for next period in the future} \\
O &= \text{ observed value for the last or most recent period} \\
F_{t-1} &= \text{ forecasted value for the last or most recent historical period}
\end{aligned}
$$

This formula indicates that the forecast for the next period will equal the observed value for the most current time period (O) times the smoothing constant (SC) plus the forecast for the most recent historical period (F_{t-1}) times 1 minus the smoothing constant. For example, if a forecast for hospital patient days for this past month (F_{t-1}) was 550 patient days, and the observed (actual) number of patient days (O) was 525, the next month's forecast arbitrarily using a smoothing constant of 0.3 would be:

$$
\begin{aligned}
F &= (SC \times O) + ((1 - SC) \times F_{t-1}) \\
&= (0.3 \times 525) + ((1 - 0.3) \times 550) \\
&= 157.5 + 0.7 \times 550 \\
&= 157.5 + 385 \\
&= 542.5 \text{ patient days}
\end{aligned}
$$

Note that this type of forecast is an expected value based upon a weighted average of two variables, the most recent actual value and a forecast. The SC is a weighting factor that influences the degree to which a forecasted value and the observed value (O) for a past period influence one another in calculating the forecast for a future period. This last example combined 30% (0.30) of the observed value for a previous month with 70% (0.70) of the forecasted value for previous month to calculate the forecast for the future month.

Table 6-11 Forecasting Using Exponential Smoothing

Month	Number of Births	Forecast Value
Smoothing Constant		0.1
July	68	
August	79	68
September	81	69.10
October	55	70.29
November	71	68.76
December	60	68.98
January	77	68.09
February	81	68.98
March	63	70.18
April	85	69.46
May	87	71.02
June	85	72.61

This forecasting technique presents certain challenges. An SC must be determined using systematic methods. This is done in much the same way as it was for moving averages. By using historical data, a forecast can be generated its accuracy determined using the forecast error. By using multiple smoothing constants, the forecast errors,summarized by the mean absolute deviations for each smoothing constant (0.1, 0.3, 0.5, etc...) can be compared and a forecast of minimum error selected, or that which generate the lowest MAD. Table 6-11 presents an exponential smoothing forecast based on the data in Table 6-6 using a smoothing constant of 0.1.

Beginning a forecast based on exponential smoothing requires that there be a value to be used as the next month's first forecast. As can be seen in Table 6-11, this requires using the actual value for the oldest period in the data as the forecast for the next period. To forecast forward, here for September, we apply the following formula:.

Using a smoothing constant of 0.1:

$$
\begin{aligned}
\text{F September} &= (\text{SC} \times \text{O for August}) + ((1 - \text{SC}) \times F_{t-1} \text{ for August} \\
&= (0.10 \times 79) + ((1 - 0.10) \times (68)) \\
&= 7.9 + 61.2 \\
&= 69.1
\end{aligned}
$$

Continuing on:

F October = (SC × O for October) + ((1 − SC) × F_{t-1} (for September))
= (0.1 × 81) + (1 − 0.1 × 69.1)
= 70.29

And so forth.

The next challenge is to select, using an appropriate method, the most appropriate SC. The principle again used is MAD. Table 6-12 shows the forecast values, forecast errors, and MAD for the smoothing constants 0.1, 0.3, 0.5, and 0.7.

The forecast with a smoothing constant of 0.3 yields the lowest MAD (10.68). In contrast, when a smoothing constant of 0.1 was used MAD equaled 11.04. When a smoothing constant of 0.5 was used MAD equaled 10.74. A 0.7 smoothing constant yielded a MAD of 10.98. Based upon the minimum MAD value, a smoothing constant of 0.3 could be used; however, one may perceive that the MAD hits a low point with a smoothing constant of 0.3, but that the MAD for the smoothing constant for 0.5 was not much higher. One might wish to examine gradations of the smoothing constant between 0.3 and 0.5 at this point. Table 6-13 shows this analysis. Examination shows that a smoothing constant of 0.35 produces the lowest MAD with these data.

To forecast July, simply extend the analysis forward using the smoothing constant of 0.35. That is:

F July = (0.35 × 87) + (0.65 × 75.22)
= 79.35

To forecast beyond July, when you are still in June, continue the same approach but substitute the forecasted value for the actual values. This is shown in Table 6-14. You will again notice that the forecasts become dampened as you progress forward in time. A second general convention is used here, and that is that the forecast should not exceed one third of the number of historical months. Given the example with 12 months, a 4-month forecast, including future July, August, September, and October, or one third of the 12 months of historical data, can be justified (see Table 6-14). As the variation in the forecast decreases, the string of numbers will eventually become totally dampened, with the forecasting formula yielding the same answer for each month. Again, this is another reason to use caution and not extend a forecast too far into the future.

When solving for a minimum MAD, a smoothing constant above 0.5 can result. Any time simple exponential smoothing yields a best constant above 0.5, it should be disregarded as a forecast, as too many variations are likely present in the data to be adequately captured with the use of a single smoothing constant. Advanced users are referred to Holt's *Method of Exponential Smoothing with Trends* and Winter's *Method of Exponential Smoothing with Seasonality*. Each of these more advanced approaches introduces multiple smoothing constants into the forecasting model to capture and use these trends in the forecast.

Table 6-12 Forecasting Using Exponential Smoothing

Month	Number of Births	Forecast Value	Forecast Error	Forecast Value	Forecast Error	Forecast Value	Forecast Error	Forecast Value	Forecast Error
Smoothing Constant		0.1		0.3		0.5		0.7	
July	68								
August	79	68	11.00	68		68		68	
September	81	69.10	11.90	71.30	9.70	73.50	7.50	75.70	5.30
October	55	70.29	15.29	74.21	19.21	77.25	22.25	79.41	24.41
November	71	68.76	2.24	68.45	2.55	66.13	4.88	62.32	8.68
December	60	68.98	8.98	69.21	9.21	68.56	8.56	68.40	8.40
January	77	68.09	8.91	66.45	10.55	64.28	12.72	62.52	14.48
February	81	68.98	12.02	69.61	11.39	70.64	10.36	72.66	8.34
March	63	70.18	7.18	73.03	10.03	75.82	12.82	78.50	15.50
April	85	69.46	15.54	70.02	14.98	69.41	15.59	67.65	17.35
May	87	71.02	15.98	74.51	12.49	77.21	9.79	79.79	7.21
June	85	72.61	12.39	78.26	6.74	82.10	2.90	84.84	0.16
MAD			11.04		10.68		10.74		10.98

Table 6-13 Forecasting Using Exponential Smoothing

Month	Number of Births	Forecast Value	Forecast Error	Forecast Value	Forecast Error	Forecast Value	Forecast Error	Forecast Value	Forecast Error
Smoothing Constant		0.3		0.35		0.4		0.45	
July	68								
August	79	68	11.00	68		68		68	
September	81	71.30	9.70	71.85	9.15	72.40	8.60	72.95	8.05
October	55	74.21	19.21	75.05	20.05	75.84	20.84	76.57	21.57
November	71	68.45	2.55	68.03	2.97	67.50	3.50	66.86	4.14
December	60	69.21	9.21	69.07	9.07	68.90	8.90	68.73	8.73
January	77	66.45	10.55	65.90	11.10	65.34	11.66	64.80	12.20
February	81	69.61	11.39	69.78	11.22	70.00	11.00	70.29	10.71
March	63	73.03	10.03	73.71	10.71	74.40	11.40	75.11	12.11
April	85	70.02	14.98	69.96	15.04	69.84	15.16	69.66	15.34
May	87	74.51	12.49	75.22	11.78	75.91	11.09	76.56	10.44
June	85	78.26	6.74	79.35	5.65	80.34	4.66	81.26	3.74
MAD			10.71		10.67		10.68		10.70

Table 6-14 Forecasting Using Exponential Smoothing

Month	Number of Births	Forecast Value
Smoothing Constant		0.35
July	68	
August	79	68
September	81	71.85
October	55	75.05
November	71	68.03
December	60	69.07
January	77	65.90
February	81	69.78
March	63	73.71
April	85	69.96
May	87	75.22
June	85	79.35
July	**79.35**	**81.32**
August	**81.32**	**80.63**
September	**80.63**	**80.87**
October	**80.87**	**80.79**

LEARNING OBJECTIVE 6: TO BE ABLE TO SELECT BETWEEN FORECASTING MODELS BASED UPON THE CALCULATED MEAN ABSOLUTE DEVIATION

Both moving averages and exponential smoothing approaches attempt to soften the variation in past data searching for a master trend and use this master trend to forecast. Moving averages do this by calculating grouped or pooled averages. A two-period ($n = 2$) moving average steps through the data in units of two. It calculates averages based upon every consecutive 2-month period. A three-period moving average does the same in groups of three. Exponential smoothing does not group data together in different combinations (e.g., $n = 2, 3, 4,$ or 5). Instead, it bases a forecast on different weighted monthly calculations, with less weight placed on observations based further in the past. A smoothing constant of 0.3, for example, bases 30% of the forecast on the actual level of the preceding time period and 70% on the forecast for the previous entire time period. Changing the smoothing constant to 0.5 bases a forecast equally (i.e., 50% and 50%) on the actual and forecast values for the preceding time period. Both moving averages and exponential smoothing are mathematical approaches used to soften the time-period to time-period variability in time series data to determine an underlying trend.

Methods other than MAD do exist as a basis for selecting specific forecasting models. For example, some use the standard error associated with many forecasts and select the specific forecasting model with the lowest standard error. Doing so provides for a slightly more specific measure of inherent variation in the data.

Using either MAD or standard error provides a systematic basis to evaluate many forecasts and select the specific forecast that best represents past events. Obviously, the belief exists that a forecast best able to represent past events will be better able than other forecasts to represent and predict the future. Either approach is acceptable.

What is perhaps most important for managers when interpreting forecasting measures and evaluating MAD values is to relate the forecast to the context of the data. When examining the MADs of both moving average forecasts and exponential smoothing forecasts, we find the results listed in Table 6-15. The lowest MAD belongs to the exponential smoothing methods with a smoothing constant equal to

Table 6-15 MAD Comparison for Moving Averages and
Exponential Smoothing Methods

Method	MAD
$n=2$	10.55
$n=3$	10.63
$n=4$	9.72
$n=5$	10.20
$n=6$	11.19
$sc = .1$	11.04
$sc = .3$	10.68
$sc = .35$	10.67
$sc = .4$	10.68
$sc = .45$	10.70
$sc = .5$	10.74
$sc = .7$	10.98

0.35. However, the smoothing constants 0.4 and 0.3 both yield MADs within 0.01 of that for 0.35. Here we are measuring the number of births; therefore, in essence, when rounded to whole births, using a smoothing constant of 0.3, 0.35, or 0.4 as well as moving averages for $n = 2$ and $n = 3$ return equally accurate forecasts. In this instance, a level of specificity to the hundredths is not required. Had this been a financial forecast, however, the hundredth place would have an impact, as a difference of a few cents when carried across the entire organization's service volume can amount to large amounts of expense or savings.

SUMMARY

Moving averages and exponential smoothing approaches provide the health services manager with robust forecasting models to extrapolate trends. Both are naive forecasting models. Each depends upon the wisdom of the health services manager to select and use these models when reasoned judgment indicates that the past may be a reasonable predictor of the future.

EXERCISES

Using the Northern College Health Services visit volume in Appendix 6-1, provide a forecast of the number of clinic visits for week **XX** using:

6-1 Extrapolation based upon Average Change
6-2 Extrapolation based upon a Confidence Interval
6-3 Extrapolation based upon Average Percent Change
6-4 Extrapolation based upon Moving Averages
6-5 Extrapolation based upon Exponential Smoothing
6-6 Of all methods used, which is best and why?

Appendix 6-1 Visit Volume for Northern College Health Services

Year	Month	Visits to Health Services	Year	Month	Visits to Health Services
2005	Jan	21	2007	Jan	32
	Feb	19		Feb	34
	Mar	16		Mar	39
	Apr	20		Apr	42
	May	15		May	41
	Jun	18		Jun	21
	July	16		July	24
	Aug	14		Aug	28
	Sept	18		Sept	47
	Oct	25		Oct	45
	Nov	30		Nov	46
	Dec	16		Dec	44
2006	Jan	22	2008	Jan	39
	Feb	26		Feb	41
	Mar	31		Mar	34
	Apr	39		Apr	39
	May	44		May	38
	Jun	17		Jun	19
	July	22		July	28
	Aug	18		Aug	29
	Sept	27		Sept	37
	Oct	33		Oct	39
	Nov	29			
	Dec	33			

Chapter 7

Regression Forecasting

LEARNING OBJECTIVES

1. To examine the foundations and components of the regression model.
2. To test the validity of the underlying assumption of linearity in the data.
3. To examine the use of time as an independent variable in regression forecasting.
4. To use regression residuals to develop a best forecast based upon mean absolute deviation (MAD).
5. To construct confidence intervals around regression forecasting estimates.

REAL WORLD SCENARIO

After finding the model with the lowest mean absolute deviation (MAD) given the methods in Chapter 6, Ms. Molly Adel would like to develop and examine a series of regression forecasting models. Because she believes that there could be an underlying linear trend, regression forecasting techniques can be highly suitable. Using the data in Appendix 7-A, she will attempt to construct a line of best fit to the historical data, or portions of it.

Regression analysis, often called ordinary least squares regression, or simple linear regression, derives from the basic algebraic notions of linearity between a set of variables, the simplest being that between two variables, X and Y. One way to examine these two variables is through correlation, in which an association or lack thereof is determined between the variables (see Chapter 2). Regression models, however, take this idea further, by examining the potential existence of a linear relationship between X and Y. Once established, such a relationship can be used to predict the change in Y as X also changes.

The purpose of this chapter is to apply linear regression to forecasting. The regression model is sufficiently robust to be used in many management applications. Regression is used as a predictive model. Models can assist the health care manager

115

in understanding the relationship between factors—typically those under the control of management and those out of management's control (e.g., models that help to understand service demands and service levels). In general, a model is a replication or simplification of reality. For example, a photograph can be considered a model because it describes reality. Although some models are merely descriptive, such as a photograph, others, like regression, can be predictive.

Generally, models are not given; they must be constructed. For example, a hospital administrator may need to know the relationship between the number of inpatient days and the number of staff hours. Managers in ambulatory care may need to know the relationship between the number of clinic visits and number of laboratory tests ordered and/or performed. Managers in nursing homes may want to know the relationship between staff hours and measures of quality of care. Knowing these types of relationships provides managers the ability to predict the number of staff hours given the forecasted hospital inpatient days for next year, the number of laboratory tests given the anticipated clinic visits for next month, or levels of patient quality in the nursing home given the anticipated number of staff hours for the next 3 months. Regression analysis provides the tools to construct these types of models in algebraic form.

The difficulty with constructing models is that care must be taken to be as thoughtful as possible about the components of the model. No model is perfect, and should not be taken as fact, even when used historically in an organization. There are two reasons for this. One is that it is rarely possible to fully understand all of the variables that create a given phenomenon. For example, if we try to create a model that determines the number of lab tests our hospital runs, we would quickly find ourselves with a very long list of contributing factors. These could be elements such as the number and severity of the patients, the number of accidents, the severity of the allergy season, the number of bee stings, etc. Even if we could measure and predict each of these things, which we cannot, our model would be too complex to be useful. This does not mean that all models are useless. Models may be constructed to include those elements that are both contributors to what we are trying to predict, and also those things we can accurately measure.

The second reason is that even when a useful model has been determined, the variables used and the relationships between them are often situational and open to change. For example, the relationship between the number of inpatient days in a hospital and the number of staff hours is different from hospital to hospital and can change over time due to technology or the population being served.

Regression models are constructed using historical data. As with other methods they utilize the primary assumption of the past being an accurate predictor of the future. Because of this, one needs to be confident that this is a sound assumption. Conversely, if a fundamental change has occurred, historical data may be less effectual for prediction and the model flawed. The proficient manager should know how to construct initial regression models and also how to update those models so they remain valid expressions of reality.

LEARNING OBJECTIVE 1: TO EXAMINE THE FOUNDATIONS AND COMPONENTS OF THE REGRESSION MODEL

The purpose of regression analysis is to construct an appropriate mathematical relationship between two or more variables. Once established, and within appropriate limits, the formula can be used to predict levels of the dependent or Y variable given values of the X or independent variable.

In regression analysis, Y is used to represent the dependent variable; the value Y takes on depends on the value of X. The X variable is the independent variable; as it changes, so too does the value of Y. Expressed algebraically as Equation 7-1, this simple relationship is the foundation for all regression modeling.

Although regression can be used to examine the relationship of many independent variables (X_1, X_2, X_3, etc.) on some dependent variable Y, this chapter restricts attention to the simple linear model using only one predictor or X variable. The linear regression model is usually expressed as:

$$Y = b_o + b_1X \qquad \text{Equation 7-1}$$

where

$$b_o = \text{the } Y \text{ intercept and}$$
$$b_1 = \text{the slope}$$

This might bear resemblance to the formula for a straight line:

Regression Model:

$$Y = b_1X + b_o$$

Generic Formula for a Straight Line:

$$Y = mX + B$$

where B and b_o are the Y intercept and b_1 and m are the slope. The two formulae are, in fact, identical.

The regression model establishes the best fit between a straight line equation and the available data which describes a relationship between X and Y. For example, imagine a set of data taken from a hospital lab over time that examines the number of lab tests over an 8-week period (Figure 7-1).

One could likely eyeball any number of lines that would "fit" these data. Figure 7-2 shows three examples. Ideally we would want to develop a line that minimizes the distance of each data point to the line.

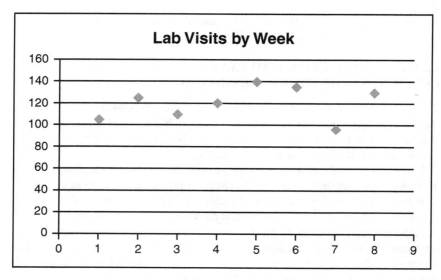

Figure 7-1 Lab Visits by Week

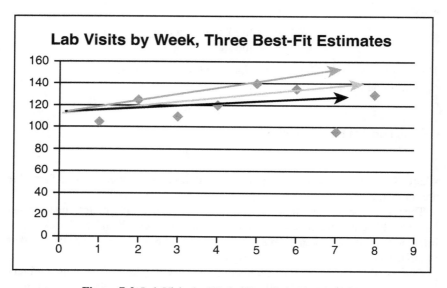

Figure 7-2 Lab Visits by Week, Three Best-Fit Estimates

Table 7-1 Clinic Visits and Lab Tests Over an 8-week Period

Week	Clinic Visits (x)	Lab Tests (y)	Lab Tests Per Visit (y/x)
1	65	105	1.62
2	65	125	1.92
3	62	110	1.77
4	67	120	1.79
5	69	140	2.03
6	65	135	2.08
7	61	95	1.56
8	67	130	1.94
Average	65.125	120	1.84

Mathematically, regression analysis does this by relying upon the least squares method to determine the coefficients of the straight line that best (but not necessarily perfectly) establishes the equation representing the relationships between X as the independent variable and Y as the dependent variable.

The least squares method minimizes the mathematical distance between the line developed using the regression model and the actual X and Y data points.

Consider a second example in Table 7-1 that describes the number of laboratory tests per week (y) as the dependent variable but now uses the number of clinic visits (x) as the independent variable.

On average, during this 8-week period, 1.84 laboratory tests were performed for each clinic visit. In some weeks, however, this level ranges from a low of 1.56 tests per visit to a high of 2.08 tests per visit. Using just the average of 1.84 lab tests per visit might mask this variation and not produce as accurate a model as provided using regression analysis.Most software programs, including Microsoft Excel, readily calculate a regression model given the ranges of data.

The Regression Equation

The regression equation can be constructed by the intercept term and the coefficient of the X variable using Equation 7-1. The y intercept is also the predicted level of y when x equals zero. Table 7-2 shows the regression output using Microsoft Excel for the data in Table 7-1, where we try to predict the number of lab tests using the number of clinic visits.

Table 7-2 Regression Output for Table 7-1

SUMMARY OUTPUT

Regression Statistics

Multiple R	0.797921174
R Square	0.636678201
Adjusted R Square	0.576124567
Standard Error	10.14599312
Observations	8

ANOVA

	df	SS	MS	F	Significance F
Regression	1	1082.352941	1082.353	10.51429	0.017629832
Residual	6	617.6470588	102.9412		
Total	7	1700			

	Coefficients	Standard Error	t Stat	P-value	Lower 95%	Upper 95%	Lower 95.0%	Upper 95.0%
Intercept	−186.4705882	94.58265084	−1.97151	0.096149	−417.905997	44.96482057	−417.905997	44.96482057
X Variable 1	4.705882353	1.451279894	3.242574	0.01763	1.154728389	8.257036317	1.154728389	8.257036317

Lab Tests = −186.47 + 4.7 × Clinic Visits

Here we find that the intercept or b_o coefficient is -186.47. The X variable coefficient, or b_1 term, is 4.71 rounded. This gives us the regression equation of lab tests $= -186.47 + 4.7 \times$ clinic visits. From this we can input any number of clinic visits to estimate the corresponding number of lab tests predicted by our model. So, for example, if we believe there would be 70 clinic visits the next month, we would expect to see approximately 143 lab tests using the equation lab tests $= -186.47 + 4.7 \times 70$. Obviously this is an estimate. In fact, the likelihood of there being exactly 143 lab tests given 70 clinic visits is quite small. However, before we can address the issue of accuracy of our prediction, we have another consideration. The regression line is that which minimizes the distance from the line to the X and Y variable points. It assumes that there is some linearity between these variables. The next section examines this assumption more closely and describes how to test to ensure it is correct before using a regression equation to forecast. The formula for constructing the b_0 and b_1 regression coefficients can be found in Appendix 7-A.

LEARNING OBJECTIVE 2: TO TEST THE UNDERLYING ASSUMPTION OF LINEARITY IN THE DATA

What do we mean when we say that we assume there is linearity in the data? Well, if we examine a scatter plot of two variables that seem to have no relationship, such as that in Figure 7-3, we could no doubt consider one or more possible lines

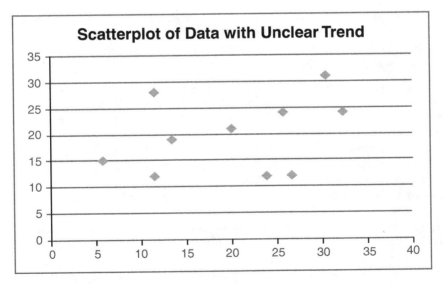

Figure 7-3 Scatterplot of Data with Unclear Trend

that might be drawn to best fit the data. In examples such as this, the data often have a cloudlike appearance, where a discernible pattern or relationship is difficult to estimate. In fact, the line of best fit here could potentially be a horizontal line or vertical line. The problem in dealing with horizontal or vertical lines is that their slopes are either zero in the horizontal case, or undefined in the vertical case. When using regression, we are primarily concerned with slopes that are potentially zero.

Relating this back to our formula a slope of zero means that as X changes, Y remains constant. This is not a good predictive equation to use for forecasting because regardless of what happens to the x-variable your prediction will always be the same. For example, if our regression formula were to be $Y = -186.1 + 0 \times X$, Y would be a constant, -186.1, regardless of whether $X = 1$, or 100, or any number. Therefore, before using the line of best fit (e.g., $y = -186.47 + 4.7x$) to describe the relationship between X and Y, a statistical test must be performed to determined whether the *predicted* slope (i.e., 4.7) is not, in truth, zero.

Many techniques exist to test a regression line. The test used in this chapter tests whether, at a 95% level of confidence, the slope of the regression line is other than zero. The test statistic we will use is the t-statistic. The question we are asking is, What is the likelihood that the predicted slope of our regression line actually equals zero in reality? Our statistical hypotheses are as follows:

> H_o = *There is no difference between the calculated slope and zero, otherwise put, $b_1 = 0$ (This is the null hypothesis.)*
> H_a = *There is a difference between the calculated slope and zero, otherwise put, b_1 does NOT = 0*

Because we have collected a sample of historical data, it is possible that in reality there is no true linear relationship between X and Y, e.g., that we would fail to reject H_o, the null hypothesis. Thankfully, the information we need to make this assessment is readily available in our regression output. Examining again Table 7-2, we see two columns; one labeled t-stat, and one labeled p-value. The t-statistic is the value of t derived from the regression equation. The p-value is the probability of that t-statistic given the appropriate t-distribution. As with any probability value, we need to identify an alpha value that we will use as a "cutoff" for determining when to reject our null hypothesis. Here we have said we will use a 95% level of confidence to assess if the slope is non zero to reject the null, or an alpha of 0.05. Thus, if our p-value is less than 0.05, we can be 95% confident our slope is not zero, and we may use this regression model for prediction. In Table 7-2, our t-statistic is 3.24 and our p-value is 0.0176. Because 0.0176 is less than 0.05, we can reject the null hypothesis and use this regression equation as a forecasting tool. If the calculated *p*-value had been greater than 0.05, the appropriate decision would be to fail to reject the hypothesis that the slope could in fact equal zero and we would have to discard the previously calculated regression equation as unusable.

Following this process provides the manager the ability to conclude whether the calculated regression equation (e.g., $y = -186.5 + 4.7x$) is a valid expression of the relationship portrayed in the data. Whether the regression equation is usable can only be determined by following this process.

LEARNING OBJECTIVE 3: TO EXAMINE THE USE OF TIME AS AN INDEPENDENT VARIABLE IN REGRESSION FORECASTING

When regression is used to forecast, time is often used as the independent (i.e., *x*) variable. Time can be expressed in any appropriate unit such as days, weeks, months, or years. To simplify calculations and provide equal units it is important to express time intervals in small numbers. For example, instead of using 1988, 1989, etc. as the *X* variable, time intervals of one integer are used, such as 1, 2, 3, etc. The reason for this is that there must be equal intervals between *x* units. This may produce slightly skewed estimates when dealing with months, because some months are of different length in days. However, it works well with days, weeks, and years, because the subunits within those larger time units are of equal length.

Consider the data in Table 7-3.

Here the *x*-values are the numeric intervals for *x* and will be entered into Excel as such. Table 7-4 shows the regression output for the data in Table 7-3. For this example, the regression model is $y = 18.87 + 7.8x$. The calculated t statistic for

Table 7-3 Hospital Births for Six Years Beginning in 2003

Time Period	Numeric Interval (x)	Births (y)
2003	1	25
2004	2	36
2005	3	43
2006	4	50
2007	5	58
2008	6	65

Table 7-4 Regression Output for Table 7-3 Data

SUMMARY OUTPUT

Regression Statistics

Multiple R	0.997
R Square	0.994
Adjusted R Square	0.993
Standard Error	1.238
Observations	9

ANOVA

	df	SS	MS	F	Significance F
Regression	1	1064.7	1064.7	694.70	1.233E-05
Residual	4	6.133	1.533		
Total	5	1070.833			

	Coefficients	Standard Error	t Stat	P-value	Lower 95%	Upper 95%
Intercept	18.867	1.153	16.366	0.000	15.666	22.067
X Variable 1	7.800	0.296	26.351	0.000	6.978	8.622

the coefficient of the *x*-variable (slope) is 26.35, and the probability of this test statistic is $p < 0.000$. This allows us to reject the null hypothesis that there is no difference between the calculated slope and zero with a 95% level of confidence (and in fact we can reject the null with a 99.9% level of confidence). Given that the regression model is useful (as shown by the *t*-test as having a non-zero slope), it can be used to forecast births (*y*).

To forecast using a regression equation, simply plug future values of *x* into the equation and solve for the corresponding predicted values of *y*. For example, if we wish to forecast the number of births that should occur in 2009, we would add 2009 to our list of data in Table 7-3 and number it in the numeric interval (*x*) column as 7. Plugging 7 into our formula of $y = 18.87 + 7.8x$ we get $y = 18.87 + 7.8 \times 7$, or $y = 73.47$. We can continue to do this into the future. Remember, however, that it is not prudent to forecast beyond one third of your data. Here we only have six points of data. One third of $6 = 2$, so we should only forecast two time periods into the future. This is shown in Table 7-5.

Testing the slope should be the first and primary test. However, the regression output provides other useful information when assessing the fit and appropriateness of the regression line. One is the F-test for significance of the overall regression equation. This tests whether the variation in *X* helps in explaining the variation in *Y*. A significance of the F-test below 0.05 is in most cases sufficient justification for using a regression equation. In Table 7-4 the F-test statistic can be seen as having a value of 694.37 with a corresponding significance of 1.23 E-5, or 0.0000123. Interpreted this means

Table 7-5 Hospital Births for Six Years Beginning in 2003 with Forecasted Values

Time Period	Numeric Interval (x)	Births (y)
2003	1	25
2004	2	36
2005	3	43
2006	4	50
2007	5	58
2008	6	65
2009	7	73
2010	8	81
regression equation: $y = 18.87 + 7.8x$		

that the model can be used. Still another is using R^2, which is the proportion of the total variance of Y explained by the regression line. In this case, our R^2 is 0.99, or 99% of the variance in Y (births) is explained by the regression line.

LEARNING OBJECTIVE 4: TO USE REGRESSION RESIDUALS TO SELECT A REGRESSION EQUATION AND DEVELOP A BEST FORECAST

Regression forecast models are based on the assumption that the past predicts the future. The question, of course, is how far into the past does the current trend hold predictive power. At some point, historical data are simply not useful or relevant to predicting the future. In relation to regression, this determines how much historical data is to be used in the model, or in other words, how many n-points of data we incorporate.

Each time we choose a new number of x data points, our regression line changes. Examine Table 7-6, which shows how incorporating an additional 2 years of historic data changes the regression output and line. Notice that the X-variables have been renumbered so that the earliest time period is labeled as time period one.

Examining the output in Table 7-7, the regression line becomes $y = 9.36 + 6.8x$.

Because the significance of the F-statistic and p-value for the t-test are both less than 0.05 we can be assured within a 95% level of confidence that the regression model has explanatory ability and also a non-zero slope. We now must determine which regression model, the one based on six points of data or the one based on eight points of data, would provide the best predictive model. Essentially, the question we are asking is, Which line fits the data points more closely? The answer to this can be determined by examining the distance from each of our actual

Table 7-6 Hospital Births for Six Years Beginning in 2003

Time Period	Numeric Interval (x)	Births (y)
2001	1	20
2002	2	23
2003	3	25
2004	4	36
2005	5	43
2006	6	50
2007	7	58
2008	8	65

Table 7-7 Summary Output

Regression Statistics

Multiple R	0.98976752
R Square	0.979639743
Adjusted R Square	0.976246367
Standard Error	2.597312408
Observations	8

ANOVA

	df	SS	MS	F	Significance F
Regression	1	1947.52381	1947.52381	288.6917647	2.65793E-06
Residual	6	40.47619048	6.746031746		
Total	7	1988			

	Coefficients	Standard Error	t Stat	P-value	Lower 95%	Upper 95%
Intercept	9.357142857	2.023809524	4.623529412	0.003602013	4.405059358	14.30922636
X Variable 1	6.80952381	0.400774005	16.99093184	2.65793E-06	5.828865148	7.790182471

historical data points, to what each line predicts. In regression terms, this is known as calculating the residuals.

A residual is defined as $Y - Y_{predicted}$. It is essentially the same as the forecast error (FE) used in previous forecasting methods. There are two ways to calculate residuals. Table 7-8 shows the addition of predicted values using the regression formula $y = 18.87 + 7.8x$. The residual column subtracts the predicted value for y at each x time period from the observed y value. By taking the absolute value of the residuals and then totaling those values gives the absolute deviation for the regression line. Taking the average of the residuals gives the mean absolute deviation (MAD) for this regression line. By calculating the MAD for each of our regression lines using different n-numbers of x-variables, we can assess which fits the data more closely. As expressed in previous chapters, the lower the MAD, the less the variance of the predictions around the regression line, and the more accurate the line is at fitting the data.

From Table 7-8, the total of the residuals is 65.08 and the MAD is 10.85. Repeating this with the model using eight historical points of data in Table 7-9 we produce a MAD of 1.50. Because the MAD is lower when using eight points of historical data, we would be better served by using this regression model for prediction as it is more accurate.

Residuals can also be produced by checking the Residuals check box in the regression function in Excel when using the data analysis tools. This method, however, will not provide the total, absolute, or mean deviation of the residuals.

Here we have calculated regression models based on two proposed lines. The "best" number of regression lines, however, is a matter of judgment on the part of the manager. Choosing the number of x-values can be a matter of examining

Table 7-8 Hospital Births for Six Years Beginning in 2003

Time period	Numeric Interval (x)	Births (y)	Predicted y	Residual (y-predicted y)
2003	1	25	23.57	1.43
2004	2	36	28.27	7.73
2005	3	43	32.97	10.03
2006	4	50	37.67	12.33
2007	5	58	42.37	15.63
2008	6	65	47.07	17.93
Total				65.08
Mean		46.17		10.85

Table 7-9 Hospital Births for Eight Years Beginning in 2003

Time Period	Numeric Interval (x)	Births (y)	Predicted y	Residual (y-predicted y)
2001	1	20	16.17	3.83
2002	2	23	22.98	0.02
2003	3	25	29.79	4.79
2004	4	36	36.60	0.60
2005	5	43	43.40	0.40
2006	6	50	50.21	0.21
2007	7	58	57.02	0.98
2008	8	65	63.83	1.17
Total	36	46.17		12.00
Average	4.5			1.50

historical trends in the data or having some knowledge about when a fundamental change may have occurred in the environment. It is important to realize, however, that predictions based on regression will always be linear as they proceed into the future. In reality, this is unlikely to be the case. It is important to assess how long these trends can be expected to continue. If using regression for short-term forecasting, it is also possible to calculate confidence intervals around the final forecasts.

LEARNING OBJECTIVE 5: TO CONSTRUCT CONFIDENCE INTERVALS AROUND REGRESSION ESTIMATES

Regardless of the type of independent variable in a regression equation, it is important that the resulting prediction be presented with a 95% confidence interval. This is because, as previously stated, a forecast is never totally accurate. Using the data from Table 7-9, x ranged from 1 to 8, and y ranged from 20 to 65. The calculated regression formula (i.e., $y = 9.36 + 6.8x$) is the line of best fit based upon the available data. Extending the line beyond the domain of the original data (i.e., $X = 8$), although appropriate, has inherent risk.

The confidence interval is not a constant width for all values of x. This is because of the way in which least squares works and the fact that the formula for regression is rooted in the values for the mean of x and mean of y. Thus, for predictions based upon values of the independent (*x*) variable close to the mean, the confidence interval is the smallest. The farther away from the mean, the less precise or wider the confidence interval becomes. Thus, the confidence interval on a predicted value of *y* depends on the value of *x* that predicts it. Table 7-10 displays the confidence intervals for the prediction.

The following formula is for the confidence interval on the mean value (expected value) of *y*.

To calculate the 95% confidence interval:

1. Calculate the mean value of *X*. Using data from Table 7-7, the mean for $X = 4.5$
2. Select a value for *Y* to be forecast. In this case, the example is based upon wanting to predict *y* for the next time interval, or $x = 7$.
3. Select the value of *X* as the basis for the 95% confidence interval.

Using data in Table 7-10, $X = 9$ (2009) has been selected as the point for which the 95% confidence interval will be calculated. Using the regression equation, solve for *Y*:

$$y = 9.36 + 6.8x$$
$$y = 9.36 + (6.8 \times 9)$$
$$y = 70.64$$

4. Solve for the 95% confidence interval (CI) using the following formula: Doing so will require values for X_o, or the predicted value of *X*, the sum of the *x*-variables, the sum of the squared values of the *x*-variables, the value of *t* (from the regression output), and the standard error of the regression (from the regression output). The first two will require two additional calculations easily attained in Excel.

$$CI\,(y) = \text{Prediction} \pm (t)\,(Se)\;\text{SQRT of}\quad \frac{1}{n} + \frac{(X_o - X\,\text{mean})^2}{n(\Sigma x^2) - (Sx)^2}$$

Using data and calculations from Table 7-10, when $X = 9$ and X mean $= 3.5$ with df $= 4$:

$$CI\,(y) = 70.64 \pm (16.99)\,(2.599)\;\text{SQRT}\quad \frac{1}{8} + \frac{(9 - 4.5)^2}{8(204) - (36)^2}$$

$$= 70.64 \pm 44.16 \times \text{SQRT}\,(0.125 + 0.0603)$$
$$= 70.64 \pm 44.16 \times \text{SQRT}\,(0.18526)$$
$$= 70.64 \pm 19.000$$
$$= 89.64 \text{ and } 51.64 \text{ when } X = 9$$

Using the 95% confidence interval provides the ability to extend the line of best fit beyond the domain of the original data. A 95% confidence interval can be

Table 7-10 Confidence Interval for the Prediction

Time period	Numeric Interval (x)	Births (y)	Predicted y	Residual (y-predicted y)	x^2	95% CI upper bound	95% CI lower bound
2001	1	20	16.17	3.83	1		
2002	2	23	22.98	0.02	4		
2003	3	25	29.79	4.79	9		
2004	4	36	36.60	0.60	16		
2005	5	43	43.40	0.40	25		
2006	6	50	50.21	0.21	36		
2007	7	58	57.02	0.98	49		
2008	8	65	63.83	1.17	64		
2009	**9**		70.64			**89.64**	**51.64**
Total	36			8.14	204		
Ave	4.5			1.36			

calculated for any level of X, including an X value included in the domain of the original data. Based upon the results of these calculations, the regression model indicates a 95% probability that births in 2009 ($x = 9$) will not exceed 90 and be no less than 51.

In any situation where the calculated regression model is used outside of the domain of the original data, a 95% confidence interval should be calculated.

SUMMARY

Regression analysis is one of the more precise forecasting tools when examining a linear relationship between variables. When used correctly, it provides the line of best fit to the data. It is based on the assumptions of the past predicting the future, and that an underlying linear trend exists within the data. Here we describe a simple relationship between two variables; however regression can be used to examine the collective effects of multiple x-variables on some dependent variable, y. Doing so, however, requires further study of multiple regression techniques, which is beyond the scope of this chapter.

EXERCISES

For the data in Table 7-e1:

7-1 Calculate the regression equation for the entire range of data.
7-2 Is this a useable regression line?
7-3 Develop two other regression lines based on 12, 24, 30, 36, and 46 months of data.
7-4 Which line would you use and why?
7-5 Develop a prediction into the future for as many months as you can. Justify why you forecasted as far as you did.
7-6 Provide confidence intervals for the predicted values.Learning Objectives

After studying this chapter, you should be able to:

1. Describe how health services managers analyze, design, and implement in a systems context.
2. Differentiate between efficiency and effectiveness as vital managerial interests.
3. Describe how quantitative methods fit into the repertoire of the health services manager.
4. Describe the general systems model in relation to health services.

Appendix 7-A Calculating the Regression Coefficients:

In order to apply the regression model, two coefficients must be calculated from data.

$$b_0 = \text{the (predicted) } y \text{ intercept.}$$
$$b_1 = \text{the (predicted) slope}$$

The y intercept is also the predicted level of y when x equals zero.

$$b_1 = \frac{n\sum(xy) - (\sum x)(\sum y)}{n\sum x^2 - (\sum x)^2}$$

where

$$n = \text{number of paired observations}$$
$$b_0 = \frac{\sum y - b_1(\sum x)}{n}$$

For example, consider Table 7-2:

$$b_1 = \frac{n\sum(xy) - (\sum x)(\sum y)}{n\sum x^2 - (\sum x)^2}$$

$$\frac{(8)(62,750) - (521)(960)}{= (8)(33,979) - (521)(521)}$$

$$\frac{(502,000) - (500,160)}{= (271,832) - (271,441)}$$

$$= 4.7$$

$$b_0 = \frac{\sum y - b_1(\sum x)}{n}$$

$$\frac{(960) - 4.7(521)}{= 8}$$

$$\frac{(960 - 2448.7)}{= 8 - 1488.7}$$

$$= 8$$

$$= -186.1$$

For the data contained in Tables 7-1 and 7-2, the regression model is:

$$y = -186.1 + 4.7x$$

If 65 clinic visits were forecasted in the future (i.e., $x = 65$), the predicted number of laboratory tests (Y) would be:

$$Y = -186.1 + 4.7 \times 65$$
$$Y = -186.1 + 305.5$$
$$Y = 119$$

Designing and Analyzing Systems

Chapter 8

Analyzing Capacity and Resources

LEARNING OBJECTIVES

1. To describe the capacity of a system.
2. To describe the relationship between costs and capacity.
3. To estimate the production capability of a specific system.

REAL WORLD SCENARIO

An occupational health clinic does two general types of visits, each involving the direct actions of a receptionist/billing clerk, a registered nurse who is also able to take simple x-rays, and a physician. No emergency care is provided. Visits include injuries paid for by workers compensation and employer paid physicals. The clinic has been asked to respond to a request for proposal (RFP) for 200 physicals per month. It has two questions. First, can the clinic, as currently staffed, do 200 more physicals per month, and if not, should it hire an additional nurse or physician to take on this added workload? Second, if the contribution margin on each of these new physicals was $100, what financial impact will this new contract have on the clinic?

LEARNING OBJECTIVE 1: TO DESCRIBE THE CAPACITY OF A SYSTEM

System capacity is finite and is created by the resources available to a system. Capacity analysis provides a quantitative methodology for establishing the production constraints of a given service system or function. Doing so, in conjunction with associated costs and revenues, allows the manager to determine the most efficient mix of resources to accomplish the service at peak operational capacity as well as ways in which the available resources can be manipulated to accomplish changes in desired output.

Capacity analysis is concerned with the efficiency of systems and subsystems. Efficiency is the ratio measure of output and input. Efficiency can be enhanced if output can be increased for the same level of inputs. It can also be increased if the level of output is held constant and input levels are reduced. Examples of inputs include worker hours, supplies, equipment, and facilities. Examples of outputs are measures used to describe specific systems, such as patient days, ambulatory care visits, meals served, and number of surgeries.

Determining the maximum capacity of a system or subsystem and the resources needed to establish a particular level of capacity are the central components of capacity analysis. Health services managers need to monitor systems to ensure that system capacity is close to the actual or forecasted demand for service. If capacity is significantly above actual or forecasted demand, then some resources may need to be subtracted to increase the efficiency of the system. If capacity is below the actual or forecasted demand, then resources may need to be added to ensure that an adequate capacity exists to provide an effective as well as efficient service. In either case, to achieve reasonable levels of efficiency, the manager needs to know when, where, and how to act and what resources need to be added or subtracted.

Health administrators manage service-oriented systems in healthcare organizations. These systems have specific properties that influence how they can be analyzed and the options available to a manager for resource allocation. Service systems used to provide medical care are usually very complex. They are multistep processes, with each step governed by procedures and protocols, and involve many service stations or servers. Even expressed in its simplest form, a typical stay at a hospital requires the coordinated interplay of multistep processes, as shown in Figure 8-1.

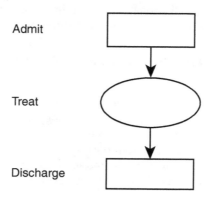

Figure 8-1 Flow of Patients Through Hospital to Produce Output

Each of these steps or phases in the multistep process is complex. Admitting a patient requires the coordinated actions of many individuals and service stations in the hospital, some of which deal directly with the patient and others that respond to patient-oriented actions. The admitting process may be significantly different for different types of patients. For example, routine admissions are different than emergency admissions.

Medical treatment is also highly complex. People come to a hospital for a medical treatment they need (as determined by the admitting physician) and expect the needed treatment to be provided in a professional high-quality manner. Treatment is a multistep process involving many servers or service stations in a hospital. The plan for the treatment also may change along the way as the physician alters the treatment plan given a change or modification in diagnosis and/or patient condition. The service systems in the hospital are expected to respond to patient needs even if these needs change. If the hospital lacks the capacity to respond to patient needs, transfer to another hospital with the needed capability is the logical action. Discharge is also a complex action. It requires decisions and actions to be made by many individuals and service stations in the hospital.

As such, medical care is a complex production process involving many steps and the coordinated interplay of many individuals and servers or service stations. The same could be said, however, for the production processes used to manufacture automobiles. Manufacturing an automobile requires the coordinated interplay of many individual service stations (e.g., molding, assembly, painting, etc.) and servers along the production line. It is also a phased process that requires that some operations precede others (e.g., assembly precedes painting). Procedures and protocols are used to govern the actions of individual service stations. Although manufacturing processes used in the automobile industry resemble production processes used in hospitals, nursing homes, and clinics, production processes used in health and medical care are different. These differences make service systems in health and medical care even more complex.

Service systems used in medical care need the ability to adjust and modify their actions based upon a patient's need, needs that change during the production process. For example, every automobile that passes through the production line requires four regular tires and one spare tire. When the manufacturing process is started, four and only four regular tires need to be available to complete the production process. Machines and workers are needed to install only these four tires on the automobile. In health and medical care, as patients pass through the process of receiving medical care, however, their needs can change. A patient admitted to a hospital for a normal vaginal delivery may need a surgical operation (i.e., Caesarean section). The hospital must have the capability to respond, as needed, to these changes.

If each wheel requires five lug nuts to install the wheels and tires on the car, the total number of lug nuts per car could be estimated. It would be 20. The analogous situation in health and medical care is much more difficult to estimate. How many laboratory tests per patient will be required? How many x-rays or scans will be required for each patient? How many meals will be required per patient? Each of these are questions that cannot be answered with the same amount of certainty associated with answering the question of how many lug nuts per car will be required.

The central point of the analogy between automobile production and medical care production is that medical care service systems must be able to respond to change during the production process and must plan for unanticipated needs. Service systems in medical care must reserve some of their capacity for these unanticipated needs. This requires that the capacity of a medical service system be established based upon anticipated as well as unanticipated needs.

People use many of the service systems provided by a healthcare organization. People have wants as well as needs and demands. Different people have different wants, as well as different needs and demands. People expect that their wants as well as their needs will be met by the medical service systems. For example, most people want to be referred to by their name, not by their medical condition (e.g., the gall bladder in room 224). People want treatment to be professional; they define "professional" to include knowing what is happening to them and why. As people, some may want more information than others. Giving a computed tomography scan to a patient for the first time may require extra time. The experienced patient may know the appropriate routine and behaviors, be better able to cooperate with the technician, and not be frightened by the machine. The amount of increased time necessary to effectively scan a first-time patient has nothing to do with the scan per se; it reflects the human dynamic associated with administering medical care to people. Similarly, younger patients may have different wants than more mature patients, even though they are in a hospital for the same service.

People evaluate their medical care and the systems used to provide the needed services based upon the outcome associated with their treatment as well as how well the service met their wants. As such, the services offered by a hospital, nursing home, or clinic must be able to respond to the wants of their patients, as well as their needs. Again, this is different than the production processes used to produce and manufacture automobiles.

As will be examined, the output of a medical service system is a unit of service as well as information. Examples of service units are a specific medical test, x-ray or scan, a meal, a prescription, and a specific surgical operation. Service systems produce these service units. They also produce information that records the action in a medical record and/or management information system. Service systems are expected to produce information as well as service units.

The last characteristics of medical service systems, similar to any production process, involves their capacity—the ability to produce service units based upon the capability and productivity of the servers as well as by the machines and other resources needed and used to produce a service unit.

Examining and determining the capacity of a system or subsystem is as much an art as a science, especially in healthcare organizations. Although some industrial engineers might find this assertion counter to dominant beliefs, it recognizes the difficulty associated with defining the boundaries of a specific system as well as assessing current capacity level given the multiple demands the systems and servers are expected to fulfill. To examine this point requires a basic review of systems theory.

Systems can be examined as processes. These processes convert input resources into outputs. The process of converting inputs into outputs adds value. Systems feed back information to adjust, as necessary, the conversion of inputs into outputs. Systems adjust how they convert resources by changing the processes used to convert inputs into outputs and/or by changing the conversion process to be able to produce either fewer or more outputs. Feedback, usually in the form of information, is the primary stimulus for managerial change in the resource input mix. Feedback is also the primary stimulus for a redefinition of the processes used to convert resources into outputs. Systems are directed by goals and objectives. Managers design, control, and modify systems to meet these goals and objectives. Any specific system is another system's subsystem. A typical system in shown in Figure 8-2.

Determining a system's capacity requires judgment. Although determining capacity and matching resources to intended and required levels of capacity must be done in a systematic manner, often using tools and approaches developed in the field of industrial engineering as well as cost analysis, the decisions that must be made are judgmental, not necessarily scientific.

Components of a Typical System

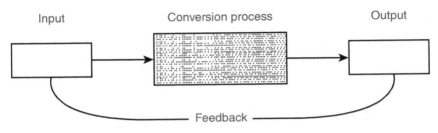

Figure 8-2 Components of a Typical System

In system terms, the health organization and its management create capacity by assigning resources to a specific service station. The service station converts these resources into services. The capacity of a service station is created by the amount and type of input resources assigned to the service station. The manager must ensure that the capacity created by the mix of input resources is appropriate. If the capacity of a service system is too high, the service system may be inefficient. If the capacity of a service station is too low, the goals and objectives of the organization that depend upon the service station are jeopardized. Service stations create feedback. One type of feedback is the quantity of outputs generated by specific service stations. Management must judge whether the resources assigned to all service stations are justified given past output performance and anticipated future requirements. In some instances, the capacity of a service station may need to be lowered to return the service station to a reasonable level of efficiency.

LEARNING OBJECTIVE 2: TO DESCRIBE THE RELATIONSHIP BETWEEN COSTS AND CAPACITY

Healthcare organizations are dominated by fixed costs. Salaries and benefits are fixed costs. The vast majority of expenses associated with physical structures are fixed costs. Equipment expenses are usually fixed costs. Interest on debt and taxes (if any) represent fixed costs. A fixed cost does not change based upon the volume of service provided. Cost analysis and the general field of financial management indicate that certain costs behave differently in terms of volume. As stated, a fixed cost does not change based upon the volume of service provided. Conversely, a unit of variable cost is added when an additional unit of service is provided. Similarly, a unit of a variable cost is avoided when a unit of service is not provided. Variable costs and total variable costs change as the volume of service changes.

The total cost of a system or subsystem is total fixed costs plus the variable costs associated with the volume of service (i.e., an output level) provided. In other words:

$$TC = FC + (VC \times U)$$

where

$$TC = \text{total costs}$$
$$FC = \text{total fixed costs}$$
$$VC = \text{variable cost per unit}$$
$$U = \text{units of service}$$

This relationship has special relevance in healthcare organizations. In general, health administrators manage organizations and systems that are dominated by fixed costs. Although some variable costs do exist, the vast majority of the costs associated with providing a personal healthcare service in a hospital, nursing home, or clinic setting are fixed. To manage a healthcare organization successfully requires the ability to manage fixed costs. Other industrial sectors that face the same challenge include schools, colleges, and airlines.

When the concept of fixed costs and variable costs are added to the relationships between volume and revenue production, the classical "break even," or cost–volume–profit relationship emerges. Figure 8-3 illustrates this relationship. It is important that features and characteristics of the break even or cost–volume–profit relationship be appreciated in this context. Note that:

1. At the break-even point in volume, total costs equals total revenue.
2. The contribution margin (CM) equals the revenue or price per service unit minus the variable cost per service unit.
3. Below the break-even point in volume, the CM is contributed to paying for the fixed costs.
4. Above the break-even point, the CM is contributed to profits—excess revenue left after all costs have been paid.

Given these relationships, the manager faced with the challenge of efficiently and effectively managing an organization or system dominated by fixed costs, has few choices. Fixed cost dominated systems require volume to be efficient.

In contrast, variable cost is managed by ensuring that the unit of variable cost is the lowest possible. For example, medical supplies are typically a variable cost. Different supplies are used to produce a patient day or used to treat a patient in a clinic. The dual challenge of efficiency and effectiveness demands that the manager ensure that the organization uses technically competent supplies (i.e., quality) and secures these supplies at the lowest unit cost possible, sometimes by purchasing supplies in bulk. To manage a variable cost, the manager strives to minimize the cost per unit.

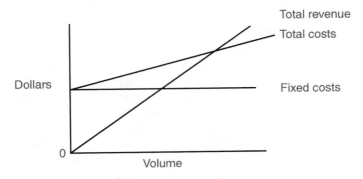

Figure 8-3 The Cost–Volume–Profit Relationship

Managing fixed costs is different. To effectively manage a system or subsystem dominated by fixed costs requires that the actual or forecasted volume of services correspond to the capacity created by the fixed costs. To accomplish this, managers have some options.

Managers have the option of changing fixed costs into variable costs by redefining certain practices. For example, changing personnel expenses from a fixed salary to a per-patient fee paid to each employee, changes a fixed cost to a variable cost. In health care, however, most professionals are compensated based upon a guaranteed salary or an hourly rate guaranteed for 37.5 or 40 hours per week. Changing the basis of compensating employees from a fixed cost to a variable cost is rarely accepted well by employees. Although this choice is always present, it is usually the most difficult choice or option to use. If used, this type of option lowers total fixed costs by transferring fixed costs into variable costs and reduces the break-even point.

Another choice is to lower fixed costs as far as possible. Paying lower salaries, providing fewer comprehensive benefits, lowering staffing levels, changing the staffing mix to include lower-paid workers, refinancing a capital debt to lower debt payments based upon lower interest charges, reducing energy costs through a conservation program, borrowing money at lower interest rates, and other related actions can be used to lower fixed costs. Because a significant majority of all fixed costs found in healthcare organizations lie in the area of personnel, lowering staffing levels and changing the staffing mix are options that usually attract most managerial interest when fixed costs need to be reduced. This option also lowers the break-even point.

Another related choice is to change a fixed cost into a semi-fixed cost. Unlike a fixed cost that does not vary or change based upon the volume of service rendered and a variable cost that does change based upon volume of service renders, a cost that is semi-fixed changes in increments or steps. It is under this option that the manager becomes especially interested in the capacity associated with specific levels of resources.

When combined, these last two choices present an interesting approach. Staffing could be held at one level when the volume is or is expected to be between X and Y units of service and increased to a higher staffing level when volume exceeds or is expected to exceed Y units of service. This type of approach, for example, changes salary costs from a fixed to a semi-fixed cost. The cost of personnel increases or decreases only when the volume exceeds the threshold established, such as Y units of service. This last option establishes a different break-even point in volume depending upon the fixed or semi-fixed costs used to create the needed capacity.

In general, the challenge of fixed costs must be met with increased volume. Actions must be taken that capacity and output are reasonably close and that when output is expected to fall, capacity is lowered. The capacity created by the fixed costs must be used for productive purposes. Having the capacity and not using it is highly inefficient. Volume is the key.

As noted, however, if volume (e.g., arrivals) is too close to capacity (services), it is likely that a patient or unit will have to wait an unacceptably long time. One can never have volume equal capacity and remain an effective healthcare delivery system.

LEARNING OBJECTIVE 3: TO ESTIMATE THE PRODUCTION CAPABILITY OF A SPECIFIC SYSTEM

The relationship between capacity and output is a measure of efficiency and is best explored using a situation analogous to healthcare organizations, the airlines and airplanes.

Airlines measure their capacity by counting the number of seats in their airplanes. The capacity of any specific flight is dependent upon the number of seats in the airplane assigned to that flight. A larger airplane may have 250 seats, a smaller airplane only 100 seats. The capacity of the larger airplane is 250 passengers; the capacity of the smaller airplane is 100 passengers. If an airline assigned a 250-seat airplane to a specific flight, no more than 250 passengers could be accommodated. If the airline assigned a 100-seat airplane to a specific flight, no more than 100 passengers could be accommodated.

The finite capacity of an airplane establishes a limit that cannot be exceeded. This limit is a production frontier. A production frontier is the upper limit of capacity. For the 250-seat airplane, it is 250 passengers. For the 100-seat airplane it is 100 passengers. Any time actual usage is less than the production frontier, inefficiency is present. Consider the concept of a production frontier, shown as Figure 8-4.

As resources are increased, more service units are possible. As the size of an airplane assigned to a specific flight increases, the number of service units

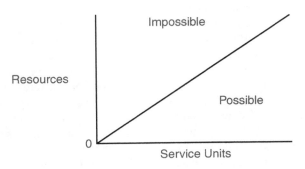

Figure 8-4 A Production Frontier

that can be generated increases. If the 250-seat airplane is substituted for the 100-seat airplane on a specific flight, capacity shifts from 100 passengers to 250 passengers.

The line on Figure 8-4 represents the maximum level of production associated with a specific level of resources. As stated, the 100-seat airplane cannot fly more than 100 passengers; 101 passengers are impossible. The 250-seat airplane cannot fly more than 250 passengers; 251 passengers are impossible. However, 250 or fewer passengers are possible. The only way capacity can be increased along the production frontier, in this case, is by substituting a larger airplane with more seats.

The line that establishes the boundary between the possible and impossible is referred to as a *production frontier*. At any specific level of resources, the production frontier cannot be crossed. The concept of production frontier establishes a quantitative measure of the upper limit of production capability at set level of resources.

Airlines measure their output based upon passenger miles. Each mile one passenger flies is one passenger mile. If an airplane flew 100 passengers 400 miles, this would generate 40,000 passenger miles. If an airplane flew 250 passengers 400 miles, the output of the flight would be 250 passengers' times 400 miles, or 100,000 passenger miles. Knowing the production frontier associated with specific levels of resources (e.g., a 100- versus 250-seat airplane), establishes the upper limit of output.

Knowing the upper limit of output provides the ability to compare actual output with potential upper limit capability to assess and manage the relationship between input resources and output. For example, if 100 passengers flew on the 250-seat airplane for the 400-mile trip, 40,000 of the potential 100,000 passenger miles were actually used, 60,000 of the passenger miles were not used. For this example, 40% of the capacity is being used. If the same airplane and load factors were experienced on a flight of 200 miles, 5000 passenger miles are possible but only 40% or 2000 passenger miles are produced.

Switching to healthcare organizations and systems, patient days are a measure of a hospital's outputs. A 100-bed hospital can produce no more than 36,500 patient days in any one non–leap year (365 days × 100 beds). Resident care days are used to express the output of a nursing home. Visits are used to express the output of a clinic or home health agency or service. Most other measures of output (and capacity) used in healthcare organizations and systems are production rates such as the number of procedures per minute, hour, day, week, or year. The number of procedures possible is the system's capacity. The number of procedures done is the system's output. Greater degrees of efficiency are achieved when the ratio measure of output divided by capacity approaches 1. If 100 procedures per hour are possible, doing 80 per procedures per hour indicates a higher level of efficiency than doing 30 procedures per hour.

The process of designing and analyzing service systems can be accomplished using a multistep process:

1. Identify the system or subsystem in question and identify the process, the steps and individual process. Typically, general system flow charting (see Chapter 3) is used to accomplish this step.
2. Determine who or what does what. Again, general systems flow charting is a useful tool to use to accomplish this step.
3. Determine the system's current capability. Determining the capability of each component in the overall production process can do this.
4. Compare the system's capability with its output.
5. Change the resource mix of the system as necessary to enhance the system's efficiency.

The critical step in this process is the determination of a system's capability.

Capacity can be measured and estimated. The time it takes staff to do a specific procedure or task can be measured. Repeated measures can be taken to ensure reliable and valid measures. Industrial engineering provides numerous approaches to measure the capacity of systems. Most involve observing a system and timing different steps.

Measuring and estimating the capacity of service systems should focus on the components of the service system. In some instances, categories of activities must be used. For example, a typical radiology department in a hospital can do in excess of 200 different x-ray procedures. The time and resources it takes to do each type of procedure can be estimated. Grouping specific procedures into resource-based categories facilitates analysis. For example, in radiology, x-rays may be able to be grouped into those that require one film or view versus those that require multiple films or views. Once categorized, the resources needed by each step in the production process can be measured and estimated by the type of procedure.

In some instances the best way to estimate capacity is to ask the professionals how many service units they can produce in a specific time period.

Capacity can be set at peak volumes. If measuring capacity cannot be done or is not feasible, the capacity of any system can be set at the level of peak volume achieved in the recent past. If a radiology department, with a specific resource mix, was able to process 150 x-rays in an 8-hour shift, then this system or subsystem has demonstrated it has this level of capacity. Using peak levels of performance to estimate capacity, whereas not as precise as capacity established based upon formal study, does provide the manager with a usable surrogate to estimate capacity.

The capacity analysis model is a quantitative model that can be used to establish the optimal or best level or resources needed to achieve a certain level of output. It is used when:

1. The same resources can be used to produce two or more types of services.
2. The problem is one of "mix;" that is, a problem that requires the most efficient optimal mix of at least two resources to produce the products or services.
3. The problem needs an optimal or best solution. A best solution is different than a good solution or acceptable solution.
4. There are constraints upon the solution. As such, certain solutions are outside the range of unable answers; they are infeasible solutions. A production frontier is an example of a constraint. These constraints are limited resources.
5. A linear relationship exists between the variables; when one variable changes, the others change in direct proportion regardless of production level.

Two methods exist: the graphical method and the algebraic method.

The graphical method establishes a graphical representation of two variables. Consider:

1. The budget is $5000 per day to support nursing salaries in a hospital. This is a constraint.
2. Registered nurses (RNs) are paid $200 per day; licensed practical nurses (LPNs) are paid $100 per day. These are constraints on the system as well.

For example:

1. Determine the nursing mix that will:
   a. Ensure at least one RN, and
   b. Will maximize the number of nurses in the hospital.
2. Determine the nursing MIX that will:
   a. Maximize the educational level of the nurses in the hospital, and
   b. Ensure at least 10 RNs and 10 LPNs.

To use this approach, a graphical model is developed that is based upon the constraints and issues in each assignment.

Consider the first constraints: budget and salary. With $10,000, one can hire 25 RNs ($10.000 ÷ $400/day) or 50 LPNs ($10,000 ÷ $200/day). This is shown graphically in Figure 7-5.

As can be seen in Figure 8-5, given the constraints associated with the assignment, 25 RNs or 50 LPNs could be hired with a budget of $10,000. Neither of these mixes of resources (25 RNs and 0 LPNs, or 50 LPNs and 0 RNs), however, satisfies all the parameters associated with the assignments. Some other mix is necessary.

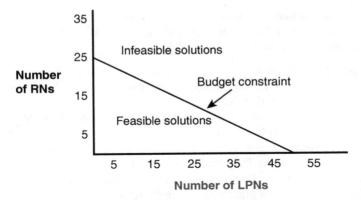

Figure 8-5 Graphical Representation of the Mix of Nursing Resources in a Hosptial

1. Determine the nursing mix that will:
   a. Ensure at least one RN, and
   b. Maximize the number of nurses in the hospital:

One RN costs $400 per day leaving $9600 to support LPNs. For $9600, at $200 per day, 48 LPNs can be retained. From Figure 8-6, the answer is one RN and 48 LPNs.

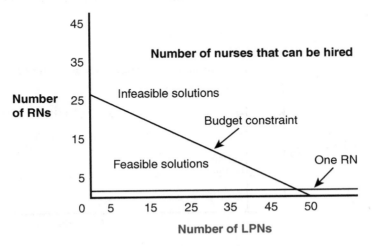

Figure 8-6 Graphical Solution to the First Part of the Nursing Task Mix

1. Determine the nursing mix that will:
   a. Maximize the educational level of the nurses in the hospital, and
   b. Ensure at least 10 RNs and 10 LPNs.

RNs have more education than LPNs. Ten (10) LPNs cost $2000 per day leaving $8000 to support RNs. At $400 per day, 20 RNs can be retained. From Figure 8-7, the answer is 10 LPNs and 20 RNs.

The graphical method of capacity analysis demonstrates the concept and the model when the mix involves mixing two variables or resources. Figures 8-5, 8-6, and 8-7 also demonstrate that some combinations of the two variables lie outside the realm of being feasible. They are infeasible solutions as long as the constraints and parameters established for the problem remain as stated or given. For example, given the constraints, it is infeasible to hire 35 RNs *and* 55 LPNs. Such a solution would violate the budgetary constraint used in this example. Solutions that are infeasible are beyond the production frontier associated with the constraints established for the specific situation.

As stated, the graphical approach is simple to use when only two resources need to be mixed and sufficient constraints and parameters are known to determine the "best" mix of resources.

The algebraic method of capacity analysis provides the same type of problem solving approach but is able to determine the best mix of more than two variables or resources. Similar to the graphical method, this method is based upon determining the production frontier and then determining the best mix of resources given specific constraints and parameters. Consider the following example involving a radiology department.

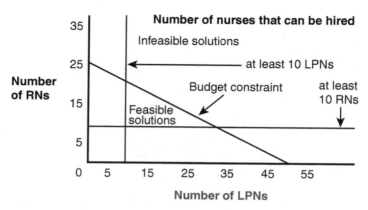

Figure 8-7 Graphical Solution to the Second Part of the Nursing Task Mix

Analysis has determined that the radiology department uses a four-step process-to-process x-rays:

1. The x-ray is *imaged*. The patient is escorted to a room with appropriate machines and the x-ray is taken. At the end of *imaging*, the patient leaves and the x-ray film is sent for processing and developing.
2. The x-ray is *developed*. The exposed x-ray is processed through a machine. After it is processed, it is usable.
3. The x-ray is *read* by a radiologist. The physician reads the x-ray and makes a clinical finding. The radiologist dictates a report.
4. The x-ray is *reported*. The report dictated by the radiologist is typed. One copy is placed in the medical record. One copy is filed in the radiology department and the other copy is sent to the physician who ordered the x-ray.

Analysis indicates that over the next 3-month period, each of these steps in the process has a finite capability or capacity. Each service station in the radiology department has a finite or limited number of work hours (assuming 80% productivity levels for all workers).

1. Imaging   = 630 work hours available
2. Developing = 600 work hours available
3. Reading   = 708 work hours available
4. Reporting   = 135 work hours available

Analysis also has determined that the radiology department does two types of x-rays:

1. General x-rays: These are simple procedures often only requiring one film.
2. Special x-rays: These are complex procedures that often require multiple films over a period of time.

Each step in the production process requires a different amount of time for each type of x-ray. Table 8-1 provides the time data for this problem.

Table 8-1 X-ray Processing Time Data (in Hours) by Type of X-ray

Stage	General X-rays	Special X-rays
Imaging	0.70	1.00
Developing	0.50	0.88
Reading	1.00	0.67
Reporting	0.10	0.25

Analysis has also determined that:

1. Each general x-ray has a $10 contribution margin
2. Each special x-ray has a $9 contribution margin

To find the mix of general and special x-rays that maximizes contribution to either profit or fixed costs, we use many of the previous relationships are established as equations:

If: GXR = the number of general x-rays
       SXR = the number of special x-rays
Then: TOTAL PROFIT (P) = $10 GXR plus $9 SXR

Fulfilling the assignment requires *maximizing* P or profit of 10 GXR plus 9 SXR, subject to the following constraints. Note that work time estimates for each step in the process are coefficients for GXR and SXR.

X-ray imaging cannot exceed 630 staff hours, so:

$$7/10 \text{ GXR} + 1 \text{ SXR must be} \leq 630 \text{ hours}$$

This should be read that the *sum* of the number of general x-rays, each of which takes 7/10th of an hour to image, times the number of general x-rays provided, plus the number of special x-rays, each of which takes 1 hour, times the number of special x-rays provided, must (in the next 3 months) be equal or less than 630 work hours. If it were more, a constraint would be violated.

X-ray developing cannot exceed 600 staff hours, so 1/2 GXR + 5/6 SXR must be equal to or less than 600 hours.

X-ray reading cannot exceed 708 staff hours, so 1 GXR + 2/3 SXR must be equal to or less than 708 hours.

X-ray reporting cannot exceed 135 staff hours, so 1/10 GXR + 1/4 SXR must be equal to or less than 135 hours. Both GXR and SXR must be numbers equal to or greater than zero.

The next step in establishing the model is to include the concept of slack (S). Slack refers to resources not used. In this example, slack would be the unused staff time or excess capacity. In each of the following equations, slack will take on the value necessary to establish the equality relationship.

IMAGING:	7/10	GXR +	1	SXR +	S_1 =	630
DEVELOPING:	1/2	GXR +	5/6	SXR +	S_2 =	600
READING:	1	GXR +	2/3	SXR +	S_3 =	708
REPORTING:	1/10	GXR +	1/4	SXR +	S_4 =	135

All slack variables must be zero or greater than zero.

Table 8-2 Limits on Capacity of Radiology Department

Stage	Maximum Number of General X-rays	Maximum Number of Special X-rays
Imaging	900	630
Developing	1,200	720
Reading	708	1,072
Reporting	1,350	540

Based upon these relationships and constraints, the production function for the multistep process can be determined. For example, for Imaging, 630 hours are available.

- At 7/10 per hour for each general x-ray, GXR can equal 900 general x-rays as long as SXR equals zero.
- Conversely, at 1 hour for each special x-ray, SXR can equal 630 special x-rays as long as GXR equal zero.

Using this approach to calculate maximum production possibilities by production stage yields Table 8-2. Given that x-ray production is a multistage process, this table indicates that only 708 general (GXR) x-rays can be produced.

Even though 900 general x-rays can be imaged, 1200 developed, and 1350 reported, only 708 can be read. Therefore, the overall production process is limited to a maximum of 708 general x-rays.

Only 540 special (SXR) x-rays can be produced. Even though 630 special x-rays can be imaged and 720 developed and 1072 read, only 540 can be reported. Therefore, the overall production process is limited to a maximum of 540 special x-rays.

Using this information, the *range* of possible maximum profits can be calculated:

- If 708 general x-rays are produced (and 0 special x-rays), profit will be 708 times $10 per x-ray or $7080.
- If 540 special x-rays are produced (and 0 general x-rays), profit will be 540 times $9 per x-ray or $4860.

At these levels of production, Table 8-3 provides a summary of excess capacity.

To know the exact mix of special and general x-rays that will maximize profits, given the production constraints and parameters, requires using a computer program that performs linear programming.

Table 8-3 Maximum Use of Resources in Radiology Department

Stage	Hours Used	Slack	Total Rate
Imaging	630	0	630
Developing	480	120	600
Reading	708	0	708
Reporting	117	18	135

If during the next 3 months, production were going to exceed a stated production frontier, then this model indicates which step or stage in the production process should receive additional resources. It also indicates where capacity could be reduced. Using the maximum ranges (708 general x-rays or 540 special x-rays), slack can be estimated (Table 8-4).

Given this approach, it would be feasible to reduce:

1. Imaging by up to 90 hours, and
2. Developing by 180 hours.

Table 8-4 Excess Capacity (Slack) in Radiology Department

Stage	Production Capability (Number of X-rays)	Production Limit (Number of X-rays)	Slack (Hours)[a]
General x-rays			
Imaging	900	708	192
Developing	1,200	708	492
Reading	708	708	0
Reporting	1,350	708	642
Special x-rays			
Imaging	630	540	**90**
Developing	720	540	**180**
Reading	1,072	540	532
Reporting	540	540	0

[a]The numbers in bold type represent excess capacity that could be eliminated without changing the mix of x-rays that could be produced in the next 3 months.

These actions would enhance efficiency and not impact any *mix* of x-rays that could be produced during the future 3-month period. If imaging hours were reduced by ninety (90), imaging would still have an excess capacity of 102 hours. Slack would be 102 (i.e., $192 - 90 = 102$). If the x-ray department was called upon to only produce special x-rays, reducing imaging by 90 staff hours would leave zero slack.

The situation with the developing stage is similar. If only general x-rays were done, reducing staffing by 180 hours over the next 3 months would still leave 312 excess hours (i.e., $492 - 180 = 312$). Reducing the developing stage by 180 staff hours would leave zero excess if only special x-rays were produced.

As demonstrated by this example, the capacity analysis model identifies the production frontier associated with multistep production processes and can be used to develop strategies to increase or reduce resources so that capacity and output are an efficient aspect of the operation of the system or subsystem. It is important to note that different services require different resources. The example classified x-rays into either general or special and states different resource requirements for each at each stage in the production process. More often than not, service stations in medical care production systems provide more than one type of service. The capacity analysis models are designed to assist when two or more variables (e.g., special versus general x-rays) are present. These models provide the ability to estimate production frontiers when faced with this type of situation.

EXERCISES

8-1 Two types of visits are provided by the Durham Health Clinic, first-time visits and return visits. Table 8-5 provides the processing time for each work station and the available staff hours per week. Determine the production frontiers for this clinic and indicate which station should be expanded to increase the overall capacity of the clinic. Which service station could be reduced?

Table 8-5 Processing Time and Staff Hours Data for Durham Health Clinic (Exercise 14-1)

	Time estimates (hours)	
Work station	*First Visit*	*Return Visit*
Reception/discharge	0.25	0.12
Nursing and testing	0.40	0.38
Medical exam and treatment	0.50	0.25

8-2 Durham Health Clinic has a contribution margin of $35 per visit. Calculate the break-even point in visits with fixed costs at $4000, $6500, and $8500 per week. Given this analysis, as a manager, what would you recommend and why?

8-3 Durham Health Clinic is considering signing a contract to perform 50 pre-employment physicals per week for a specific corporation. In terms of staff time, a pre-employment physical requires 0.20 hours in Reception/Discharge, 0.45 hours in Nursing and Testing, and 0.20 hours in Medical Examination. By work-station, determine how many work hours per week will be needed to perform these physicals.

8-4 Currently the clinic does 250 visits per week, with 50% of all visits as return visits. Each employee (physician, nurse, and receptionist) is scheduled to work 35 hours per week.

    a. How many employees by type does the clinic currently need?

    b. How many employees by type will the clinic need if it signs the contract for pre-employment physicals?

    c. If return visits shift to 10% of all regular visits, how many employees by type will the clinic need with and without the contract for pre-employment physicals?

    d. How will the answers to "b" and "c" change if the number of physicals is modified to 35 pre-employment physicals per week?

Throughout these analyses, specify all assumptions, including assumptions concerning worker productivity.

8-5 How would your answers change for problem 8-1 if nursing and testing time was increased to 0.50 hours for both first and repeat visits, and medical exam and treatment time was reduced to 0.30 hours for a first visit and 0.20 hours for a return visit?

Chapter 9

Managing Waiting Lines

LEARNING OBJECTIVES

1. To describe service systems and waiting lines using appropriate terms and concepts.
2. To analyze service systems and waiting lines using queuing theory.
3. To use queuing theory calculations to manage the relationship between waiting and the resources needed to provide service.

REAL WORLD SCENARIO

A walk-in clinic is experiencing significant patient waiting and is considering adding staff and examination rooms. Its goal is that patients do not wait more than 20 minutes to enter service. Analysis reveals that the hourly arrival rate averages 12 per hour on weekdays during the 12-hour shift from 8 AM to 8 PM. The current service rate with two examination rooms is 6.67 patients per hour. Management wants to know whether this system as designed should be experiencing excessive wait. What are the implications of expanding the number of examination rooms to four rooms with the ability to continue to service 6.67 patients per hour? Management needs answers.

LEARNING OBJECTIVE 1: TO DESCRIBE SERVICE SYSTEMS AND WAITING LINES USING APPROPRIATE TERMS AND CONCEPTS

We have all been there—waiting in line for service. Lines waiting for service are everywhere, including throughout health care. For example, laboratory specimens wait in line for processing. Bills wait in line for payment. Prescriptions wait in line for filling in a pharmacy. Computed tomography (CT) scans wait in line for interpretation. Patients wait to be seen by their primary care provider. Waiting in lines and health care today are ubiquitous.

This chapter focuses on waiting lines and service systems, and the quantitative models that can be used to balance the waiting time of units (e.g., people, laboratory specimens, bills, prescriptions, etc.) with the resources used to provide the service. Throughout this chapter, anything or anyone that waits in a line is referred to as a unit. The service provided to the unit is referred to as a unit of service.

Most people find waiting lines, especially waiting lines they consider too long, somewhat obnoxious, as well as a contemporary fact of life. People generally do not like to wait. For the patient, waiting is nonproductive time and is referred to as *idle time*. From a service system perspective, however, a line represents a demand for service. As long as a line of units, such as people or patients, is present, the server has the ability to engage in productive activity, such as serving the (next) unit, patient, resident, or client. In situations that use lines, when no line exists, the server is idle until the next unit arrives. Idle servers are not productive elements of the organizations. Units, such as people waiting in line for service, suggest that a server is productive. If no unit is on line, the server is idle, just waiting for a unit to enter the line and proceed to be serviced.

This last point is significant to your understanding of waiting lines. Servers, such as physicians, benefit from long patient waiting lines in their "waiting" rooms. When lines exist, the physician has no idle or nonproductive time between patients. When finished with one patient the physician is able to immediately move on to the next patient in line.

Providing a service requires and consumes resources. For example, filling a prescription requires a pharmacist's time as well as the supplies necessary to satisfy the demand expressed in the prescription. It also requires adequate space and, in some instances, specialized equipment. How long a specific unit, such as a prescription, waits in a line for service depends upon the number of pharmacists on duty to fill prescriptions as well as the time it takes the pharmacist to fill prescriptions that arrived earlier. In principle, adding more pharmacists and/or other resources can lower the time a unit waits in line. More pharmacists are able to process more prescriptions. Being able to process more units should lower the time any one unit has to wait in line for service. If, however, demand fluctuates and too many pharmacists are assigned, some will be idle and not engaged in productive activity.

Any service system has a finite (processing) capacity. Maybe one professor can grade five short papers per hour. Twelve minutes per paper or five papers per hour would be the (average) service rate of a system that relied upon one professor to grade short papers. As such, faced with a stack or line of 40 papers, it should take one professor 8 hours to process all the papers. Two professors should be able to complete the same task in approximately 4 hours, each devoting 4 hours to grading. Although the total amount of service time did not change, it remained at 8 hours; the time any one paper had to wait in line was shortened because all papers were graded in 4 hours. In other words, with one professor, the last paper in the line of stack had to wait 8 hours minus 12 minutes, or 7 hours and 48 minutes to be processed. With two professors, the last papers only had to wait 4 hours minus the 12 minutes necessary to process any one paper, or 3 hours and 48 minutes. By adding resources to the service system, such as adding an additional professor, the speed of the service system to process or serve units can be increased. A service rate (per hour) is defined as the amount of time it takes to provide service to one unit. In the previous example, the service rate per short paper was (on average) 12 minutes.

However, service systems have a finite, not an infinite, capacity to provide a unit of service. In some instances, the limitation of the service system is a physical limit. A hospital with three surgical suites can perform only three surgical operations at any one time. If the demand for surgery is more than three at any one time, patients wait. Machines also have limitations. For example, the CT scanner may be technically capable of no more than 100 individual scans per hour regardless of the staffing used to support the machine. In still other instances, management establishes a limitation of a service system based upon the number and type of servers assigned to the service system. By assigning one, in contrast to more than one, pharmacist to the pharmacy, management has defined the service capacity of the pharmacy. If one pharmacist is able to fill 10 prescriptions per hour, assigning only one pharmacist to the pharmacy limits the pharmacy's ability to service prescriptions to no more than 10 prescriptions per hour.

Management needs to balance waiting time with the resources used to provide a service. Health administrators face a dual and potentially conflicting concern. On one hand, health administrators are concerned about efficiency and worker productivity. Idle staff, machines, and surgical suites do not benefit the organization, its financial position, or its potential patients or clients. On the other hand, health administrators want to provide a quality service when it is needed. They want to minimize, for example, the amount of time a patient must wait for surgery, a laboratory test, or a specific treatment. Delay in providing a service is never therapeutic. Long delays may lead to a change or deterioration in the condition of the patient or a laboratory specimen awaiting a test. Although short delays are usually acceptable from a clinical perspective, the definition of what constitutes a long and or short delay is very circumstantial. Twenty (20) minutes may constitute too long or an unacceptable delay for a special medical test or procedure, given the condition of the patient. Twenty (20) minutes may, however, be a short or acceptable delay for a patient to be seen by the physician in an ambulatory care clinic. The clinical acceptability or unacceptability of the delay in the service system to provide the demanded (and needed) service varies based upon the specific service in question as well as other clinical and medical considerations. The client's acceptance of a delay may affect a patient and participation in the service. Too long a wait may decrease clientele.

To have an efficient organization as well as efficient service systems and sub-systems, managers must balance acceptable waiting times with the input resources used to provide the service. This balancing can be referred to as *managing the service system.*

A system's arrival rate is the rate (per hour) in which a unit arrives for service. Upon arrival, a unit either waits for service or, if the service system is idle, is served immediately and experiences no waiting time. Most lines work using first in, first out (FIFO). Units that arrive first are serviced first. Some exceptions exist.

In some instances, service systems are managed using scheduling and appointment systems to predetermine when units arrive. For example, most physicians in private practice provide appointments to their patients. Most patient admissions to a hospital are scheduled by providing an appointment for a given day. Surgeons are provided appointments for using a specific surgical suite in the hospital. Providing an appointment attempts to minimize the wait for service by establishing a constant demand over time for a service that can be met within existing resource levels.

In still other situations, special procedures are used to manage service systems. For example, in hospitals, a physician can order *stat* processing of a medical test, meaning that the test will be rushed to the laboratory and processed ahead of any other tests waiting service. In hospital emergency rooms, patients are seen and evaluated, and then placed in the service line based upon their medical needs, not based upon the order in which they arrive for service. Referred to as medical triaging, in this type of service system, one's place in the service line is not necessarily established by the order of arrival. Thus, in a hospital emergency room, the order of units in the line is determined and redetermined every time another patient arrives based upon the new patient's medical need. A patient will remain last in line as long as patients with more pressing medical needs continue to arrive and demand service.

Many analytical models exist to assist the manager to analyze service systems and balance the capacity of the system to provide a unit of service with the time a unit must wait for service. In other words, quantitative models exist to help managers make decisions concerning the design and operation of waiting lines. Some of these models can be found in queuing theory, the formal study of waiting lines. *Queue* is the English term for a waiting line.

LEARNING OBJECTIVE 2: TO ANALYZE SERVICE SYSTEMS AND WAITING LINES USING QUEUING THEORY

Queuing theory provides the ability to quantitatively describe lines, waiting, and the overall characteristics of service systems. To use this approach requires that the line and service system meet certain criteria. For example, units (e.g., patients, tests, prescriptions) must arrive for service randomly; they are not scheduled. When a unit arrives is not influenced by when previous units arrived or exited the system. The number of units waiting also must have no influence upon when a unit will arrive. If the average number of units that arrive in 1 hour is six, this does not mean that a unit arrives every 10 minutes. It means that in any 1 hour, six units on average will arrive. This is very different than a unit arriving every 10 minutes, even though both could be expressed as an arrival rate of six per hour. With an (average) arrival rate of six per hour there is a probability that all will arrive at any one time during the hour. There is also the probability that each will arrive every 10 minutes. Random arrivals mean that probabilities govern when units arrive in the specified time period.

Another defining criterion is FIFO line behavior. FIFO means first in, first out, as a characteristic of how units wait in a line. In a FIFO situation, the order of service is determined by the order of arrival. FIFO is present when the order of arrival determines the order the service system services the unit.

Using queuing requires channels and servers. Channels are the number of lines formed by the units. Supermarkets usually have many channels at the checkout stations. Some banks use one channel to feed multiple service windows or tellers. Channels are lines. Some systems are designed to have a single channel, and other systems are designed to have multiple channels. Servers provide the service. The checkout clerk in the supermarket is a server. The bank teller is a server. The physician in the walk-in ambulatory care clinic is a server. The pharmacist is a server. Sometimes a service team is composed of a number of healthcare providers (e.g., physician, nurse, and medical assistant) working together to provide the actual service. Some systems have one server or service team, whereas other systems have multiple servers or service teams. Common situations are one channel, one server and one channel, many servers.

If waiting never occurs, then queuing theory is not appropriate. Queuing theory assumes that, on average, at least some of the units wait. This does not mean that every unit waits. It means that every unit, when it arrives for service, has some probability of waiting. Depending upon the situation, some or many may wait. In other words, the probability of a unit waiting for service is greater than zero. *Wait* is defined as the amount of time between when a unit arrives and enters the line or queue and when the unit begins to receive service.

Given these characteristics, analytical models can be used to analyze the operation of the line and assist the manager to make decisions concerning the line and service system. Any analytical model is intended to assist the manager make a decision, not to make the decision. Making the actual decision is the prerogative and role of the manager, not the analytical model or technique. At best, the model informs the manager and clarifies alternatives and implications.

Other common terms and concepts from queuing theory are:

- Balking: When a unit seeing the length of the line decides it is too long and refuses to enter the queue.
- Reneging: When a unit waiting in line decides the wait has been too long, and leaves the queue.
- Batching: When more than one unit enters service at a time (e.g., family photo, well-child clinic).
- Jockeying: When the unit chooses one line and then decides another is shorter, and so changes queue.

LEARNING OBJECTIVE 3: TO USE QUEUING THEORY CALCULATIONS TO MANAGE THE RELATIONSHIP BETWEEN WAITING AND THE RESOURCES NEEDED TO PROVIDE SERVICE IN DIFFERENT TYPES OF SYSTEMS

Queuing theory uses the Poisson data distribution to describe arrivals to the service facility and the exponential data distribution—the inverse of the Poisson distribution—to describe service times. These are different than the binomial distribution. Arrivals and service times are random within the context of these two probability distributions. Based upon using these data distributions and specific formulae, queuing theory can be used to determine:

1. The percent of the time that a service facility is idle
2. The probability of a specific number of units in the service system
3. The average number of units in the system
4. The average time each unit spends in the system (waiting + service time)
5. The average number of unit in the waiting line or queue
6. The average time each unit spends in the waiting line
7. The percent of time or probability that an arriving unit will have to wait

This information together with additional information on the cost of providing a service and patient waiting line limitations (e.g., space) provides the manager with ample information to analyze, design, and redesign waiting lines and associated service systems.

A service "system" includes the line for service and the actual service facility. In a walk-in ambulatory care clinic, the "system" includes the waiting room and the examination room used by the nurses and physicians to diagnose and treat the patient.

Basic queuing theory uses a Poisson probability distribution to estimate the pattern in which units arrive for service. Studies generally indicate that the Poisson distribution is a most appropriate estimate of random arrival patterns. Unlike the binomial probability distribution, which is symmetrical and bell-shaped, Poisson distribution has a long tail (on the right), and the distribution is not symmetric. Unlike binomial distribution, which gives equal probabilities to values on either side of a mean, Poisson distribution recognizes that random arrival rates cluster about mean but cannot be less than zero. Arrival rates also have a (low) probability of being much higher than the mean. The queuing theory models presented in this chapter are based upon the Poisson distribution being used to estimate the random arrival pattern.

Queuing theory also offers a probability distribution to describe service times. A service time probability distribution is needed to estimate how long it takes to provide a unit of service. The exponential probability distribution, unlike the binomial data distribution, suggests that service times will be greater than zero and more frequently short than long.

It is important to note that the field of operations research indicates that using the Poisson probability distribution to describe and estimate random arrivals and the exponential probability distribution to describe and estimate service times, is usually the "best" approach to use in modeling and analyzing waiting lines. It provides the most conservative estimates; that is, the longest waiting time. This does not mean that this model is always the best. In some instances, even these probability distributions fail to capture the essence of arrivals and service times. In such situations, other probability distributions are used or waiting line models are developed using computer simulations.

For the purposes of this chapter, it is assumed that:

1. The Poisson probability distribution is considered an appropriate representation of arrivals.
2. The exponential probability distribution is considered an appropriate representation of service times.
3. The lines to be analyzed are governed by FIFO.
4. There is no balking, reneging, or jockeying.
5. There are no batch services.
6. The client population is infinite (i.e., sample with replacement).

Based upon these assumptions, queuing models are available to describe waiting lines based upon the number of channels (lines) and the number of servers. In general, as the arrival rate gets numerically closer to the service rate, the line will get longer while the idle time in the system will decrease. As the arrival rate gets numerically farther away (and less than) from the service rate, the line will get shorter but the idle time in the system will increase.

If for some reason the arrival rate is greater than the service rate, the queue will be infinitely long. In other words, all systems need to be designed with the service rate (per hour) greater than the arrival rate (per hour). Queue theory provides the consequences when the service rate is higher than the arrival rate.

Single Server Single Channel Queue Theory Models

This type of model has one server. To use this model requires estimating:

λ =   The expected number of arrivals per time period (mean arrival rate)
μ =   The expected number of services possible per time period (mean service rate)

(Note: For any system to work, λ must be less than μ.)
For purposes of this example, Let

λ =   arrival rate   =   3 per hour, and
μ =   service rate   =   4 per hour

Given these estimates, the following formulas can be used to calculate the probability that the service facility is idle (P_0); that is, no units are in the system.

The probability that the service facility is idle (P_0), and that no units are in the system:

$$P_0 = 1 - \left(\frac{\lambda}{\mu}\right)$$

$$= 1 - \left(\frac{3}{4}\right)$$

$$= 0.25 \text{ or } 25\%$$

The average number of units in the system (L):

$$L = \frac{\lambda}{(\mu - 1)}$$

$$= \frac{3}{(4 - 3)}$$

$$= 3 \text{ units}$$

The average time (in hours) a unit spends in the system (W); that is, waiting plus service time:

$$W = \frac{L}{\lambda}$$

$$= \frac{3}{3}$$

$$= 1 \text{ hour}$$

The average number of units in the queue waiting for service (L_q):

$$L_q = \frac{\lambda^2}{(\mu(\mu - 1))}$$

$$= \frac{3^2}{(4(4 - 3))}$$

$$= \frac{9}{4}$$

$$= 2.25 \text{ units}$$

The average time (hours) a unit spends in the queue waiting (W_q):

$$W_q = \frac{L_q}{\lambda}$$

$$= \frac{2.25}{3}$$

$$= 0.75 \text{ hours or 45 minutes}$$

The probability that a unit has to wait (P_w):

$$P_w = \frac{\lambda}{\mu}$$

$$= \frac{3}{4}$$

$$= 0.75 \text{ or } 75\%$$

Notice that P_w is $1 - P_0$, because a unit only waits for service if the server is busy. In a single channel, single server system, an idle system means an idle server, and a busy server means a unit must wait for service.

Given this model, additional estimates can be made based upon different values for λ, the rate of arrivals per hour, and μ, the service rate per hour (Table 9-1).

Table 9-1 Sample Performance Measures for Single-Server, Single-Channel Model

Service rate per hour (μ)	4	5	6	7	8
Arrival rate per hour (λ)	3	3	4	4	4
P_0	25.00%	40.00%	33.33%	42.86%	50.00%
L (units)	3.00	1.50	2.00	1.33	1.00
W (hours)	1.00	0.50	0.50	0.33	0.25
L_q (units)	2.25	0.90	1.33	0.76	0.50
W_q	0.75	0.30	0.33	0.19	0.12
P_w	75.00%	60.00%	66.67%	57.14%	50.00%

It is interesting to note that based upon these calculations:

- As the service rate (μ) increases 25%, from four to five service units per hour, estimated wait (W) decreases 50%, from 1.00 hour to 0.50 hours.
- As the rate of arrivals (λ) increases 33%, from three to four per hour, and the service rate (μ) increases 100%, from three to six per hour, wait (W) decreases 50% from 1.00 hour to 0.50 hours.

Note that the closer μ is to λ, the higher W will be.

These types of calculations and observations highlight the Poisson and exponential probability distributions at work and the type of tradeoffs managers can consider.

Any service system (usually) can increase its service rate by adding servers plus space, equipment, and other items needed to provide an additional service facility. Each of these costs can be estimated.

- Hourly wage rates can be used to estimate the cost of a service team.
- The cost of equipment can be estimated based upon its useful life, expressed in units of service and purchase + operational costs or its rental costs.
- The cost of space can be estimated based upon operational and capital costs, expressed on a square foot or market rental cost basis.

In this section, a single server system was analyzed using different service rates (e.g., service rate (μ) = 4, 5, 6, 7, and 8 units per hour). Increasing a service rate requires additional input resources. The critical managerial question is the *value* associated with adding additional resources to the service system given the characteristics of the service system. Consider the following example:

The cost per hour of a 1 MD + 1 RN service team for the ambulatory care clinic is $80 per hour. The 1 MD + 1 RN service team can service on average up to four patients per hour. If a physician's assistant (PA) is added to the team for an additional $12 per hour, the service team can service on average up to six patients per hour (i.e., 1 MD, 1 RN, 1 PA). If an additional RN is added to the team for an additional $20 per hour, the service team can service on average up to eight patients per hour (i.e., 1 MD + 2 RNs). The arrival rate is estimated to be three patients per hour. Consider Table 9-2. Is it worth an additional $12 or $20 per hour to alter this system?

To answer this question requires managerial judgment. The queue theory model plus some basic cost estimates provide the manager the information that is necessary to evaluate the situation and make an insightful decision based upon the circumstance.

Multiple Server, Single Line Systems

Multiple server systems have more than one server. They work differently than single server systems. In a multiple server system, when a unit gets to the head

Table 9-2 Performance Measures for Ambulatory Care Clinic with Single-Server Model

Service rate per hour (μ)	4	5	6	7	8
Service teams (S)	1	1	1	1	1
Arrival rate per hour (λ)	3	3	4	4	4
Staff cost per hour ($)	80	92	92	100	100
P_0	25.00%	40.00%	50.00%	57.14%	62.50%
L (units)	3.00	1.50	1.00	0.75	0.60
W (hours)	1.00	0.50	0.33	0.25	0.20
L_q (units)	2.25	0.90	0.50	0.32	0.22
W_q	0.75	0.30	0.17	0.11	0.07
P_W	75.00%	60.00%	50.00%	42.86%	37.50%

of the (single) line, the unit is served by the next available server. To use multiple server queuing models, let

S = the number of servers
    For example, let S = 2 servers
λ = Mean arrival rate for the system
    For example, let λ = 3 units per hour
μ = Mean service rate for the system
    For example, let μ = 4 units per hour

The actual formula for this analytical model is complex when S > 2. They are excluded to avoid confusion.

A table of the values for P_0, the probability that the service facility is idle, for the multiple-server model may be found at the end of the chapter (Table 9-7). This table also provides the calculations for L_q, the average waiting time in the queue. Table 9-7 uses two inputs:

1. The ratio of λ/μ
2. The number of channels

For example, if the arrival rate (λ) is eight clients per day and the service rate (μ) is 10 clients per day, the ratio of λ/μ is 0.80. If three servers are present, examine the cell value in the row for 0.8 and the column for three (see Table 9-7). These values are:

- 0.4472
- 0.0189

The result indicates that the system is idle (empty) 44.72% of the time and that the average number of units waiting for service is 0.0189, much less than one unit.

All other measures of performance can be calculated from these two values. Returning to the previous example, if $\lambda = 3$, $\mu = 4$, and $S = 2$, then $P_0 = 0.4545$, and $L_q \cong 0.125$ (interpolating between 0.7 and 0.8 for 3/4). Thus, the average number of units in the system (L), both waiting and being served:

$$
\begin{aligned}
L &= L_q + \left(\frac{\lambda}{\mu}\right) \\
&= 0.125 + \left(\frac{3}{4}\right) \\
&= 0.125 + 0.75 \\
&= 0.875 \text{ units}
\end{aligned}
$$

The average time a unit spends in the system (W):

$$
\begin{aligned}
W &= \frac{L}{\lambda} \\
&= \frac{0.875}{3} \\
&= 0.29 \text{ hours} \\
&= 0.29 \text{ hours} \times 60 \text{ minutes per hour} \\
&= 17.5 \text{ minutes}
\end{aligned}
$$

Another formula for W is:

$$
W = W_q + \left(\frac{\lambda}{\mu}\right)
$$

The average time a unit spends in the queue waiting for service (W_q):

$$
\begin{aligned}
W_q &= \frac{L_q}{\lambda} \\
&= \frac{0.125}{3} \\
&= 0.041 \text{ hours.}
\end{aligned}
$$

The probability that an arriving unit has to wait for service is equal to the probability that all servers are busy when a unit arrives. This means that the number, n, in the system is equal to or greater than the number of channels. This probability, P_w, can be obtained from the last table in this chapter, Table 9-8. In this table, the number of channels is identified as S, the number of servers.

For the last example, the ratio λ/μ is 3/4 = 0.75 and S = 2. Thus, P_w is found to be 0.2045. That is, more than 20% of the time, a unit has to wait to be served.

In the second example with the arrival rate of eight units per day and service rate of 10 units per day, the ratio λ/μ is 0.8. With three servers, the table value is 0.0520; that is, approximately 5% of the time a unit has to wait for service.

Using the multiple server queue theory model provides the ability to expand the economic analysis. In this case, the option is to establish additional service teams, not just add resources to an existing single service team.

Recalling the previous example, it was stated that the cost per hour of a 1 MD + 1 RN service team for the ambulatory care clinic is $80 per hour. A team with 1 MD + 1 RN can service on average up to four patients per hour. Therefore, one team can be expected to average up to four patients per hour; two teams can be expected to average up to eight patients per hour, etc. If a PA is added to the team (i.e., 1 MD + 1 RN + 1 PA) for an additional $12 per hour, then each service team can service on average up to six patients per hour. If an additional RN is added to the original team (i.e., 1 MD + 2 RNs) for an additional $20 per hour, the service team can service on average up to eight patients per hour. The arrival rate is estimated to be three patients per hour.

When an additional service team is added, costs also include expenses associated with the physical plant and equipment. For example, an additional service team may need additional offices, examination rooms, and/or treatment rooms. Additional equipment will be required so the new service team will not need to borrow from the original service team. The cost of adding a supplementary service team may be significantly different than adding salaries. For the example used, assume the estimate of these other costs is $5 per hour.

Given the example used throughout this chapter, the economic implications of different staffing levels for a single server model can be compared with the economic implications of using two (S = 2) service teams. Table 9-3 contains estimates concerning both types of service systems. As this example continues to unfold, queuing theory calculations and cost estimates provide the manager the ability to examine line and system characteristics and, by adding cost estimates, consider different configurations of the service system, associated lines, and the economic implications associated with different configurations.

Table 9-3 contains sufficient information for the manager to use to do a comprehensive analysis of the walk-in ambulatory clinic example using the cited parameters. For example,

- If the manager wanted to minimize the probability that a patient waits when he or she arrives at the walk-in ambulatory clinic, given the parameters cited in the example, two service teams would be used. The probability of waiting (P_w) is lowest under this option ($P_w = 20.45\%$). However, the cost of this option is the highest, at $165 per hour.
- If the manager wants to minimize costs, the best option would be to use a single server system with a staffing configuration of 1 MD and 1 RN. Under

Table 9-3 Performance Measures for Ambulatory Care Clinic with Single-Server Model and Multiple-Server Models

Service rate per hour (μ)	4	5	6	7	8	5
Service teams (S)	1	1	1	1	1	2
Arrival rate per hour (λ)	3	3	3	3	3	8
Staff cost per hour	80	92	92	100	100	165
P_0	25.00%	40.00%	50.00%	57.14%	62.50%	11.11%
L (units)	3.00	1.50	1.00	0.75	0.60	4.44
W (hours)	1.00	0.50	0.33	0.25	0.20	0.56
L_q (units)	2.25	0.90	0.50	0.32	0.22	2.80
W_q	0.75	0.30	0.17	0.11	0.07	0.36
P_W	75.00%	60.00%	50.00%	42.86%	37.50%	71.11%

this option, the cost per hour is $80. However, the probability of patient waiting (P_w) is the highest under this option ($P_w = 75\%$).

Marginal costs and marginal benefits can be compared using all the estimates included in Table 9-3. For example, is an increase of $85 per hour ($165 − $80 = $85), an increase of 106% worth a 73% decrease in the probability that a patient will wait (75% to 20.45%)? This depends on the value placed on patient time.

Queuing theory models provide the manager with a rich and comprehensive ability to analyze and design service systems, including the evaluation of lengths of lines and the potential for waiting. Based upon the goals and objectives of the system, the manager uses this information to trade off economic considerations with service system characteristics and considerations in arriving at the preferred configuration.

Appointment-Based Systems

Most appointment-based systems used in health care resemble a single server system. For example, a patient is given an appointment to see a specific physician, even though the physician may be one of many employed in a clinic. As a single

Table 9-4 Performance Measures for an Ambulatory Care Clinic with an Appointment-Based System

Service rate per hour (μ)	3	4	4	5	5	6
Arrival rate per hour (λ)	2	2	3	3	4	4
P_0	33.33%	50.00%	25.00%	40.00%	20.00%	33.30%
L (units)	2.00	1.00	3.00	1.50	4.00	2.00
W (hours)	1.00	0.50	1.00	0.50	1.00	0.50
L_q (units)	1.33	0.50	2.25	0.90	3.20	1.33
W_q	0.67	0.25	0.75	0.30	0.80	0.33
P_W	66.67%	50.00%	75.00%	60.00%	80.00%	0.67

server system, appointment-based systems can be analyzed using the single server queue theory model. Appointment systems fix the mean arrival rate, but not necessarily the inter-arrival times.

- An arrival rate (λ) = two units per hour means granting appointments every 30 minutes.
- An arrival rate (λ) = three units per hour means granting appointments every 20 minutes.
- An arrival rate (λ) = four units per hour means granting appointment every 15 minutes.

The service rate (μ) is estimated in the same manner as estimated using the queue models (e.g., μ = three or four units per hour). Table 9-4 presents the queue theory calculations for different service rates and arrival rates.

Using Queuing Theory for Staffing

A critical rule in queuing theory is that the arrival rate must be less than the system's service rate. The system service rate is the rate the entire system, potentially made up of many servers, can provide services. In a single server system the system's service rate is equal to the service rate of the one server. In a multiple server system, the service rate of the system is equal to the service rate of each server times the number of servers. Consider a clinic in which 280 patients arrived on average during the 7 hours the clinic was open. This would be calculated as an arrival rate of 40 patients per hour. Service time was estimated to be, on average 12 minutes per patient per service team or server. This is a service rate of five patients per hour per server. If this was designed as a single server system, with an arrival rate of 40 patients per hour and a service rate of five patients per hour, the system would create very long lines.

To calculate the minimum number of servers needed so that the arrival rate, on average, is less than the system service rate, divide the arrival rate (40 per hour) by the service rate per server (five per hour). This yields the answer eight. With eight servers, the arrival rate (40 per hour) now equals the systems service rate (i.e., five patients per hour × eight servers = a system service rate of 40 patients per hour). To be an efficient system, however, the system's service rate must be larger (not just equal to) the arrival rate. In this example, adding a ninth server can increase the service rate. With nine servers, the service rate is 45 patients per hour. As a system with nine servers, an arrival rate of 40 patients per hour and a service rate of 45 patients per hour, appropriate calculations can be made to examine the characteristics of the system. Perhaps a tenth server will be desired. This is a general way to estimate the number of servers needed to staff a service system.

In situations in which arrival rates vary dramatically, such as by time of day or day of the week, the analysis needs to examine the system during its peak and slow times using the standard queuing theory calculations.

Table 9-5 summarizes the equations and analytic approaches for waiting lines described in this chapter. The appropriate use of these models is dependent upon a series of assumptions involving the application of specific probability distributions. In instances in which these assumptions are not met, other approaches, such as computer simulations, must be used to develop and then use appropriate probability distributions that best fit the circumstances. Analytical models such as these can be used to analyze the operation of (waiting) lines and assist the manager in making informed decisions concerning the line and service system.

REAL WORLD SCENARIO REVISITED

This chapter began with a real world situation involving an urgent care clinic. In this clinic a physician and nurse or medical assistant work multiple examination rooms. The number of examination rooms being used to serve patients is equal to S, the number of servers. It is a multiple server single line system. The arrival rate (λ) is 12 patients per hour. The service rate (μ) is 6.67 patients per hour with S = 2. Note that λ/μ = 12/6.67 = 1.8. Consider this system's attributes:

Using Tables 9-7 and 9-8:

- When S = 2 (current system)
- The probability that a patient must wait when λ/μ = 1.8 and S = 2 is 85.26%.
- The probability that the system is empty (p_0) = 5.26%.
- The expected number of patients waiting in line for service (L_q) is 7.67.

Table 9-5 Queuing Theory Equations and Analytical Approaches

Parameter	Symbol	Single-server, single line	Multiple-server, single line
Service rate per hour (hr)	μ		
Arrival rate per hour (hr)	λ		
Probability (%) the service system is idle	P_0	$1 - \lambda/\mu$	See Table
Average number of units in the system	L	$\lambda/(\mu - \lambda)$	$L_q + (\lambda/\mu)$
Average time (hrs) a unit spends in the system	W	L/λ	L/λ
Average number of units waiting in line for service	L_q	$\lambda^2/(\mu(\mu - \lambda))$	See Table
Average time (hrs) unit spends in line waiting	W_q	$L_q/(\mu(\mu - \lambda))$	$W_q = L_q/\lambda$
Probability (%) a unit must wait on arrival	P_w	λ/μ	See Table

When S = 4 (expanded system):

- The probability that a patient must wait when $\lambda/\mu = 1.8$ and S = 4 is 12.85%.
- The probability that the system is empty (p_0) = 16.16%.
- The expected number of patients waiting in line for service (L_q) is 0.11.

Additionally, the average number of patients in the system (L), both waiting and being served:

$$L = L_q + \left(\frac{\lambda}{\mu}\right)$$

When S = 2
$$= 7.67 + 1.8$$
$$= 9.47 \text{ patients}$$

When S = 4
$$= 0.11 + 1.8$$
$$= 1.91 \text{ patients}$$

The average time a unit spends in the system (W):

$$W \quad = \frac{L}{\mu}$$

When S = 2

$$= \frac{9.47}{6.67}$$

$$= 1.42 \text{ hours or } 85.2 \text{ minutes}$$

When S = 4

$$= \frac{1.91}{6.67}$$

$$= 0.29 \text{ hours or } 17.4 \text{ minutes}$$

The average time a patient spends in the queue waiting for service (W_q):

$$W_q \quad = \frac{L_q}{\lambda}$$

When S = 2

$$= \frac{7.67}{12}$$

$$= 0.64 \text{ hours or } 38.4 \text{ minutes}$$

When S = 4

$$= \frac{0.11}{12}$$

$$= 0.009 \text{ hours or } 0.54 \text{ minute}$$

The proposed expansion to four examination rooms seems justified. It will better balance this system's service capabilities with patient waiting.

EXERCISES

9-1 Alpha Walk-in Clinic operates as a single channel single server system. On Tuesdays, its average arrival rate (μ) per hour is 7.0. Analysis indicates that its service rate (λ) is 8.5 patients per hour. Using queuing theory, describe this service system. What is:

    a. The probability that the clinic is idle—no patients waiting or being served?

    b. The average number of patients in the system?

    c. The average time (hours) a patient spends in the system (waiting + service time)?

d. The average number of patients in the queue waiting for service?
e. The average time (hours) a patient spends in the queue waiting?
f. The probability that the patient, upon arrival, must wait?

9-2 The following data have been collected from a hospital pharmacy. This service system operates as a single server, single channel system.

	7–3 PM	3–11 PM	11–7 AM
Service rate per hour	200	100	50
Arrival rate per hour	60	50	40

The service rate can be increased or decreased in increments of 50 prescriptions per hour. The expense associated with each 50-prescription increment is $100. In other words, to be able to process 50 additional prescriptions will cost an additional $100 per hour. If the current rate of processing or service is lowered by 50 prescriptions per hour, the savings are $100 per hour. Using queuing theory, describe this service system. What is:

a. The probability that the clinic is idle—no patients waiting or being served?
b. The average number of patients in the system?
c. The average time (hours) a patient spends in the system (waiting + service time)?
d. The average number of patients in the queue waiting for service?
e. The average time (hours) a patient spends in the queue waiting?
f. The probability that a patient, upon arrival, must wait?

Given the associated costs, should the service rate be changed? What are the financial implications associated with your recommendations?

9-3 Consider the data in Table 9-6. This table reports the number of a specific lab test received for processing at an outpatient medical lab over a 10-day period of time. Based on machine capabilities and staffing, the service rate for the day shift (7 AM–3 PM) must be constant even though the arrival rate changes during this time period. The system currently operates as a single channel single server system.

a. What service rate do you recommend for the day shift (7 AM–3 PM)? Remember that the service rate must be greater than the arrival rate. Use queuing parameters to describe this system with different service rates.
b. What are the implications of changing this system from a single server to a multiple server system in which S = 2. Show the queuing theory parameters. How would management make this decision?

Table 9-6 Data on Outpatient Medical Laboratory

Day / Time	Number of lab tests received by day and time			
	7–11 AM	11–3 PM	3–7 PM	7–7 AM
1	156	105	44	355
2	155	110	48	363
3	160	121	59	390
4	154	127	32	320
5	180	127	50	370
6	170	120	32	322
7	155	126	30	380
8	167	129	30	430
9	148	130	40	320
10	155	105	35	350
Average tests	160	120	40	360
Average per hour	40	30	10	30
Service rate per hour	60	60	20	40

9-4 One expectant mother arrives at a birthing center, on average, every 12 hours. She uses a birthing suite (and all associated services) for approximately 18 hours. How many suites should there be? Why? Assume one waiting area in the center and use days as the unit of time.

a. Probability that a unit must wait (P_w) in queuing system with Poisson arrivals and exponential service times.

b. Probability of an empty system (P_0) and expected number of units in the queue (L_q) for queuing systems with Poisson arrivals and exponential arrival times.

Table 9-7 Probability That a Unit Must Wait for Service (P_w) in Queuing Systems with Poisson Arrivals and Exponential Service Times.

Number of Servers in the Queuing System

λ/μ^a	1	2	3	4	5	6	7	8	9	10
.1	.1000	******	******	******	******	******	******	******	******	******
.15	.1500	.0104	******	******	******	******	******	******	******	******
.2	.2000	.0181	******	******	******	******	******	******	******	******
.25	.2500	.0277	******	******	******	******	******	******	******	******
.3	.3000	.0391	******	******	******	******	******	******	******	******
.35	.3500	.0521	******	******	******	******	******	******	******	******
.4	.4000	.0666	******	******	******	******	******	******	******	******
.45	.4500	.0826	.0113	******	******	******	******	******	******	******
.5	.5000	.1000	.0151	******	******	******	******	******	******	******
.55	.5500	.1186	.0195	******	******	******	******	******	******	******
.6	.6000	.1384	.0246	******	******	******	******	******	******	******
.65	.6500	.1594	.0304	******	******	******	******	******	******	******
.7	.7000	.1814	.0369	******	******	******	******	******	******	******
.75	.7500	.2045	.0441	******	******	******	******	******	******	******
.8	.8000	.2285	.0520	******	******	******	******	******	******	******

(*continues*)

Table 9-7 (*Continued*)

λ/μ^a	Number of Servers in the Queuing System									
	1	2	3	4	5	6	7	8	9	10
.85	.8500	.2535	.0606	.0117	******	******	******	******	******	******
.9	.9000	.2793	.0700	.0143	******	******	******	******	******	******
.95	.9500	.3059	.0801	.0171	******	******	******	******	******	******
1.0	******	.3333	.0909	.0204	******	******	******	******	******	******
1.2	******	.4499	.1411	.0370	******	******	******	******	******	******
1.4	******	.5764	.2033	.0603	.0153	******	******	******	******	******
1.6	******	.7111	.2737	.0906	.0258	******	******	******	******	******
1.8	******	.8526	.3547	.1285	.0404	.0111	******	******	******	******
2.0	******	******	.4444	.1739	.0597	.0180	******	******	******	******
2.2	******	******	.5421	.2267	.0839	.0274	******	******	******	******
2.4	******	******	.6471	.2870	.1135	.0399	.0125	******	******	******
2.6	******	******	.7588	.3544	.1486	.0558	.0187	******	******	******
2.8	******	******	.8766	.4286	.1895	.0754	.0270	******	******	******
3.0	******	******	******	.5094	.2361	.0991	.0376	.0129	******	******
3.2	******	******	******	.5964	.2885	.1271	.0508	.0184	******	******
3.4	******	******	******	.6893	.3466	.1595	.0669	.0256	******	******
3.6	******	******	******	.7877	.4103	.1965	.0862	.0346	.0127	******

3.8	******	******	.8914	.4795	.2382	.1088	.0456	.0175	******
4.0	******	******	******	.5541	.2847	.1351	.0590	.0237	******
4.2	******	******	******	.6337	.3359	.1650	.0749	.0313	.0121
4.4	******	******	******	.7183	.3919	.1988	.0935	.0407	.0164
4.6	******	******	******	.8077	.4525	.2365	.1150	.0518	.0217
4.8	******	******	******	.9016	.5177	.2783	.1395	.0650	.0282
5.0	******	******	******	******	.5875	.3241	.1672	.0805	.0361
5.2	******	******	******	******	.6616	.3740	.1982	.0983	.0455
5.4	******	******	******	******	.7401	.4279	.2330	.1186	.0565
5.6	******	******	******	******	.8227	.4859	.2706	.1415	.0694
5.8	******	******	******	******	.9094	.5479	.3120	.1673	.0843
6.0	******	******	******	******	******	.6138	.3569	.1959	.1012
6.2	******	******	******	******	******	.6836	.4055	.2275	.1204
6.4	******	******	******	******	******	.7572	.4576	.2622	.1420
6.6	******	******	******	******	******	.8345	.5133	.2999	.1660
6.8	******	******	******	******	******	.9155	.5725	.3408	.1925
7.0	******	******	******	******	******	******	.6353	.3849	.2217
7.2	******	******	******	******	******	******	.7015	.4322	.2536
7.4	******	******	******	******	******	******	.7711	.4827	.2882
7.6	******	******	******	******	******	******	.8441	.5363	.3256

(continues)

Table 9-7 (*Continued*)

Number of Servers in the Queuing System

λ/μ [a]	1	2	3	4	5	6	7	8	9	10
7.8	******	******	******	******	******	******	******	.9204	.5932	.3659
8.0	******	******	******	******	******	******	******	******	.6533	.4091
8.2	******	******	******	******	******	******	******	******	.7165	.4552
8.4	******	******	******	******	******	******	******	******	.7828	.5042
8.6	******	******	******	******	******	******	******	******	.8522	.5561
8.8	******	******	******	******	******	******	******	******	.9246	.6110
9.0	******	******	******	******	******	******	******	******	******	.6687
9.2	******	******	******	******	******	******	******	******	******	.7293
9.4	******	******	******	******	******	******	******	******	******	.7927
9.6	******	******	******	******	******	******	******	******	******	.8590
9.8	******	******	******	******	******	******	******	******	******	.9281

[a] In the relationship λ/μ, λ = arrival rate to the queuing system and μ = service rate for each server. For example, if λ = 6 and λ = 5, then λ/μ = 6/5 = 1.2. With the number of servers = 2, P_w = 0.4499. That is, the system with these characteristics has all servers busy almost 45% of the time, so there is a 45% probability that a unit must wait for service.

Table 9-8. Probability of an Empty System (P_0) and Expected Number of Units in the Queue (L_q) for Queuing Systems with Poisson Arrivals and Exponential Arrival Times

Number of Servers in Queuing System

λ/μ[a]	1	2	3	4	5	6	7	8	9	10
0.1	0.9000[b]	0.9048	0.9048	0.9048	0.9048	0.9048	0.9048	0.9048	0.9048	0.9048
	0.0111[b]	0.0003	0.0000	0.0000	0.0000	0.0000	0.0000	0.0000	0.0000	0.0000
0.2	0.8000	0.8182	0.8187	0.8187	0.8187	0.8187	0.8187	0.8187	0.8187	0.8187
	0.0500	0.0020	0.0001	0.0000	0.0000	0.0000	0.0000	0.0000	0.0000	0.0000
0.3	0.7000	0.7391	0.7407	0.7408	0.7408	0.7408	0.7408	0.7408	0.7408	0.7408
	0.1286	0.0069	0.0004	0.0000	0.0000	0.0000	0.0000	0.0000	0.0000	0.0000
0.4	0.6000	0.6667	0.6701	0.6703	0.6703	0.6703	0.6703	0.6703	0.6703	0.6703
	0.2667	0.0167	0.0013	0.0001	0.0000	0.0000	0.0000	0.0000	0.0000	0.0000
0.5	0.5000	0.6000	0.6061	0.6065	0.6065	0.6065	0.6065	0.6065	0.6065	0.6065
	0.5000	0.0333	0.0030	0.0003	0.0000	0.0000	0.0000	0.0000	0.0000	0.0000
0.6	0.4000	0.5385	0.5479	0.5487	0.5488	0.5488	0.5488	0.5488	0.5488	0.5488
	0.9000	0.0593	0.0062	0.0006	0.0001	0.0000	0.0000	0.0000	0.0000	0.0000
0.7	0.3000	0.4815	0.4952	0.4965	0.4966	0.4966	0.4966	0.4966	0.4966	0.4966
	1.6333	0.0977	0.0112	0.0013	0.0001	0.0000	0.0000	0.0000	0.0000	0.0000

(*continues*)

Table 9-8 (Continued)

				Number of Servers in Queuing System						
λ/μ^a	1	2	3	4	5	6	7	8	9	10
0.8	0.2000	0.4286	0.4472	0.4491	0.4493	0.4493	0.4493	0.4493	0.4493	0.4493
	3.2000	0.1524	0.0189	0.0024	0.0003	0.0000	0.0000	0.0000	0.0000	0.0000
0.9	0.1000	0.3793	0.4035	0.4062	0.4065	0.4066	0.4066	0.4066	0.4066	0.4066
	8.1000	0.2285	0.0300	0.0042	0.0005	0.0001	0.0000	0.0000	0.0000	0.0000
1.0	******	0.3333	0.3636	0.3673	0.3678	0.3679	0.3679	0.3679	0.3679	0.3679
	******	0.3333	0.0455	0.0068	0.0010	0.0001	0.0000	0.0000	0.0000	0.0000
1.1	******	0.2903	0.3273	0.3321	0.3328	0.3329	0.3329	0.3329	0.3329	0.3329
	******	0.4771	0.0664	0.0106	0.0016	0.0002	0.0000	0.0000	0.0000	0.0000
1.2	******	0.2500	0.2941	0.3002	0.3011	0.3012	0.3012	0.3012	0.3012	0.3012
	******	0.6750	0.0941	0.0159	0.0026	0.0004	0.0001	0.0000	0.0000	0.0000
1.3	******	0.2121	0.2638	0.2712	0.2723	0.2725	0.2725	0.2725	0.2725	0.2725
	******	0.9511	0.1303	0.0230	0.0040	0.0006	0.0001	0.0000	0.0000	0.0000
1.4	******	0.1795	0.2360	0.2449	0.2463	0.2466	0.2466	0.2466	0.2466	0.2466
	******	1.3451	0.1771	0.0325	0.0060	0.0010	0.0002	0.0000	0.0000	0.0000
1.5	******	0.1429	0.2105	0.2210	0.2228	0.2231	0.2231	0.2231	0.2231	0.2231
	******	1.9286	0.2368	0.0448	0.0086	0.0016	0.0003	0.0000	0.0000	0.0000
1.6	******	0.1111	0.1872	0.1993	0.2014	0.2018	0.2019	0.2019	0.2019	0.2019
	******	2.8444	0.3129	0.0605	0.0122	0.0023	0.0004	0.0001	1.0000	1.0000

1.7	******	******	0.0811	0.1657	0.1796	0.1821	0.1826	0.1827	0.1827	0.1827	0.1827
	******	******	4.4261	0.4095	0.0803	0.0168	0.0034	0.0006	0.0001	0.0000	0.0000
1.8	******	******	0.0526	0.1460	0.1616	0.1646	0.1652	0.1653	0.1653	0.1653	0.1653
	******	******	7.6737	0.5321	0.1052	0.0288	0.0048	0.0009	0.0002	0.0000	0.0000
1.9	******	******	0.0256	0.1278	0.1453	0.1487	0.1494	0.1495	0.1496	0.1496	0.1496
	******	******	17.5870	0.6884	0.1360	0.0303	0.0066	0.0014	0.0003	0.0000	0.0000
2.0	******	******	******	0.1111	0.1304	0.1343	0.1351	0.1353	0.1353	0.1353	0.1353
	******	******	******	0.8889	0.1739	0.0398	0.0090	0.0019	0.0004	0.0001	0.0000
2.1	******	******	******	0.0957	0.1169	0.1213	0.1222	0.1224	0.1224	0.1225	0.1225
	******	******	******	1.1488	0.2204	0.0515	0.0121	0.0027	0.0006	0.0001	0.0000
2.2	******	******	******	0.0815	0.1046	0.1094	0.1105	0.1107	0.1108	0.1108	0.1108
	******	******	******	1.4909	0.2772	0.0659	0.0159	0.0037	0.0008	0.0002	0.0000
2.3	******	******	******	0.0683	0.0933	0.0987	0.0999	0.1002	0.1002	0.1003	0.1003
	******	******	******	1.9511	0.3464	0.0835	0.0207	0.0049	0.0011	0.0002	0.0000
2.4	******	******	******	0.0562	0.0831	0.0889	0.0903	0.0906	0.0907	0.0907	0.0907
	******	******	******	2.5888	0.4306	0.1048	0.0266	0.0065	0.0015	0.0003	0.0001
2.5	******	******	******	0.0449	0.0737	0.0801	0.0816	0.0820	0.0821	0.0821	0.0821
	******	******	******	3.5112	0.5331	0.1304	0.0339	0.0086	0.0021	0.0005	0.0001
2.6	******	******	******	0.0345	0.0651	0.0721	0.0737	0.0742	0.0742	0.0743	0.0743
	******	******	******	4.9328	0.6582	0.1610	0.0427	0.0111	0.0027	0.0006	0.0001

(continues)

Table 9-8 (*Continued*)

					Number of Servers in Queuing System					
λ/μ^a	1	2	3	4	5	6	7	8	9	10
2.7	******	******	0.0249	0.0573	0.0648	0.0666	0.0671	0.0672	0.0672	0.0672
	******	******	7.3535	0.8115	0.1976	0.0533	0.0142	0.0036	0.0009	0.0002
2.8	******	******	0.0160	0.0502	0.0581	0.0601	0.0606	0.0607	0.0608	0.0608
	******	******	12.2735	1.0020	0.2412	0.0660	0.0180	0.0047	0.0012	0.0003
2.9	******	******	0.0077	0.0437	0.0521	0.0543	0.0548	0.0550	0.0550	0.0550
	******	******	27.1927	1.2345	0.2929	0.0812	0.0227	0.0061	0.0015	0.0004
3.0	******	******	******	0.0377	0.0466	0.0490	0.0496	0.0497	0.0498	0.0498
	******	******	******	1.5283	0.3542	0.0991	0.0282	0.0078	0.0020	0.0005
3.1	******	******	******	0.0323	0.0417	0.0441	0.0448	0.0450	0.0450	0.0450
	******	******	******	1.9019	0.4269	0.1203	0.0349	0.0098	0.0026	0.0007
3.2	******	******	******	0.0273	0.0372	0.0398	0.0405	0.0407	0.0407	0.0408
	******	******	******	2.3857	0.5130	0.1453	0.0428	0.0123	0.0034	0.0009
3.3	******	******	******	0.0227	0.0330	0.0358	0.0366	0.0368	0.0369	0.0369
	******	******	******	3.0273	0.6152	0.1745	0.0522	0.0153	0.0043	0.0011
3.4	******	******	******	0.0186	0.0293	0.0322	0.0331	0.0333	0.0334	0.0334
	******	******	******	3.9061	0.7367	0.2086	0.0633	0.0190	0.0054	0.0015
3.5	******	******	******	0.0148	0.0259	0.0290	0.0298	0.0301	0.0302	0.0302
	******	******	******	5.1650	0.8816	0.2485	0.0762	0.0232	0.0068	0.0019

3.6	******	******	******	0.0113	0.0228	0.0260	0.0269	0.0272	0.0273	0.0273
	******	******	******	7.0898	1.0553	0.2948	0.0913	0.0283	0.0085	0.0024
3.7	******	******	******	0.0081	0.0200	0.0233	0.0243	0.0246	0.0247	0.0247
	******	******	******	10.3471	1.2646	0.3488	0.1089	0.0343	0.0105	0.0031
3.8	******	******	******	0.0051	0.0174	0.0209	0.0219	0.0222	0.0223	0.0224
	******	******	******	16.9370	1.5187	0.4116	0.1293	0.0413	0.0129	0.0038
3.9	******	******	******	0.0025	0.0151	0.0187	0.0198	0.0201	0.0202	0.0202
	******	******	******	36.8595	1.8302	0.4846	0.1529	0.0495	0.0157	0.0048
4.0	******	******	******	******	0.0130	0.0670	0.0178	0.0182	0.0183	0.0183
	******	******	******	******	2.2165	0.5695	0.1801	0.0590	0.0190	0.0059
4.1	******	******	******	******	0.0111	0.0149	0.0160	0.0164	0.0165	0.0166
	******	******	******	******	2.7029	0.6685	0.2115	0.0701	0.0229	0.0072
4.2	******	******	******	******	0.0093	0.0132	0.0144	0.0148	0.0149	0.0150
	******	******	******	******	3.3273	0.7839	0.2476	0.0828	0.0275	0.0088
4.3	******	******	******	******	0.0077	0.0117	0.0130	0.0134	0.0135	0.0136
	******	******	******	******	4.1494	0.9191	0.2890	0.0975	0.0328	0.0107
4.4	******	******	******	******	0.0063	0.0104	0.0117	0.0121	0.0122	0.0123
	******	******	******	******	5.2682	1.0778	0.3365	0.1143	0.0389	0.0129
4.5	******	******	******	******	0.0050	0.0091	0.0105	0.0109	0.0110	0.0111
	******	******	******	******	6.8624	1.2650	0.3910	0.1336	0.0460	0.0155
4.6	******	******	******	******	0.0038	0.0080	0.0094	0.0098	0.0100	0.0100
	******	******	******	******	9.2893	1.4869	0.4535	0.1556	0.0542	0.0185

(continues)

Table 9-8 (*Continued*)

λ/μ^a	\multicolumn{10}{c}{Number of Servers in Queuing System}

λ/μ^a	1	2	3	4	5	6	7	8	9	10
4.7	******	******	******	******	0.0027	0.0070	0.0084	0.0089	0.0090	0.0091
	******	******	******	******	13.3821	1.7520	0.5251	0.1807	0.0636	0.0220
4.8	******	******	******	******	0.0017	0.0061	0.0075	0.0080	0.0081	0.0082
	******	******	******	******	21.6408	2.0711	0.6073	0.2093	0.0744	0.0261
4.9	******	******	******	******	0.0008	0.0053	0.0067	0.0072	0.0074	0.0074
	******	******	******	******	46.5655	2.4593	0.7017	0.2418	0.0867	0.0307
5.0	******	******	******	******	******	0.0045	0.0060	0.0065	0.0066	0.0067
	******	******	******	******	******	2.9376	0.8104	0.2788	0.1006	0.0361
5.1	******	******	******	******	******	0.0038	0.0053	0.0058	0.0060	0.0061
	******	******	******	******	******	3.5363	0.9357	0.3207	0.1165	0.0423
5.2	******	******	******	******	******	0.0032	0.0047	0.0052	0.0054	0.0055
	******	******	******	******	******	4.3009	1.0805	0.3683	0.1345	0.0493
5.3	******	******	******	******	******	0.0027	0.0042	0.0047	0.0049	0.0050
	******	******	******	******	******	5.3028	1.2486	0.4222	0.1549	0.0573
5.4	******	******	******	******	******	0.0021	0.0037	0.0042	0.0044	0.0045
	******	******	******	******	******	6.6611	1.4444	0.4833	0.1779	0.0664
5.5	******	******	******	******	******	0.0017	0.0032	0.0038	0.0040	0.0040

x									
5.6	******	******	******	******	8.5902	1.6736	0.5527	0.2039	0.0767
	******	******	******	******	0.0013	0.0028	0.0034	0.0036	0.0037
5.7	******	******	******	******	11.5185	1.9438	0.6314	0.2332	0.0884
	******	******	******	******	0.0009	0.0025	0.0030	0.0032	0.0033
5.8	******	******	******	******	16.4462	2.2643	0.7208	0.2662	0.1016
	******	******	******	******	0.0006	0.0021	0.0027	0.0029	0.0030
5.9	******	******	******	******	26.3732	2.6482	0.8226	0.3033	0.1165
	******	******	******	******	0.0003	0.0018	0.0024	0.0026	0.0027
6.0	******	******	******	******	56.2996	3.1130	0.9385	0.3451	0.1332
	******	******	******	******	******	0.0016	0.0021	0.0024	0.0024
6.1	******	******	******	******	******	3.6830	1.0709	0.3920	0.1519
	******	******	******	******	******	0.0013	0.0019	0.0021	0.0022
6.2	******	******	******	******	******	4.3937	1.2226	0.4447	0.1730
	******	******	******	******	******	0.0011	0.0017	0.0019	0.0020
6.3	******	******	******	******	******	5.2981	1.3968	0.5039	0.1966
	******	******	******	******	******	0.0009	0.0015	0.0017	0.0018
6.4	******	******	******	******	******	6.4796	1.5977	0.5705	0.2230
	******	******	******	******	******	0.0007	0.0013	0.0015	0.0016
6.5	******	******	******	******	******	8.0771	1.8306	0.6455	0.2525
	******	******	******	******	******	0.0006	0.0012	0.0014	0.0015
	******	******	******	******	******	10.3406	2.1019	0.7298	0.2855

(continues)

Table 9-8 (*Continued*)

						Number of Servers in Queuing System				
λ/μ^a	1	2	3	4	5	6	7	8	9	10
6.6	******	******	******	******	******	******	0.0004	0.0010	0.0012	0.0013
							13.7701	2.4200	0.8249	0.3223
6.7	******	******	******	******	******	******	0.0003	0.0009	0.0011	0.0012
							19.5323	2.7960	0.9323	0.3634
6.8	******	******	******	******	******	******	0.0002	0.0008	0.0010	0.0011
							31.1272	3.2446	1.0536	0.4092
6.9	******	******	******	******	******	******	0.0001	0.0007	0.0009	0.0010
							66.0548	3.7856	1.1911	0.4603
7.0	******	******	******	******	******	******	******	0.0006	0.0008	0.0009
								4.4472	1.3473	0.5174
7.1	******	******	******	******	******	******	******	0.0007	0.0007	0.0008
								5.2697	1.5253	0.5810
7.2	******	******	******	******	******	******	******	0.0004	0.0006	0.0007
								6.3138	1.7289	0.6521
7.3	******	******	******	******	******	******	******	0.0003	0.0005	0.0006
								7.6747	1.9627	0.7315
7.4	******	******	******	******	******	******	******	0.0003	0.0004	0.0006
								9.5111	2.2325	0.8204

7.5	******	******	******	******	******	******	******	0.0002	0.0004	0.0005
	******	******	******	******	******	******	******	12.1088	2.5457	0.9198
7.6	******	******	******	******	******	******	******	0.0002	0.0004	0.0004
	******	******	******	******	******	******	******	16.0392	2.9118	1.0314
7.7	******	******	******	******	******	******	******	0.0001	0.0003	0.0004
	******	******	******	******	******	******	******	22.6357	3.3432	1.1566
7.8	******	******	******	******	******	******	******	0.0001	0.0003	0.0004
	******	******	******	******	******	******	******	35.8982	3.8563	1.2976
7.9	******	******	******	******	******	******	******	0.0000	0.0002	0.0003
	******	******	******	******	******	******	******	75.8269	4.4736	1.4567
8.0	******	******	******	******	******	******	******	******	0.0002	0.0003
	******	******	******	******	******	******	******	******	5.2226	1.6367
8.1	******	******	******	******	******	******	******	******	0.0002	0.0002
	******	******	******	******	******	******	******	******	6.1608	1.8411
8.2	******	******	******	******	******	******	******	******	0.0001	0.0002
	******	******	******	******	******	******	******	******	7.3444	2.0740
8.3	******	******	******	******	******	******	******	******	0.0001	0.0002
	******	******	******	******	******	******	******	******	8.8845	2.3406
8.4	******	******	******	******	******	******	******	******	0.0001	0.0002
	******	******	******	******	******	******	******	******	10.9597	2.6474
8.5	******	******	******	******	******	******	******	******	0.0001	0.0001
	******	******	******	******	******	******	******	******	13.8914	3.0025

(continues)

Table 9-8 (*Continued*)

λ/μ^a	1	2	3	4	5	6	7	8	9	10
									Number of Servers in Queuing System	
8.6	******	******	******	******	******	******	******	******	0.0001	0.0001
8.7	******	******	******	******	******	******	******	******	18.3226	3.4166
	******	******	******	******	******	******	******	******	0.0000	0.0001
8.8	******	******	******	******	******	******	******	******	25.7532	3.9032
	******	******	******	******	******	******	******	******	0.0000	0.0001
8.9	******	******	******	******	******	******	******	******	40.6832	4.4807
	******	******	******	******	******	******	******	******	0.0000	0.0001
9.0	******	******	******	******	******	******	******	******	85.6127	5.1742
	******	******	******	******	******	******	******	******	*******	0.0001
9.1	******	******	******	******	******	******	******	******	*******	6.0186
	******	******	******	******	******	******	******	******	*******	0.0001
9.2	******	******	******	******	******	******	******	******	*******	7.0644
	******	******	******	******	******	******	******	******	*******	0.0000
9.3	******	******	******	******	******	******	******	******	*******	8.3873
	******	******	******	******	******	******	******	******	*******	0.0000
	******	******	******	******	******	******	******	******	*******	10.1066

9.4	******	******	******	******	******	******	******	******	0.0000
	******	******	******	******	******	******	******	******	12.4204
9.5	******	******	******	******	******	******	******	******	0.0000
	******	******	******	******	******	******	******	******	15.6861
9.6	******	******	******	******	******	******	******	******	0.0000
	******	******	******	******	******	******	******	******	20.6179
9.7	******	******	******	******	******	******	******	******	0.0000
	******	******	******	******	******	******	******	******	28.8825
9.8	******	******	******	******	******	******	******	******	0.0000
	******	******	******	******	******	******	******	******	45.4799
9.9	******	******	******	******	******	******	******	******	0.0000
	******	******	******	******	******	******	******	******	95.4101

[a] In the relationship $\frac{\lambda}{\mu}$, λ = arrival rate and μ = service rate for each server.

[b] Cells show the values for P_0 (top value) and L_q (bottom value) for each λ/μ and number of servers. For example, if $\lambda = 3$ and $\mu = 2$, then $\lambda/\mu = 3/2 = 1.5$. With the number of servers = 2, $P_0 = 0.1429$ and $L_q = 1.9286$. That is, the system with these characteristics is empty of units less than 15% of the time and, on average, there are almost two units waiting for service.

SECTION IV

Project Analysis

Chapter 10

Decision Analysis

LEARNING OBJECTIVES

1. To be able to construct and use decision trees as a method to examine decision alternatives.
2. To be able to calculate expected payoff and select a decision based upon maximum payoff using specific examples.

REAL WORLD SCENARIO

Hayes Markham is the administrator for the Amherst Clinic, one of ten clinics in the Hancock Medical System. Recently the clinic has been realizing higher than average visit volumes. Hayes examined this using statistical control charting (discussed in Chapter 14), and found evidence to suggest that a fundamental change had occurred. Upon further investigation, it was found that the population in the clinic's service area had increased by 5%, largely because of the relocation of a large employer, Bayside Systems, to the neighboring town of Gardner, which the Amherst Clinic serves. In talking to management from Bayside, they conveyed that further growth was likely, as they had plans to relocate two additional divisions to the Gardner facility. This would add an additional 400 employees. They could not, however, provide a definite assurance of this, or timeline for the addition. At the clinic, wait times have increased, appointment times have been extended to the future, and the staff has begun to hear rumblings of patient dissatisfaction. Hayes must decide on a course of action for the clinic, examining all possible options.

Managerial life is full of decisions. Managers must decide, given available resources, how best to meet their organization's mission. Often, managers must adjust organizational goals and objectives based upon changes in internal capacity or the external environment. They often investigate ways to enhance the efficiency and effectiveness of their organization, which often requires making decisions involving the reallocation of resources that in turn affect the work and process flow within the organization. And most important, they have to make decisions in a systematic way that relies on informed assessments and not purely on gut reactions and incomplete or false information.

195

This chapter examines the art and science of decision analysis. Although it is a process influenced by many qualitative factors, such as organizational culture, precedents, and the values of the managers, it is also a process in which quantitative analytic frameworks can be effectively applied.

LEARNING OBJECTIVE 1: TO BE ABLE TO CONSTRUCT AND USE DECISION TREES AS A METHOD TO EXAMINE DECISION ALTERNATIVES

Most decisions are made under conditions of uncertainty. It is rare that one knows with full certainty the consequences of his or her decisions. Some decisions are simple, having only two outcomes, but others are complex, having any number of potential outcomes. The outcomes associated with decision alternatives are further governed by unknown probabilities. At times the decision maker will have some insight into these probabilities, such as the chance of rain from a weather forecast. Other times, decisions must be made in an environment of complete uncertainty. How to handle both is examined here. Finally, all decisions carry implications. A decision might mean that a fewer or greater number of resources are used in the future. It might mean extending the types of services currently being offered, or offering them at a new location. For the purposes of this analytic method, all outcomes are assessed in terms of some monetary cost. What is the value of adding 10 more appointment slots to a clinic? What is the cost? And thus, what is the net revenue? Here these are termed *payoffs*, and they can be either negative or positive. It is important to note, however, that in practice not all payoffs are monetary. In the medical professions these can also be expressed as years of life gained, or quality adjusted life years (QALYs) to name a few. Decision analysis of this type, falling under the category of cost-effectiveness analysis, is beyond the scope of this text.

There are three parts to any decision, only two of which are under the control of the decision maker. They are:

1. Stating the *alternatives* from which a decision can be made. These are the decision options, and they *are* under the control of the decision maker. Examples are whether to hire more staff or not, or to invest in equipment or not.
2. Conceptualizing the *state of the world* that will occur in the future. These are unknowns at the time the decision is made. These are *not* under the control of the decision maker. Examples are whether or not visit volume increases or a new technology is developed.
3. Determining the potential *payoffs* of the decision combined with the potential states of the world that may or may not occur. These *are* within the control/consideration of the decision maker and should be assessed in the most complete manner possible. This means using as much relevant information as

is available. An example is the potential net revenue that would come from adding service hours, minus resource cost, within reasonable estimates of potential volume increases.

Managers are expected to consider alternatives before making a decision. Some alternatives are different strategies intended to realize the same outcome or payoff. In other instances, managers consider very different alternatives given their assessment of the payoffs and outcomes associated with each alternative; for example, to carry an umbrella on a given day. Intuitively, each person makes this decision using reasoned judgment. We listen to the weather reports and then think about how far we have to walk. We also might think about what we are wearing that day. In this example, the alternatives are either to carry the umbrella or not. The states of the world will be either that it will rain or it will not. States of the world are unknown in that they occur in the future. So, regardless of which alternative we choose, there is a chance that any of the states of the world could occur. In decision analysis, we list our alternatives for each state of the world. We then determine the payoff for each interaction of alternative and state of the world. For this example, let us determine the payoffs as the cost of an umbrella, should we carry one, but lose it or break it and the cost of ruined clothes, should we not choose to carry an umbrella and get rained upon. There are obviously others, but we will use these for simplicity.

There are always as many possible payoffs as the product of the number of alternatives times the number of states of the world. In this case, for example, there are two alternatives and two states of the world for a total of four payoffs (Table 10-1).

This example demonstrates the basic decision analytic approach covered in this chapter—the explicit identification of decision alternatives, states of the world, and comparison of outcomes and payoffs. Missing from this simple analysis, however, is an assessment of the likelihood of rain. It is rarely the case that we have no information on the day's weather. Decision analysis allows for us to assign each

Table 10-1 Two Alternatives and Two States of the World for a Total of Four Payoffs

Alternative	State of the world	Payoff
Carry an umbrella	It rains	Lose umbrella: –$1
	It does not rain	Lose umbrella: –$1
Don't carry an umbrella	It rains	Ruin Clothes: –$50
	It does not rain	No loss: $0

state of the world a probability of occurrence to better assess the payoffs. It is a formal process very similar to the intuitive processes we use every time we hear of the chance of showers. The difference, however, is that the explicit approach has the power to assist health services managers identify alternatives and select among the alternatives.

One way of looking at the chronology and payoffs of a decision is to construct a decision tree. A decision tree looks like a tree with branches for each decision alternative and each state of the world. A square is used for a choice node and a circle is used for the states of the world nodes. The decision tree for the previous example is shown in Figure 10-1. Note that this tree shows the decision being made first and the weather condition occurring second. When you choose to carry the umbrella, you are choosing under conditions of uncertainty; you do not know for certain whether it will rain or not. If it is raining when you leave the house, you are choosing under conditions of certainty; you know the payoff for sure so you choose correctly every time. On a day when it is not raining as you leave the house, you do not know the state of the world later that day *for certain* so you cannot *be certain* of choosing correctly. In this instance, you would no doubt consult a weather forecast for assistance. In our example, let us suppose that there is an 80% chance of rain. You will notice that in our decision tree diagram, this probability is added after each state of the world in Figure 10-2. From this information we can calculate our total expected payoffs for each decision.

Expected Payoff as the Decision Making Criterion

From statistics, recall the idea of the expected value of some outcome, x. Here, x is our payoff. The formula of the expected value of x, $E(X)$ is:

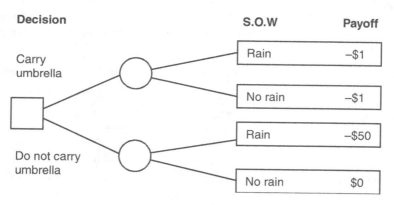

Figure 10-1 Decision Tree for Carrying an Umbrella

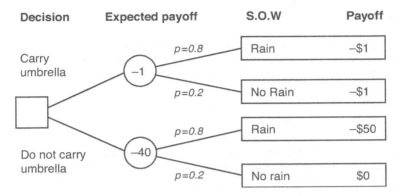

| Decision | Expected payoff | S.O.W | Payoff |

Figure 10-2 Decision Tree for Carrying an Umbrella Part 2

$E(X)$ = probability of (X_1) × payoff of (X_1) + probability of (X_2) × payoff of (X_2) + probability of (X_3) × payoff of (X_3) + ... probability of (X_n) × payoff of (X_n)

where the Xs are the possible outcomes.

Each decision alternative has an expected payoff. When the expected payoffs have been calculated, you would then choose the alternative whose expected payoff is best. With monetary outcomes, this is often the expected value that is greatest. In the example of carrying the umbrella, we examine the expected cost, or financial consequences for each alternative. Table 10-2 shows the expected payoffs for this example.

We stated our probability of rain at 80%. Knowing that the probabilities of states of the world must add up to one, if there is an 80% chance of rain, then there is a 20% chance it will not rain.

This is also illustrated in the decision tree in Figure 10-2. Note that the expected payoffs are written inside the state of the world nodes.

If we carry the umbrella, there is a chance of leaving it somewhere, but that cost is low (loss of $1) compared with not carrying the umbrella and ruining our clothes (loss of $40).

We should choose, under these probabilities of rain, to carry an umbrella as the expected cost to us is lowest.

Table 10-2 Expected Payoffs Umbrella Example

Expected payoff [carry]	= (0.8 × −$1) + (0.2 × −$1) = −$1
Expected payoff [not carry]	= (0.8 × −$50) + (0.2 × $0) = −$40

Break Even Analysis

Thinking about the preceding example, one question that may come to mind would be, How low does the probability of rain have to be before we leave our umbrella at home? In essence we are asking at what probabilities for future states of the world we are indifferent to our decision choices. This is a break even question, presented in Chapter 8. Expressed as a break even question, with the payoffs we have estimated, what probability value will give an expected payoff if we do not carry an umbrella equal to the expected payoff if we do?

In this case, we would set the expected payoff of not carrying an umbrella be equal to −$1, which is the value of the expected payoff for carrying an umbrella. We can state this algebraically:

$$-\$1 = (p \times -\$50) + [(1 - p) \times 0)]$$

Here p represents the probability of rain. Remembering that all probabilities add up to 1, we use p to represent the probability of rain and $1 - p$ to represent the remaining probability of no rain.

Solving this equation, we find:

$$-1 = p \times -50$$

and thus

$$p = 1/50$$

$$= 0.02 \text{ or } 2\%$$

Given the parameters used in this example, when the chance of rain equals 2%, we are indifferent as to whether we carry an umbrella or not. If the chance of rain is less than 2% we choose *not* to carry our umbrella.

Again it is important to realize that our payoff amounts for losing an umbrella or the value of our clothes are often estimates. At times we may need to alter those estimates and reassess our analysis. If, for example, we estimate the value of our clothes to be equal to $20 rather than $50 when our clothes got wet, then the break even probability for carrying an umbrella changes to:

$$-1 = p \times -20$$

and thus

$$p = 1/20$$

$$= 0.05 \text{ or } 5\%$$

Changing the value of our expected loss from ruined clothes from $50 to $20, changes the break even point for our decision alternatives—in such an example the probability of rain must be 5% or less for us not to carry an umbrella.

LEARNING OBJECTIVE 2: TO BE ABLE TO CALCULATE EXPECTED PAYOFF AND SELECTING A DECISION BASED UPON MAXIMUM PAYOFF USING SPECIFIC EXAMPLES

Health services managers make decisions under conditions of uncertainty all the time. In some instances, uncertainty may be relatively low. For example, purchasing a new imaging device to meet existing volume demands more efficiently involves a low level of uncertainty. Conversely, purchasing a new imaging device to meet an unknown demand, or to compete with another similar service provider, might represent a situation characterized by a high level of uncertainty. Consider the following examples.

Clinic Renovation

An ambulatory care clinic administrator is trying to decide whether to renovate to accommodate possible increased demand. The manager could plan a major renovation costing $700,000 that would allow 50 patients per day to be served, or a minor renovation costing $225,000 that would allow 35 patients a day to be served. The final alternative is to do nothing, thus keeping the status quo by not renovating. This continues the existing capacity of accommodating the current 20 patients per day, but no more. Presently the clinic earns $75 per patient served. Assume that the clinic is open 300 days per year and that management wants to cover the costs of the renovation from first-year earnings.

To begin quantitatively analyzing our decision options, we first go back to the three decision steps listed previously. The first step is to state the alternatives. These are to do nothing, undergo a minor renovation, or undergo a major renovation. The second step is to determine the future states of the world. These are the unknowns in our decision. Here they are the estimates of future demand. Because our decisions limit future capacity, we will use these limits as estimates of future demand. Thus, let us describe the potential for 20 patients per day, 35 patients per day, or 50 patients per day to be served, defined by current capacity, capacity given a minor renovation, and capacity given a major renovation.

There are three alternatives and three possible states of the world. This means that there are *nine* possible outcomes. These are listed in Table 10-3. The third step is to determine the payoffs for each of the potential outcomes.

Earnings are based upon patients served; therefore, part of the payoff involves earnings. For each state of the world of future demand, there are different potential maximum patients who can be seen. Each of these brings in revenue of $75. This amount is then multiplied by the 300 days the clinic is open yearly to calculate the total revenue per year. The maximum revenue generated in each state of the world can be seen in Table 10-4.

Table 10-3 Expected Outcomes for Clinic Renovation

Alternative	State of the world (future demand forecasts)	Outcome
No renovation/do nothing	Demand remains at 20 patients per day	Demand is met
No renovation/do nothing	Demand increases to 35 patients per day	Demand is not met
No renovation/do nothing	Demand increases to 50 patients per day	Demand is not met
Minor renovation	Demand remains at 20 patients per day	Demand is met
Minor renovation	Demand increases to 35 patients per day	Demand is met
Minor renovation	Demand increases to 50 patients per day	Demand is not met
Major renovation	Demand remains at 20 patients per day	Demand is met
Major renovation	Demand increases to 35 patients per day	Demand is met
Major renovation	Demand increases to 50 patients per day	Demand is met

Table 10-4 Potential Monetary Payoffs by States of the World

Future demand forecasts (patients per day)	Payment per patient	Days open	Total yearly payment
20	$75.00	300	$450,000.00
35	$75.00	300	$787,500.00
50	$75.00	300	$1,125,000.00

In addition to revenue, however, clinic renovations cost money that must be charged against these earnings. Remember that doing nothing carries no renovation expense, whereas minor and major renovations cost $225,000 and $700,000 respectively. Table 10-5 lists the revenue, cost, and payoff for each decision alternative.

It is important to remember that the potential demand is uncertain. The clinic does not know for certain whether the demand will continue to be 20, 35, or 50 patients per day. It is quite possible that if a major renovation is undertaken, only 35 patients per day show up or are booked. At this point in this example, one management approach would be to use expert opinion or mathematical forecasting to predict the future demand and base the subsequent analysis upon the "certainty" associated with the forecast. Such insight may help determine how probable future demand might be and could assist in choosing an alternative.

Another approach is to assume that all states of the world are equally likely to occur. In this example doing so would mean that the probability of current demand (20 patients per day) would be 0.3333, moderate demand (35 patients per day) would be 0.3333, and high demand (50 patients per day) would be 0.3333, thus setting them equal.

Remember that states of the world are future unknown events. They are beyond the power of the decision maker to know. However, there may be data or other information that can assist in altering our probabilities of a future event, such as the case with the decision to carry an umbrella earlier in the chapter. In that instance, a weather forecast could have provided valuable information about setting the probabilities of rain. When the future is truly unknown, setting probabilities equal is a good starting rationale. Once probabilities for each state of the world have been determined, the expected total payoff for each can be determined. Remember again that each state of the world in this example has three potential outcomes (see Tables 10-3 and 10-5). Only one of these *will* occur. Thus for each state of the world all probabilities must add up to 1 (or 100%). To calculate the expected total payoff for each state of the world, we simply multiply each outcome's payoff by its probability of occurrence, and sum them.

Table 10-5 Revenues, Expenses, and Expected Payoffs for Clinic Renovation

Alternative	State of the world (future demand forecasts)	Earnings	Renovation expense	Payoff
No Renovation/Do Nothing	20	$450,000	0	$450,000
No Renovation/Do Nothing	20	$450,000	0	$450,000
No Renovation/Do Nothing	20	$450,000	0	$450,000
Minor Renovation	20	$450,000	$225,000	$225,000
Minor Renovation	35	$787,500	$225,000	$562,500
Minor Renovation	35	$787,500	$225,000	$562,500
Major Renovation	20	$450,000	$700,000	($250,000)
Major Renovation	35	$787,500	$700,000	$87,500
Major Renovation	50	$1,125,000	$700,000	$425,000

Using equal probabilities our expected total payoff (ETP) for each decision payoff in Table 10-5 we find:

1. Expected Payoff [no renovation] = (0.33) × $450,000 + (0.33) × $450,000 + (0.33) × $450,000 = $450,000

2. Expected Payoff [minor renovation] = (0.33) × 225,000 + (0.33) × $562,500 + (0.33) × $562,500 = $445,500

3. Expected Payoff [minor renovation] = (0.33) × $250,000 + (0.33) × $87,500 + (0.33) × $425,000 = $86,625

In this case, the clinic management would choose the higher of the expected total payoffs, or the decision associated with $450,000—to do nothing and continue at present capacity. What is important to note, however, is how close the ETP values are for decision alternatives one and two. One might wonder, as we did in the umbrella example, what probability would cause us to make a different decision. Because we are dealing with three and not two decisions, we cannot calculate a break even set of probabilities per se. What we can do is alter our probabilities slightly to assess the changes in our ETP and thus our choice.

Perhaps the clinic management anticipates they would conduct marketing in the community concurrent with construction to increase demand. Let us say that they think there is a 10% chance that demand will remain at 20 per day and there is a 50% chance that demand will increase to 35 per day. This means they are implicitly assigning the probabilities of 0.1 to low future demand, and 0.5 to moderate future demand, leaving 0.4 left over for high future demand, or a 40% chance.

Expected Payoff [no renovation] = (0.1) × $450,000 + (0.5) × $450,000 + (0.4) × $450,000 = $450,000

Expected Payoff [minor renovation] = (0.1) × 225,000 + (0.5) × $562,500 + (0.4) × $562,500 = $528,750

Expected Payoff [major renovation] = (0.1) × −$250,000 + (0.5) × $87,500 + (0.4) × $425,000 = $238,750

In this case, the clinic management would change their decision to choose a minor renovation strategy because the expected payoff is the greatest. Notice that this is true *even though* the probability of high demand is less than that of moderate demand. Thus, all conditions before the decision being equal, decision analysis tells the manager to choose a minor renovation.

Example 2: Bid for Services

You are part of a consulting firm that is considering bidding on a project to set up a pricing plan for cardiovascular treatment procedures. You will determine the cost for each procedure—based upon provider time, materials and supplies, lab work, anesthesia, etc.—that will become the standard price that a specialty practice group bills for these procedures. If you get the bid, it will cost you $300,000 to complete the pricing project. Merely preparing the proposal, however, will cost you $100,000. Your challenge is to determine how much to bid.

You have competitors who also want this project. Because the project will go to the lowest bidder, you cannot bid too high. However, the lower you bid, the lower will be your profit. You know something about your competitors and decide that you have four alternatives:

1. Bid $800,000.
2. Bid $575,000.
3. Bid $500,000.
4. Do not submit a bid.

The states of the world are:

1. There is no other bid less than $800,000.
2. There is no other bid less than $575,000.
3. There is no other bid less than $500,000.
4. At least one bid is less than $500,000.

Because this is a complicated situation, the information is presented in Table 10-6. Remember that it will cost $400,000 to complete the project if you get the bid ($100,000 for the proposal and $300,000 to perform the actual work of the project), and it will cost the consulting firm $100,000 to bid on the project even if it does not win the project.

The next step is to assign probabilities to each state of the world. If you have no reason to think that any one state is more likely than another, you would assign equal probabilities to each state. Because there are four states, each has a 25% chance of occurring.

In this case, in which each probability is 0.25, the expected total payoffs will be:

Expected payoff [bid $800,000] = (0.25) × $400,000 + (0.75) × −$100,000
= $25,000

Expected payoff [bid $575,000] = (0.50) × $175,000 + (0.50) × −$100,000
= $37,500

Expected payoff [bid $500,000] = (0.75) × $100,000 + (0.25) × −$100,000
= $50,000

Expected Payoff [No bid] = $0

You should choose to bid $500,000 under these conditions, because that alternative has the highest expected payoff (Table 10-6).

Table 10-6 Alternative in Bid for Services Example

	Payoff for alternatives (bid)			
	Assumes costs of bid and project of $400,000			
States of the world	Bid $800,000	Bid $575,000	Bid $500,000	Do not bid
No bid < 800,000	$400,000	$175,000	$100,000	$0
No bid < 575,000	−$100,000*	$175,000	$100,000	$0
No bid < 500,000	−$100,000*	−$100,000**	$100,000	$0
At least one < 500,000	−$100,000	−$100,000	−$100,000	$0

*assumes at least one bid was less than $800,000
**assumes at least one bid was less than $575,000

Example 3: Medical Treatment Versus Prevention

Mammography does not prevent breast cancer, but can avert a more advanced stage of cancer, thus preventing premature mortality from breast cancer. Assume the average mammogram, including technician, equipment, and radiologic assessment, costs $200 to perform. Additional costs associated with false-positive screening, such as biopsies, add an additional expected cost to each mammographic screening of $25.

The medical treatments for advanced breast cancer are assumed to be $150,000. Mammography can reduce the chance of advanced breast cancer by 40% with proper screening.

Given these parameters, should we screen for breast cancer? The decision tree for this example is shown in Figure 10-3.

The incidence of breast cancer is approximately 4 per 1000 women over age 50 in the United States. If we assume that, without screening, the incidence of advanced breast cancer is 4 per 1000. Introduction of screening would reduce this 40% to 2.4 per 1000. That is, 1.6 cases of advanced stage breast cancer per 1000 women would be potentially averted. In this simplified example, the expected total payoffs for screening women over 50 years old are:

For every 1000 women screened,

$$\text{Expected Payoff [screen]} = \$225 \times 1000 \text{ women} + \$150,000 \times 2.4 \text{ cases} = \$825,000$$

$$\text{Expected Payoff [not screen]} = \$150,000 \times 4 \text{ cases} = \$600,000$$

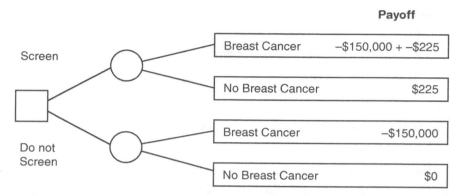

Figure 10-3 Breast Cancer Screening Decision Tree

Although the difference is small, the expected payoff rule says that we would choose to screen women over 50. The savings from advanced cases averted compensate for the costs associated with screening.

CONCLUSION

Decision analysis provides a quantitative method for choosing among options in the face of uncertainty. It allows us to specify alternatives and estimate payoffs of decisions based on our assessment of their likelihood of occurrence. It further allows the health care manager to assess how different probabilities of future states of the world affect decision making. Decision analysis has three core component parts: the alternatives, the anticipated or forecasted state of the world that will occur after the decision is made, and the payoffs assigned to each. It is important to note, however, that in healthcare management decision making, expected payoff is not always the only criterion we use for assessing choices. It is important to consider patients' quality of life and other values important to the community, because it is not just the decision but the consequences of that decision that are ultimately most important.

EXERCISES

10-1 Draw a decision tree for the bid for services example.

10-2 In the clinic renovation example, what if management thinks that the likelihood of current demand remaining is 30%, the likelihood of a moderate increase is 25%, and the likelihood of a large increase is 45%? What should they do, according to the expected total payoff?

10-3 In the clinic renovation example, what if management thinks that the likelihood of a moderate increase is twice as likely as either current demand remaining or high demand occurring? What should they do?

Chapter 11

Economic Analysis

LEARNING OBJECTIVES

1. To understand the balance/conflict that may be involved in making project decisions.
2. To understand what is meant by economic analysis and differentiate among the different types of economic analyses.
3. To understand the basic elements of a cost-effectiveness (CE) analysis.
4. To be able to calculate the CE of a specific project or intervention.

REAL WORLD SCENARIO

Christine Hammond is Senior Benefit Design Manager of the Merriwell Business Group, a major coalition of businesses contracting for healthcare services from St. Clements–Mercy Medical Center. St. Clements has proposed a number of potential screening and immunization programs as part of a battery of services to be offered to employees represented by the coalition. All of the services have the potential to identify risk factors or early stages of disease, but the coalition cannot afford to offer all of them to employees. In discussions with St. Clements, Ms. Hammond has indicated that she is looking for some way of comparing the different programs against each other so that she can select the ones with the greatest benefit, while also taking into account the cost of the programs. Seeking advice, she contacts Dr. Robert Woodworth, an economist at the local university. Dr. Woodworth suggests that Ms. Hammond can get the information she needs to make her decision by using a tool from economics, such as cost-benefit or cost-effectiveness analysis. Dr. Woodworth explains that these are ways in which to compare the programs against each other, taking into account monetary or economic factors. Intrigued, Ms. Hammond hires Dr. Woodworth to assist the coalition.

211

LEARNING OBJECTIVE 1: TO UNDERSTAND THE BALANCE/CONFLICT THAT MAY BE INVOLVED IN MAKING PROJECT DECISIONS

Based upon the goals of the organization, a health services manager must make decisions and recommendations regarding what services to provide. Changing needs, demands, and wants, along with changing organizational goals and objectives, require the manager to revise existing services, add new services, and eliminate existing services. New technology consistently redefines the medical care frontier. The health services manager approaches these issues with two potentially conflicting perspectives and one stark realization.

The realization is that community and organizational resources are scarce and must be used wisely. Value or benefit is expected from every resource used in a service. Patients expect value. Healthcare organizations expect value. Communities expect value. Healthcare organizations and financing sources also continue to stress exactly how scarce resources are, and that resources used for healthcare preclude using those same resources for other purposes, such as economic development, transportation, education, amusement, and defense. Being scarce, resources need to be allocated to meet prioritized goals and objectives. Personnel budgets, organizational budgets, and governmental budgets reflect how resources are allocated between and among competing needs, demands, and wants. Markets allocate resources based upon the interplay of supply and demand. The need to allocate resources is a given; the question becomes, On what basis will resources be allocated?

The health services manager, as an employee of a healthcare organization, feels the potentially competing perspectives of the "community" and the "organization." From an organizational perspective, any decision or recommendation must be evaluated based upon its impact on the organization. Organizational performance, as reflected by profits and losses, is real and is an important criterion used to evaluate a manager and his or her actions. From a community perspective, however, the health services manager is challenged to use organizational resources to improve the health status of the community served by the healthcare organization. From this perspective, the health status of the community is the dominant criterion used to evaluate the manager and the healthcare organization. Although these criteria can be compatible, they can also be mutually exclusive. Organizational benefit and community benefit can range from being the same to being opposite. Each is a dominant, real, and an important perspective that every health services manager must feel and consider whenever making a decision or recommendation involving new or revised projects.

The purpose of this chapter is to equip health services managers with the ability to formulate project recommendations that include community benefit. This does not imply that the manager should be insensitive to organizational profit and loss; indeed, the manager *must* be sensitive to these factors. It merely implies that the health services manager must examine *both* the organizational and community benefit associated with any project recommendation.

Health services managers are retained to exercise reasoned judgment. Their actions are expected to benefit their organization and the community served by their organization. Reasoned judgment requires that the health services manager is able to evaluate project alternatives from many perspectives, including an economic perspective, that values community benefit as well as organizational costs and benefits. Sometimes, however, considerations other than economic will be the dominant influence on the health services manager (i.e., a political perspective based upon stakeholder interests). To exercise reasoned judgment, the health services manager must be conversant in these many perspectives. This chapter expands the ability of the health services manager to consider the community implications associated with project recommendations.

LEARNING OBJECTIVE 2: TO UNDERSTAND WHAT IS MEANT BY ECONOMIC ANALYSIS AND DIFFERENTIATE AMONG THE DIFFERENT TYPES OF ECONOMIC ANALYSES

There are many ways to evaluate potential projects. For example, management decisions and recommendations can be made on the basis of anticipated costs compared with anticipated benefits associated with the project. To evaluate project alternatives, analyses must assess the costs and benefits associated with each, including the alternative of doing nothing. Analysis can be used to determine whether a proposed project is better in terms of the relationship of benefits to costs than any project alternatives. This concept is critical in managerial decision making in the healthcare field, because it incorporates into the analysis the impact the project alternatives should have upon clientele served by the healthcare organization.

Every healthcare organization intends to improve the health status of the populations it serves. This distinguishes healthcare organizations and their managers from other types of organizations and managers in the services sector. In particular, community health status is important to healthcare organizations.

A *community* can be defined as a group of individuals with common attributes. These attributes can be demographic, behavioral, geographic, or disease specific. Health status is influenced by prevention programs and medical treatments available to the community, as well as by factors involving behavior, genetics, and the environment. For example, an immunization program should decrease the numbers of infectious diseases, thus increasing health status. An anticholesterol drug that lowers blood cholesterol associated with cardiovascular disease can decrease the number of heart attacks in a community of "users" compared with "nonusers," thus increasing health status. A neonatal intensive care unit in the community hospital can enhance the likelihood of survival for low birth weight babies. All these programs use healthcare resources.

As health status in a community improves due to the prevention of adverse health outcomes (i.e., a heart attack), fewer healthcare resources should have to be spent in this community on treatment of the same health outcomes. When health status decreases, it is likely that more healthcare resources will be expended on treating avoidable adverse health events. The major question in healthcare economic analysis is how do *increased* expenditures on projects to improve health status compare with the *decreased* expenditures on healthcare resources resulting from averted health related events (HRE)? This question is particularly relevant today. For example, it is a fundamental question used in decisions regarding health insurance coverage, especially in managed care plans. It is also a basic question used to evaluate the actions and community benefit of healthcare organizations. It is also a classical question from the field of public health: Would society be better served by preventing a disease or treating a disease?

Given this perspective and questions, the management decision regarding the initiation of a new project or service or the evaluation of existing services must include three parts.

1. *What is the total cost—per unit—of providing a particular service?* What is the cost per person screened or per MRI performed or per immunization? Costs include fixed and variable costs associated with all resources consumed in the provision of this service. Analysis based upon a true determination of the costs of resources consumed in providing the service must be used to determine the total or full cost associated with providing the particular unit of service associated with the existing program or project alternative. Service units also must be specified.

2. *What are the benefits (payoffs)—per unit—of this service?* Analysis also must determine the benefits associated with each unit of service. Estimating benefits, especially when trying to express all benefits in terms of dollars, is not always easy to do. For example, it is possible to estimate the costs of medical care averted by treating one case of a disease, injury, pregnancy, or other HRE, or the costs associated with increased job absenteeism as a result of averting a particular disease. In other instances, estimating the economic value associated with a particular service is more difficult; examples include estimating the value of averted deaths and disabilities or increased quality of life.

3. *What proportion of individuals receiving this service will actually benefit?* This proportion represents the probability of an individual payoff and usually

requires knowledge of the effect of the service on reducing the risk of an adverse health event. For example, a relatively high percentage of cervical cancer can be averted through early detection using Pap screening. Another example is that 50% of neural tube defects could be prevented if women of childbearing age took 0.4 mg of folic acid every day. The scientific literature can provide a reasoned basis to make these types of estimates.

Once these three pieces of information are collected and analyzed, one can proceed to the determination of the value of the service to the organization and community. Using the technique of decision analysis, which allows the comparison of alternative strategies—using costs, payoffs, and probabilities—one can choose the project alternative that is best. One alternative is always to do nothing; that is, do not provide the service.

There are three evaluation techniques for projects:

- Cost-benefit analysis (CBA)
- Cost-effectiveness analysis (CEA)
- Cost-utility analysis (CUA)

This chapter focuses on CEA. For completeness, however, a brief discussion of CBA and CUA is provided.

CBA evaluates all project inputs (i.e., costs) and outcomes (i.e., benefits) of a service in *monetary terms*. This means that not only are service costs calculated, but that all benefits are also calculated in terms of costs, even including the cost of a life saved. This is very difficult, especially because our society cannot come to any agreement on the value of a human life. For example, is life of any quality of the same value? In many cases, the benefit of a life saved is calculated as the present value of the individual's future income stream. This approach, however, values the lives of a young productive population and discounts the value of those either retired from productive labor or unable to be productive. Until we can address this issue as a society, CBA in its complete form generally cannot be used across all services and health interventions.

CUA also compares project costs and benefits. Benefits, however, are expressed in terms of consumer preferences. This is an economic and operations research concept that recognizes that individuals prefer certain goods to others and thus are assumed to *prefer* certain health states to others. Many investigators have spent and continue to spend many years interviewing people, then calculating and refining these measures called "relative weights." For example, a year of life after a heart attack has been said to be worth 80% of a healthy year of life. Thus, years after adverse health events are valued less than years before these events. The application of cost-utility analysis is relatively limited and fraught with highly value-laden assumptions.

LEARNING OBJECTIVE 3: TO UNDERSTAND THE BASIC ELEMENTS OF A COST-EFFECTIVENESS ANALYSIS

In CEA, project and service costs are calculated in monetary terms. Benefits, however, are calculated in their *natural units*, such as the number of cases of heart disease or cancer averted. CEA compares alternative interventions (i.e., project A versus project B) whose outcomes (benefits) are measured in identical *units*. This chapter uses examples of interventions and projects whose purpose is to prevent some specific disease, injury, or other health event that consumes healthcare resources.

Basic Elements

To use CEA, a manager must be able to determine the cost of the intervention or project, the cost of adverse health related events (i.e., HREs) averted or other benefits, and the estimated proportion of current HREs averted by the intervention or project.

Project Costs

Every project intervention requires resources to implement and maintain. These include labor for services rendered, facilities and utilities, equipment and supplies, and administrative support. Direct and indirect project costs must be estimated.

Intervention Side Effects

All interventions have an effect or one would not implement them. Some interventions have adverse side effects as well as beneficial results. As for all interventions, the benefits must exceed the risks for the intervention to be implemented ethically. Costs associated with these risks must be included. Thus, the extremely small risk of severe vaccine reactions must be included in a mass vaccination program, because in a million doses the cost associated with an adverse effect may occur. Diagnostic procedures to rule out false-positives in a screening intervention also must be included in a CEA.

Direct Medical Costs of Health Related Events Averted

A prevention program is undertaken to avert an adverse HRE. For every adverse HRE averted, the direct medical costs associated with that event do not occur. When sufficient numbers of HREs are averted, the cost savings may exceed the cost of the prevention intervention.

Personal Costs of a Health Related Event Averted

Personal costs are the economic impacts associated with an adverse HRE. Examples include earnings (productivity) losses to society as a whole because of the premature morbidity and mortality of persons who become ill with an adverse HRE. Thus, if one can avert adverse health outcomes, one averts the morbidity and mortality that occur with that health outcome and retains the productivity of the potentially afflicted individual.

Two methods of costing this morbidity and mortality are the *human capital* and the *willingness-to-pay* approaches. The human capital approach values personal loss as the income not earned by the individual who experienced the HRE. The willingness-to-pay approach values this loss as what someone might spend to avert this particular event; for example, how much an individual was willing to pay to install automobile seat belts or air bags in a car to avert death or injury. Although many cost-effective analyses include these personal costs, sometimes referred to as *indirect cost factors*, the approach used in this chapter concentrates on the resources used and direct benefits associated with averting a specific HRE.

Determining Resource Costs

Resources are those project inputs to the prevention intervention without which the intervention would not exist. To determine the resource costs, the following steps should be followed:

1. Choose a time period for the intervention analysis.
2. Choose the service unit of the intervention.
3. List the resources required for all activities comprising the intervention.
4. Measure or count the units of each resource used in the time period.
5. Determine the cost per unit of each resource.
6. Multiply the cost/unit by the number of units (this will equal the total cost of each resource).
7. Determine the cost of any resources not measured per unit of service.
8. Add up all total resource costs to determine the total cost for the intervention—for a specific period and based upon an anticipated level of service.
9. Divide the total cost by number of service units to determine the *expected* cost per service.

Following these steps will yield an estimate of the cost per unit of service and the total cost of the project.

Time Period

The time period for the cost analysis is important. It is recommended that at least 1 year of resource data be used to determine the cost of the intervention itself, unless that year includes start-up time. In that case, a 3-month period for start-up should be omitted from data collection; the 1 year of data collection should begin after that start-up period.

Service Unit

The choice of the appropriate service unit(s) in advance of data collection is critical because it may drive the way in which data are collected. The CE calculation is predicated upon a denominator of effectiveness; thus, the unit of this denominator must be chosen in advance.

Resource Inputs

The list of resources to be collected may include the following:

- Direct provider time for each type of service or activity, by provider type, and their salary and fringe benefit expenses
- The supplies and materials for each type of service provided and their costs
- The type of laboratory or other tests for each service provided and their costs
- Lab controls, etc.
- Additional facilities, including rent and utilities required for this intervention
- Additional equipment
- Maintenance of facilities and equipment
- Additional support staff
- Additional administrative staff
- Other direct costs of providing services, such as courier services, cars and vans, uniforms or badges, additional insurance or permits, travel reimbursement, and computer database development/maintenance

Not all interventions will include all of these items. A table of unit costs should be constructed, based upon this list.

In addition, information on the participant may need to be collected. Participation in prevention activities may be influenced by the time it takes and the extra expenses it entails. This is a form of personal or indirect costs, costs not associated with direct use of medical or health resources, but with participation. Participant costs include:

- Participant time—travel, wait, actual service
- Participant expenses for travel, child care, etc.

These costs can be determined by a survey of the participants as they enter the facility and by collecting time information about arrival and service time.

Measuring Resources Consumed and Provider Time and Costs

There are five methods of estimating provider time:

1. Direct observation of services
2. Random observations of activities
3. Time diaries
4. Patient records
5. Provider surveys

Because of the variable nature of service times, a large number of observations may have to be collected.

Regardless of the technique chosen, a histogram of service times should be produced. If service times are clustered about one number and look symmetric, a sample of 30 may be sufficient as a basis for estimating mean service time. However, if the times are variable and asymmetric, a larger sample (e.g., $n = 100$) will be needed. The Poisson distribution has a mean equal to the standard deviation. This is the most conservative case and yields a sample size calculation of $n = 96$, for a 95% confidence level.

Direct Observation

Direct observation of services requires a trained observer who can determine what type of service is happening at a particular time. Data would be collected on each type of service included in the intervention. For example, in breast cancer screening, the time for counseling, the mammogram, the radiologist's interpretation, and the clinical breast examination would be collected. If direct observation of the service is not possible, the time a woman enters and then leaves the examination or consultation room can be measured, and an estimate could be made of the time spent on the various service components.

Random Observation

Random observation is a technique based upon the proposition that the proportion of time spent on an activity is equal to the proportion of observations made of that particular activity during the work day. To do this, each provider is assigned a code number. Before the beginning of the observation period, a schedule of observations is drawn up. A random number table is used to determine which provider is to be observed every *t* minutes. Time interval *t* is based on how far apart these providers are; that is, how long it will take to go from one to another. When a particular provider's code number comes up on the schedule, the observer goes to find him or her and notes what the provider is doing at that instant. This technique requires at least 100 observations of each type of service to obtain a confident estimate of the proportion of time spent on each activity.

To determine the time for each activity, the frequency of each activity is noted. Each activity frequency is a proportion of the total observations taken during the work day. Thus, that proportion equals the proportion of time spent in that activity during the work day.

Time Diaries

Time diaries are a provider-based technique. Each provider is given a sheet to fill out during his or her work day that requires the notation of the time each activity begins. Because this is an intrusive method for the provider, it is important to study the types of activities the provider is usually engaged in and to construct a checklist on the form for the provider. Personal time should always be a choice to be checked. If the time diary option is used, the providers need to be assured of the confidentiality of the diaries. The diaries should be collected in sealed envelopes and analyzed offsite.

Patient Record

The *patient record* method requires that each patient be tracked through the intervention. The exact time the patient enters a new service and leaves an old service must be noted. This type of following can yield information about patient flow and patient waiting time. Each patient carries a form upon which each provider can note the time the patient begins and ends the service by that provider.

A Survey of Providers

A survey of providers is the least accurate data collection method. Individuals generally do not remember how long they spend on a particular activity. Contemporaneous collection; that is, collection of data each day, may work, but asking a provider how much time he or she spent immunizing a child during a routine visit will not elicit an accurate response.

LEARNING OBJECTIVE 4: TO BE ABLE TO CALCULATE THE COST-EFFECTIVENESS OF A SPECIFIC PROJECT OR INTERVENTION

Determining Resource Costs per Unit: Calculation of Provider Time Costs

The following formula is used to estimate the cost of service providers:

Cost = each provider type × [salary + fringe] × duration of service × number of services provided in time period   Equation 11-1

Example: What is the cost per week for nutritionist services?

Nutritionist service cost per hour = ($35,000 per year + 15% fringe = $40,250) = $20.64 cost per hour

Thus, the nutritionist service cost in a time period of 1 week =

($20.64 per hour) × (0.42 hours per service) × 118 services during the week of data collection = $1022.92 cost per week

Calculation of Other Resource Costs per Unit of Service

Materials, supplies, tests, and other resources per unit of service are associated with particular services. Using expert opinion, a list of these is constructed. Costs should reflect those that are actually paid by the intervention program. This avoids confusion for other users of the data.

The following equation is used to calculate costs in a time period:

Cost = materials and supplies per unit of service × number of units
          Equation 11-2

Example: What is the cost per week for per-unit resources to provide a cholesterol screening service?

	Cost
Materials handed out to clients:	$1.27
Finger-prick supplies:	$0.75
Laboratory test:	$3.50
Total cost per client for per-unit items:	$5.52

Thus, the total cost of resources per week of data collection =

($5.52 per client × 118 service units) $651.36 per week

Calculation of Resource Costs Not Expressed per Unit of Service

Resources such as facilities, equipment, administrative support, and other overhead costs may not be expressed per unit of service within a particular range of service volume. For example, an x-ray machine sits idle some proportion of every work day. The same equipment accrues costs whether 100 or 200 patients are screened per day. (Note that the x-ray film is a per-person expense.) Thus, the following calculations are suggested.

For facilities, determine whether additional facilities will be acquired for the project. If so, use the cost of this space plus utilities. If not, determine whether additional facility time is required. If so, calculate the additional facility time for this intervention as a proportion of the total time the facility is in use. Use this proportion to multiply by the total cost of space plus utilities. If neither additional facilities nor additional time is used, then the facility cost may be ignored.

For equipment, determine the useful lifetime of the equipment in years, the total cost of the equipment plus maintenance, and the proportion of that lifetime the equipment will be used by the project. This proportion of equipment lifetime should include the proportion of the useful life in years multiplied by the proportion of time in any year that the equipment is in use. The total cost is divided by the estimated lifetime of the equipment and then multiplied by the estimated proportion of that lifetime that the equipment is used in the intervention.

Administrative and staff support costs are calculated as a proportion of their time spent on this particular project. The salary and fringe for each person providing support is multiplied by the proportion of their time spent in support.

Other direct costs are collected through expert opinion. Only resources directly used by the project should be included. In an incremental (marginal) cost analysis, the fixed costs may be irrelevant because facilities and equipment are already in place and no additional costs are associated with the intervention.

To calculate the fixed cost in time period, determine:

- Additional facility space × [cost of rent + utilities] for that space or additional facility time × [cost of rent and utilities] for that proportion of time spent on the intervention
- [Total cost of equipment and maintenance ÷ estimated lifetime of equipment] × proportion of that lifetime for this intervention
- Proportion of administrator's time spent on intervention × [salary + fringe]
- Proportion of support staff time spent on intervention × [salary + fringe]
- Other direct costs of providing the intervention, e.g., travel, courier, outside agency charges

Example: What are the facility costs associated with this project per week?

$$\text{Cost per year for rent and utilities} = \$22{,}500$$
$$\text{Cost per week} = (\$22{,}500 \div 52)$$
$$= \$432.69$$

The project will be associated with 36% of the time the organization spends on all programs.

$$\text{Program facilities costs} = (\$432.69 \times 0.36)$$
$$= \$155.77 \text{ fixed facilities cost}$$
$$\text{per week for this project}$$

Example: What are the equipment costs associated with this intervention per week?

Cost of computer + software	= $1900
Lifetime of computer	= 3 years
Salvage value of computer	= $250
Computer cost	= ($1900 − $250) ÷ 3 years
	= $550 per year
Maintenance contract	= $45 per month
Proportion of time computer used for project	= 25%
Computer costs per week	= ($550/year ÷ 52 weeks/year)
	= $10.58 per week + ($45/month ÷ 4.3 weeks/month
	= $10.47 per week)
	= $21.05
Computer costs to the project	= ($21.05 × 0.25)
	= $5.26 fixed computer costs per week for this project

Example: What are the travel costs associated with this project per week?

$$\text{Cost of travel} = 217 \text{ miles per week reimbursed}$$
$$= \$60.76 \text{ travel costs per week}$$

Example: What are the administrative and support costs associated with this project, per week?

Proportion of time administration and support
staff are involved in this intervention   = 5% and 13%

Administration and support costs	=	($52,375 + 23% fringe) × 0.05
	=	$3221.06 +
		($12,500 + 15% fringe) × 0.13
	=	$1868.75
	=	$5089.81 per year
Cost per week	=	$97.88 fixed support costs per week

To calculate participant costs a participant survey should be conducted. Data collected should include how far participants travel (miles) and expenses incurred, such as bus fare, tolls, mileage, and child care. The cost of participant time is based upon average wages. Regional wage rates may be obtained from Bureau of Labor Statistics publications.

Example: What are the participant costs?

Participant time for travel, waiting, and service	=	115 minutes
Average participant expenses	=	$2.59 per client
Participant costs	=	(115 minutes = 1.92 hours) × $10/hour
Median wage	=	$19.17 time cost + $2.59 for expenses
	=	$21.76 per participant
Total costs associated with participation	=	$21.76 × 118 participants/week
	=	$2567.29 participant costs per week

Intervention side effects costs also must be determined or estimated. These can be adverse vaccine reactions, diagnostic workups on positive screening results, psychologic support for persons told they have a positive HIV test, or presumed injuries associated with seat belt use. The scientific literature should be consulted for the costs associated with these events, or expert opinion can be used to determine the costs to deal with these eventualities. Then, the probability of the occurrence of side effects must be determined. For example, if a vaccine reaction occurs in 1 out of every 10,000 persons vaccinated and the project vaccinates 5000 children, the project can expect to incur one half of the cost of the vaccine reaction (5000 ÷ 10,000). These costs are added to the total costs of the intervention.

For example, suppose that for every 500 persons provided a cholesterol screening service, one person needs immediate medical attention. The time it takes the nutritionist to refer the patient is approximately 35 minutes and the phone call costs are approximately $1.24. Therefore, the total cost of one referral = ($20.64/hour × 0.58 hour) + $1.24 = $13.28. In 118 services per week, one would expect less than one side effect. The expected number = (118/500) = 0.236 persons with a side effect. The expected cost per week then is $3.13 ($13.28 × 0.236). This cost, $3.13, is a legitimate part of the cost of the project.

Total Costs for the Time Period

To calculate or estimate total costs, the manager must:

1. Sum the resource costs for the time period.
2. Sum the participant costs for the time period.
3. Sum any costs for side effects associated with the intervention.
4. Calculate the number of service units provided in the time period.
5. Calculate the total costs associated with the intervention = (1) + (2) + (3).
6. Divide the total costs by (4) to determine the cost per unit of intervention.

The total costs for the cholesterol screening program described in the preceding for one week can be calculated as follows.

Summary of resources and costs per week:

Provider time	$1022.92
Materials, supplies, lab	$651.36
Facilities	$155.77
Computer	$5.26
Travel	$60.76
Administration and Support	$97.88
TOTAL PROJECT	$1993.95
Participation	$2567.29
Side effects	$3.13
TOTAL COST PER WEEK	$4564.37
TOTAL COST PER SERVICE	= $4564.37 ÷ 118
	= $38.68
TOTAL COST TO PROGRAM, PER PARTICIPANT	= $1997.08 ÷ 118
	= $16.92

Direct Medical Costs of Health Related Events Averted

To calculate or estimate the direct medical costs of health event averted:

1. List the HREs to be averted.
2. Determine the rate of occurrence, per year, in a "treated" compared with "untreated" community. For example, the rate of severe injury may be 2.3 per 1000 with the intervention but 4.2 per 1000 without. Thus, the difference is 1.9

per 1000. These are the expected number of health related events averted in 1000 people participating in the intervention (i.e., the rate of HRE averted).

3. Multiply the rate of health related events averted by the number of persons participating in the project or intervention. That is, if 1500 individuals participated, then one would expect $1.9 \div 1000$ multiplied by 1500 events averted $= 2.85$ HREs averted.

4. Consult the scientific literature or obtain expert opinion on the healthcare costs associated with treating this HRE.

5. Multiply the expected number of HRE averted by the costs associated with each HRE to obtain the direct medical costs averted through the project.

For example, the medical care costs associated with cholesterol-related diseases that could be averted through intervention can be calculated as follows:

Hypothetical medical care costs associated with nutrition-related diseases, per case	= $55,000
Rate of nutrition-related disease	= 1/1000
Rate of disease among participants In 10,000 persons screened	= 0.75/1000
Diseases averted	= 1 − 0.75
	= 0.25 in 1000
	2.5 in 10,000
Medical costs of disease averted	= $55,000 × 2.5
	= $137,500

The Cos-Effectiveness of an Intervention

Now to combine all the components of the analysis, the CE ratio of the intervention is calculated using the following formula. The cost-effectiveness of an intervention is defined as:

CE = net costs divided by benefits	Equation 11-3

where net costs = (intervention costs + side effects costs) − direct medical care costs saved and benefits are the effectiveness measure chosen, such as the specific HRE averted. Some managers present the net costs calculation as the measure of cost effectiveness. Most analyses, however, go one step further and calculate the net costs per *unit* of effect. For example, the cholesterol screening intervention described in the preceding calculated a cost of $38.68 per screen. For 10,000 participants, the net cost is:

$$\text{Net cost} = \$386,800 - \$137,500 = \$137,113$$

If participant costs are *not* considered in this analysis, the net cost is:

$$\text{Net cost} = \$169,200 - \$137,500 = \$31,700$$

Finally, the CE ratio, i.e., net costs ÷ effect, is:

$$\$137,113/2.5 \text{ cases averted} = \$54,845 \text{ per case}$$

Timing of Costs and Benefits

This entire discussion presumes that the costs of the intervention and the benefits from the intervention occur in the same year. If this is not the case, discounting must be used to compare dollars spent in one period with dollars saved in future periods. For example, a dollar cost this year is of different value than a dollar saved 20 years from now. See Chapter 6 for a review of this concept.

EXERCISES

Use the following information to do a cost-effectiveness analysis of a work site screening program.

Serum cholesterol is a major predictor of coronary heart disease. As the value of serum cholesterol increases, the risk of heart disease increases, particularly for those individuals with values over 200 mg/dl as a percent of total blood.

Coronary heart disease (CHD) treatment is expensive. For example, assume that a CHD death costs $19,321 and a nonfatal case of CHD costs $58,025. For purposes of this analysis, assume that the expected lifetime benefits from coronary heart disease averted, for persons less than 60 years old who lower their serum cholesterol by 5% are as follows. Costs are:

Initial cholesterol level mg/dl	Present value of dollars saved
260	$72–$93
300	$90–$120
340	$118–$161

These figures represent the *present value* of healthcare dollars saved because of cases of CHD averted in the population lowering their cholesterol by 5%. Because most individuals do not suffer from CHD, the average cost saved over many people is relatively low. These lifetime costs can be compared with the costs of a cholesterol lowering intervention.

One way of reducing the costs of prevention interventions is to provide an intervention at the work site. This consists of two parts: an initial screening for all participants and a special intervention for those whose cholesterol is found to be equal to or greater than 200 mg/dl. Use the following data for an initial screening only.

	Hours	Numbers	Dollars
Preparation time for screening	12.4		
Contact work site	7.3		
Collect equipment and supplies	1.8		
Arrange staff	2.1		
Train staff	1.2		
Travel time to site	1.3		
At site for screening	6.4		
Follow-up time of screening	7.8		
Mailings	2.3		
Telephone	1.5		
Checking forms	4.0		
Average number of screenees, per site		51	
Average number of hospital providers per site		9.3	
Average provider salary plus fringe			$25,000
Miles to site from hospital		23	
Supplies per participant			$3.70
Mail and phone charges per participant			$0.19

Costs for the special intervention were calculated to be an additional $27.55 per participant. This includes both fixed and variable costs at the site.

Effects on serum cholesterol, obtained from the baseline and 12-month rescreening of all participants whose initial values were equal to or greater than 200 mg/dl were:

Initial intervention only: 1.9% reduction
Initial plus special intervention: 5.3% reduction

Use the following worksheet Table 11-1 to answer the subsequent questions:

11-1 How much did it cost, per person screened, for the initial cholesterol testing? Remember that each provider on site incurs costs to travel from the health department to the site and back.

11-2 How much did it cost per person who participated in the special intervention as well as the initial screening?

11-3 What is the cost per percent reduction in cholesterol for the initial screening only and for the initial plus special group?

11-4 What is the marginal cost per percent additional reduction in cholesterol attributable to the special intervention?

11-5 How does this compare with the lifetime coronary heart disease cost savings from reducing serum cholesterol?

WORKSHEET

	Who	$/Unit	# Units	$ cost
Cost of activities for service				
Site preparation time				
Contact work site	Clerk	____	7.3 hr	____
Collect equip/supplies	Nutr	____	1.8 hr	____
Arrange staff	Nutr	____	2.1 hr	____
Train staff	Nurse	____	1.2 hr	____
Travel time to/from site	Nutr	____	8×1.3 hr	____
Time at site for screening	Nutr	____	8×6.4 hr	____
Follow-up time				
Mailing	Clerk	____	2.3 hr	____
Phone	Nutr	____	1.5 hr	____
Check forms	Nurse	____	4 hr	____
Materials and supplies				
Preparation		____	____	____
At site		____	51	____
Follow-up		____	51	____
Travel reimbursement		____	____	____
Postage		____	____	____
Phone		____	____	____

Table 11-1 Worksheet

Service	Time (min)	Provider	Salary/ Fringe ($)	Other costs ($)
ID Patient	15	Med Records	3.69	
Find Patient	20	Nurse	5.63	
Obtain Consent	5	Nurse	1.23	$1 Consent Form
Pretest Counseling	15	Counselor	3.03	$1 Pamphlet
Test	5	Phlebotomist	0.79	$75 per test series
Find Patient	30	Med Records	7.38	$1.50 per phone call
Post test counseling				
Positive	60	Counselor	12.13	
Negative	10	Counselor	2.02	

Chapter 12

Program Evaluation Review Technique: PERT

LEARNING OBJECTIVES

1. To define the scope and tools of project management.
2. Understanding the components of PERT analysis.
3. To understand how to use PERT for project management.

REAL WORLD SCENARIO

As the administrator of the Sunrise Care Center, a long-term care facility, Michael Sharp is preparing to add on a new assisted living wing. The wing will be built as an addition to the existing facility. There are many steps involved with building the addition, and care must be taken to fully prepare for all of them. Further, timing is vitally important, as units have already been sold to prospective patients. If the project takes longer than anticipated, there are financial implications. Mr. Sharp also needs to be aware of disruptions to ongoing care being provided in the facility. A project of this scope requires that each step be mapped out in detail and estimates be developed for completion time for each. Mr. Sharp has elected to use PERT analysis to manage the project.

This chapter presents Program Evaluation and Review Technique (PERT) and its application as a planning, scheduling, and control system to use with large scale projects. PERT was developed to support complex research and development projects. PERT provides the manager with a method to identify and sequence the many activities that comprise a complex project. It allows the manager an analytic tool to assess impacts when a change to the sequence or timing of required activities is needed. Such changes occur to finish the project by a specific date or as adjustments to changing circumstances once the project has begun.

Here we present single time estimate PERT, although other forms exist. Single time estimates create a "most probable" completion time when assessing proposed tasks. Other methods use multiple time estimates, such as optimistic and pessimistic time ranges. These may be desirable when project tasks are detailed, or when environmental factors could be an issue, such as cold weather or shipping time uncertainty. Here we examine single time estimate PERT to more easily develop the concept.

LEARNING OBJECTIVE 1: TO DEFINE THE SCOPE AND TOOLS OF PROJECT MANAGEMENT

A *project* is an activity done once. Building a new nursing home or modernizing a part of an existing hospital are examples of projects. Installing a new machine in a laboratory is a project. Developing a new capability, such as installing labor and delivery rooms in a hospital, is also a project. Installing a new computer system or a new computer capability to process patient accounts is a project. A project is a one-time activity intended to change the capabilities or capacity of the organization.

The antonym of a project is a *program*. A program is a repetitive activity. So while developing and installing a system for mothers to give birth in the same hospital room that they will use for the duration of their maternity stay is a *project*, using this new capability over and over again for many mothers is a *program*. Doing surgery in a newly renovated same day surgical suite is a program.

A project has defining attributes. It usually seeks to achieve a desired capability or capacity, and when that capability is achieved the project is, by definition, completed. As such, projects have formal beginning and ending points and do not continue past the point when the desired capability has been achieved.

Projects also evolve through many phases. Any project must move through at least three phases of development. The first is the concept phase. During this phase different ways to achieve the desired capabilities are considered and evaluated. Broadly defined project options are identified. Usually one or two of these conceptual options are taken further by gathering information and examining alternative methods to achieve the capability. Some projects spend hours or days in this phase, whereas others spend years depending on scope.

During the second, or definition phase, managers define exactly what resources are needed to achieve the desired capabilities associated with the specific project option chosen. These resources are defined in as much detail as possible. Usually a business plan or similar type of report is developed. At the completion of this phase, some type of organizational approval is sought to continue the project into its next phase. This approval may be based upon a detailed economic and/or financial analysis. In health care, some projects must also secure regulatory approvals, such as approval granted in the form of a Certificate of Need. If approvals are not received to move the project into the next phase—the project implementation phase—managers are expected to repeat the definition phase using different parameters, return to the concept phase, or are told that the organization no longer desires the capability.

The third phase is the implementation phase. During this phase of project management, resources and capabilities are installed in the organization in keeping with the intent of the overall project. It is during this phase that a project may involve new construction, buying new equipment, training staff, hiring new staff, revising job descriptions, and any other activities needed to implement the desired capability. This phase may also include an evaluation component to ensure the outcomes achieved were those planned, and if not, how the two differ and by how much. PERT is used in all phases of a project.

Projects typically involve altering existing capabilities as well as installing or implementing new capabilities. For example, expanding the capacity of a nursing home by 20% will require more rooms, beds, and staff to administer to the needs of additional residents. However, such a project may also require altering the nursing home's existing capacity to park cars (e.g., more visitors and staff), process laundry (e.g., increased amount), feed patients and staff (e.g., more meals), and store heating oil.

As a project manager, you will have total system (or subsystem) performance responsibility (TSPR). TSPR characterizes all project management activities. As the project manager, you will be expected to install the "total package" of capabilities necessary to complete the project. Installing a new computer system that exceeds the capability of existing electrical circuits violates TSPR. Installing the equipment to do laser surgery without training the operating room staff to use the equipment violates TSPR. Consider the following example: An organization that specializes in eye and ear sub specialties contracts to provide those services to another major hospital's emergency department. A cart containing all of the necessary equipment is installed in that hospital's ED with the appropriate security measures (locks, etc...) and the key locations are known by all staff who would need access to the cart. Upon first use, the cart is wheeled to the hospital's sanitation room for sterilizing which is required after each use. There it is found that the existing sterilization service volume does not accommodate a new cart and because the cart originates from an outside facility, the staff are even more reluctant to attempt to rework the schedule. In this instance the manager with project responsibility at the eye and ear facility violated TSPR by failing to consider the need for sterilization of the cart. As a result, the cart had to be transported back to the eye and ear facility after each use, which carried added cost and potential quality issues if during that time, other patients were in need of the cart. Having total system performance responsibility means defining the project to include all the capabilities needed to fully complete the project, which in turn also entails the effective integration of the project into existing work flows and capacity of the organization, or in the above example, the contracted organization.

Some projects are complex, involving many action steps, significant resources, and a number of people. However, the definition of complex is often situational. What may be complex to one organization may not be to another. Complex can also refer to the duration of a project. A project that will require 2 years to complete may be complex; a project that takes 1 day may not be considered complex.

Formal project management methods, such as PERT, are reserved for complex projects. Often these projects have significant financial implications created by the expenses associated with installing the new capability as well as the expense (e.g., lost revenue) associated with any delay in achieving the capability. Using PERT to meet the deadline to submit a Certificate of Need application may be justified by the implications associated with being late or unprepared.

Generally project activities are performed in a predetermined sequence. Some steps must occur before others can begin. For example, the framing of an addition must be complete before electrical work can begin. Further, some sequences are more efficient than others. In other instances, the timing of activities is also very important. For a project that requires a significant amount of time, it may be inappropriate to train staff as an initial step. Training needs may change over the course of the project. Some trained staff may leave before the project comes on-line. Staff may forget their training given the long gap between when training occurred and when they begin to use the skills acquired. Similarly it would be inappropriate to hire new staff for an expanded nursing home months before the staff was actually needed. PERT assists managers in identifying and sequencing all the activities that must be completed to complete the project.

Consider the project to expand a nursing home by 20%. The initial list of the needed activities or steps could include the following:

1. Get Certificate of Need (CON) approval.
2. Get zoning approval.
3. Hire an architect and approve plans.
4. Get the necessary construction financing.
5. Hire a construction company.
6. Build it.
7. Advertise for staff.
8. Interview staff.
9. Select staff and train.
10. Revise existing insurance policies.
11. Change the operating budget to reflect the project.
12. Determine the necessary new equipment, issue bids, and select the equipment.
13. Get the equipment delivered, unpack it, and set it up. Test equipment and secure replacements for any defective equipment.

When the steps necessary to implement project capabilities are defined, they should be listed in sequential order to the extent possible. For example, for this project we would seek CON approval before obtaining construction financing, etc. However, although some activities must be accomplished in a sequential order, other activities can be accomplished simultaneously or in parallel with others. Accomplishing activities in parallel can shorten the total time between when a project is begun and when it is completed. By authorizing and managing activities to proceed in parallel, projects can become more efficient, but also more difficult to manage and coordinate. PERT facilitates managing parallel activities, especially when the order of activities influences the overall time a project will take.

The Work Breakdown Structure

Before using PERT, any complex project must be first broken down into its component parts. Each piece of the project must be identified. A Work Breakdown Structure (WBS) is used to divide the project into appropriate and logical components and then subdivide each component of the project into even more specific parts. The WBS is a comprehensive listing of the components of the project listed in outline form. Some use a numbering system to ensure that macro as well as micro components of the project are identified and ordered. For example, the project to increase the capacity of the nursing home by 20% could be broken down into the following work breakdown structure:

1.0 Regulatory Approvals
    1.1 Certificate of Need
    1.2 Zoning
    1.3 Fire Department
    1.4 Highway Department
    1.5 Building Inspection
    1.6 Certificate of Occupancy
2.0 Physical Addition
    2.1 Design
        2.1.1 Building Design—New Space
            2.1.1.1 Resident Rooms and Baths
            2.1.1.2 Hallways and Storage
            2.1.1.3 Work Stations
            2.1.1.4 Common Areas
            2.1.1.5 Other New Space
        2.1.2 Changes to Existing Mechanical Systems
            2.1.2.1 Heat
            2.1.2.2 Fire Alarm

            2.1.2.3 Electric
            2.1.2.4 Telephone
            2.1.2.5 Water
            2.1.2.6 Air
            2.1.2.7 Other Mechanical Systems
    2.2 Build
3.0 Staff
    3.1 Professional Staff
        3.1.1 Registered Nurses
        3.1.2 Licensed Practical Nurses
        3.1.3 Social Workers
        3.1.4 Therapists
    3.2 Nonprofessional Staff
    3.3 Consultants

This example only begins to illustrate the concept of a work breakdown structure. It is not the comprehensive WBS for this specific project.

Project managers, with input from many sources, create a WBS to define the project in terms of its scope and detail. A comprehensive WBS insures a comprehensive project. To create the comprehensive WBS, project managers ask what is necessary to achieve the desired project capability, categorize their answers into logical top level tasks (e.g., regulatory approvals, building design, staff, financing, etc.), and then continue to define subcomponents of each task until they feel that the project has been adequately defined in scope and detail. For example, building design could be further broken down into the subtasks of architect plans and contractor schedule. The latter could be further broken down into the subtasks of framing, plumbing needs, electrical work, dry walling, etc.

How much detail is included in the WBS is a product of managerial judgment. The WBS must be sufficiently comprehensive to include all necessary components and contain sufficient detail to guide the continued definition, implementation, and management of the project. In short, a good WBS lists *all* the pieces of the project.

Before the advent of PERT and similar methods in the 1960s, project managers used such a list of project activities to schedule activities. Gantt Charts, for example, listed all the activities associated with a project (i.e., WBS) on the vertical axis of a chart and used lines across a horizontal time axis to indicate when the specific activity was to begin and end. Figure 12-1 is one simplified form of a Gantt chart.

Gantt charts provide the manager with a list of project activities and the estimated duration of each activity. These charts also provide the estimated start date as well as completion date for each activity. From a project management perspective, these charts have one serious flaw—they do not represent the relationship between and among activities. A Gantt chart does not indicate—although it does imply—which activities *must* precede other activities. Although these types of chart do indicate

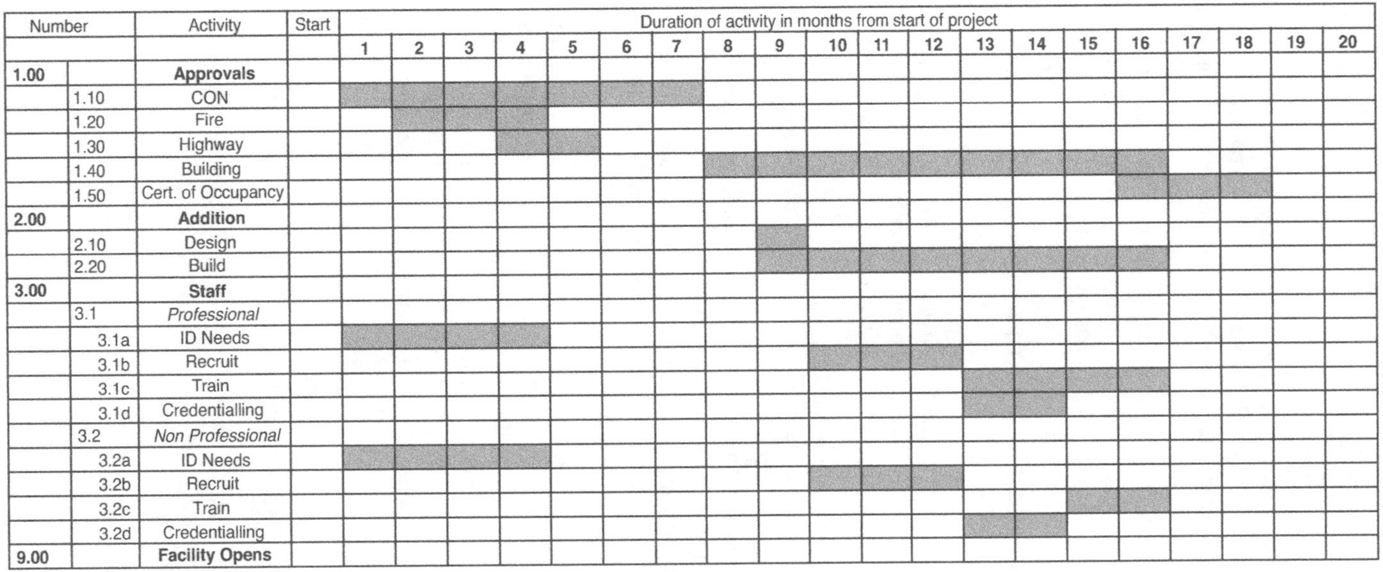

Number	Activity	Start	1	2	3	4	5	6	7	8	9	10	11	12	13	14	15	16	17	18	19	20
1.00	**Approvals**																					
1.10	CON			▩	▩	▩	▩	▩	▩													
1.20	Fire			▩	▩	▩																
1.30	Highway						▩															
1.40	Building									▩	▩	▩	▩	▩	▩	▩	▩	▩	▩	▩		
1.50	Cert. of Occupancy																					
2.00	**Addition**																					
2.10	Design										▩	▩	▩	▩	▩	▩	▩	▩				
2.20	Build														▩	▩	▩	▩				
3.00	**Staff**																					
3.1	*Professional*																					
3.1a	ID Needs		▩	▩	▩	▩																
3.1b	Recruit											▩	▩	▩	▩	▩	▩	▩				
3.1c	Train														▩							
3.1d	Credentialling																					
3.2	*Non Professional*																					
3.2a	ID Needs			▩	▩	▩																
3.2b	Recruit												▩	▩								
3.2c	Train															▩	▩	▩				
3.2d	Credentialling																					
9.00	**Facility Opens**																					

Duration of activity in months from start of project

Figure 12-1 Gantt Chart for Expansion Project

which activities *can* precede other activities, they fail to indicate which activities *must* precede other activities. PERT was developed to overcome this shortcoming.

Gantt charts nonetheless remain an effective project planning and control approach for relatively simple projects. These charts provide the manager with appropriate scheduling information and a yardstick to use to compare actual experience with planned actions. Although easily created in any spreadsheet program, Gantt charts have been included in many specialized project management software packages available today.

LEARNING OBJECTIVE 2: UNDERSTANDING THE COMPONENTS OF PERT ANALYSIS

Although misnamed a "Program Evaluation Review Technique," when it actually deals with projects, PERT is a formal method to define projects and support project management. Specifically it helps project managers to determine:

1. When the project will be completed.
2. What the scheduled start and completion date for each specific activity included in the project will be.
3. What activities are "critical" and must be completed exactly as scheduled to keep the project on schedule. This feature of PERT makes PERT a much more robust project planning and control system than Gantt charts.
4. How long "noncritical activities" can be delayed before they cause a delay in the total project.

Based upon timing and the specific activities, PERT segregates all activities into critical and noncritical activities. By definition, if the completion date of a critical activity is delayed, the completion date for the overall project will be delayed. If the completion date of a critical activity is earlier than estimated, the date for the completion of the overall project may be earlier than originally planned. Noncritical activities, by definition, do not affect the scheduled completion date of the overall project. As projects evolve and circumstances change, noncritical activities can become critical activities and vice versa.

Developing the Network Table and Diagram

When completed, a PERT network table and diagram are tabular and graphical representations that show the relationships between project activities and the time estimated for individual activities as well as for the total project.

Step 1. List All Project Activities Using the Work Breakdown Structure

Each activity should be expressed using an action verb, such as "secure a Certificate of Need," "build the new addition," or "train new staff." The list needs to be

Table 12-1 Activity List for Project of Opening a New Clinic

Office:	
	Identify site and lease
	Make modifications to site
	Install equipment
	Aquire supplies
Staff:	
	Hire staff
	Train staff

comprehensive and indicate all the activities needed to complete the project. In Table 12-1 each project activity has been modified by the addition of an action verb. Using this approach, the work breakdown structure becomes an activity list that includes all the activities that must be completed.

Step 2. For Each Activity, Indicate Its Immediate Predecessor Activity

In this step, the order of activities is determined. Each activity should be considered separately to determine which activity or activities *must* occur immediately before the next. This step begins to identify the essential sequence of activities of the project. The immediate predecessor for each activity is then listed (Table 12-2). For example, it is *essential* that the organization hires staff (E) before it trains staff (F). It is also possible that a step will have more than one immediate predecessor, such as with step D in Table 12-2, Acquire supplies.

Table 12-2 Activity List with Immediate Predecessors

Activity		*Predecessor*
A	Identify site and lease	–
B	Make modifications to site	A
C	Install equipment	B
D	Acquire supplies	A,C
E	Hire staff	A
F	Train staff	E,D

Table 12-3 Activity List with Immediate Predecessors and Time Estimates

Activity		Predecessor	Time estimate (weeks)
A	Identify site and lease	–	3
B	Make modifications to site	A	3
C	Install equipment	B	2
D	Acquire supplies	A,C	2
E	Hire staff	A	3
F	Train staff	E,D	1

Step 3. Estimate the Time It Will Take to Complete Each Activity

When estimating the time each activity will take a common unit of time such as days, weeks, or years should be used. The estimate should be a reasonable estimate and not based on "best-case" or "worst-case" scenarios (Table 12-3).

Step 4. Create a Network Diagram That Includes Time Estimates

After identifying the immediate predecessor activities, project "paths" can be determined. Because some activities have more than one predecessor, separate paths must be mapped out. An example of this from Table 12-2 would be the following. All paths start at the beginning or at activity A. Activity A must precede activity B, thus a path would start A to B. However, activity A also precedes activities D and E. Here, two other paths must be started, one that runs from A to D, and one that runs from A to E. Following the A to B path, we look for activities that require B as a predecessor. We see that step C lists step B as a predecessor. This path now reads A to B to C. We continue down each path in this way until step F is reached, which is the end of the project. Table 12-4 lists out all the paths for this

Table 12-4 PERT Project Paths and Times

Path	Path Time
A-B-C-D-F	11
A-E-F	7
A-D-F	6

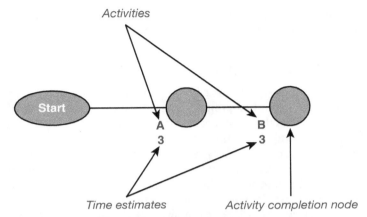

Figure 12-2 PERT Diagram Components

project. A PERT network diagram considers each path separately and places them visually in one diagram. Figure 12-2 shows the components of a PERT network diagram. PERT requires the use of specific symbols. Circles indicate the completion of a predecessor activity and the beginning of the next activity and lines are used to indicate relationships between activities. These are shown in Figure 12-2. Figure 12-3 shows the completed network diagram for this project. The activities are labeled using their designated letter between the activity completion nodes.

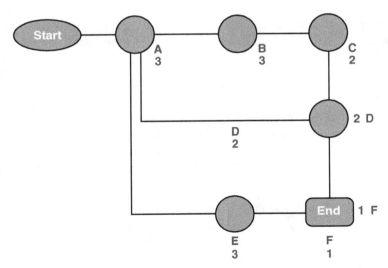

Figure 12-3 PERT Network Diagram for New Clinic Project

The time estimates for each activity are placed below. It is important that each project, and thus network diagram, have only one start and one end. Visually, all paths lead to these two nodes.

Step 5. Determine the Critical Path

The critical path is the longest time path through the network and is determined by adding all of the individual project step time estimates for each path. From Table 12-4, we find that the critical path is the pathway represented by activities A, B, C, D, and F. Adding the times for each of these activities yields a total minimum project time of 11 weeks. The path containing activities A, E, and F has a total minimum completion time of 7 weeks, and the path with activities A, D, and F has a total minimum completion time of 6 weeks. The critical path is thus 11 weeks, or the longest. This means that given the time estimates of the various activities, the project cannot be done in any less than 11 weeks. If any of the activities on the critical path becomes delayed, or take longer than anticipated, the overall time of completion for the entire project will also be delayed.

Given the sequence of activities included in a PERT network, each activity has an earliest start date, which is simply the earliest time the activity can start after the project has begun. For example, activity B has an earliest start of 3 weeks and can only start after activity A has completed. Activity A is estimated to take 3 weeks to complete. Activity A, the first step in any project, by definition always has a start time of zero. The latest start time is the latest time the activity can begin without jeopardizing the total time estimated for the project. For activities on the critical path, the latest start time and the earliest start time are always the same. There is no flexibility in these start times, as any delay would delay the entire project. For activities not on the critical path, however, there may be flexibility in start times, and the earliest start time and latest start time can differ. For example, Activity E could begin as late as the seventh week without jeopardizing the 11 weeks estimated for the entire project. To calculate the latest start time for noncritical path activities, it is often easier to work backward from the end of the project. To stay within the estimated project time of 11 weeks, we would calculate the time needed to complete those steps to the end of the project, *including the activity we are estimating*. To do this we select the path the activity is on, because it is not on the critical path. Activity E is followed by activity F, which ends this project. Activity F takes 1 week to complete. This means that it must start at week 10 to stay on time. Activity E takes 3 weeks to complete. Therefore, the latest it can start and still end by the tenth week would be week 7.

The difference between the earliest and latest start times is called a slack time. Slack is the amount of timing flexibility that exists within an activity. It conveys the amount of time that an activity can increase without changing the

Table 12-5 Activity Times and Slack

Activity	Critical path?	Earliest start time (EST)	Latest start time (LST)	Slack
A	Y	0	0	0
B	Y	3	3	0
C	Y	6	6	0
D	Y	8	8	0
E	N	3	7	4
F	Y	10	10	0

estimated completion date of the overall project. Along the critical path slack equals zero. When slack is greater than zero, the activity is not on the critical path. Table 12-5 has been updated to show slack time as well as a column designating whether the activity is on the critical path or not, a helpful, but not necessary, convention.

PERT establishes the sequential schedule of activities that constitute the overall project. By sequencing the activities in an appropriate order and adding time estimates, the overall time necessary to complete the project can be estimated. Equally important is the identification of those activities that must be monitored to complete the overall project on schedule—activities on the critical path.

LEARNING OBJECTIVE 3: TO UNDERSTAND HOW TO USE PERT FOR PROJECT MANAGEMENT

Once developed as a project planning technique, PERT provides the manager the ability to evaluate and control the project. In projects with many activities and paths, PERT focuses the attention of the manager on those activities on the critical path. Although all activities are important and essential for the completion of the project, PERT indicates those special or critical activities that the manager must monitor and manage to complete the project within the original time estimate. If the manager can shorten the time associated with these critical activities, the completion date of the project can be shortened.

Once a project is begun, managers monitor all activities by comparing the estimated time for each activity with the actual time taken to complete an activity. The difference between the time estimated and the actual time is the variance. When the actual time is less than the original time estimate, a positive variance occurs. When the actual time is more than the original time estimates, a negative variance occurs.

Negative variances on the critical path delay the overall project. A delay is referred to as a slip or slippage. Managers must evaluate any negative variance to determine if it is associated with a critical or noncritical path activity. If slippage is related to a critical activity, the overall completion date of the project will be affected as will the date subsequent activities begin. If it is not on the critical path, then the manager must determine the impact of the activity slippage. It is important to remember that extreme slippage of an activity from the original critical path sifts the entire critical path of the network.

Some managers use "rolling wave" PERT for projects that involve long time durations. Under this approach, managers continue to update and change the original network based upon project experience (what actually happens) and new information about completion times and estimates. For example, if a snowstorm delays lumber shipments from Canada early in the project, all subsequent activities must be adjusted accordingly. Rolling wave estimates add more detail than was originally included in the network. To ensure appropriate project management, it breaks macro activities into many micro activities and monitors adherence to the revised schedule of activities.

PERT networks and charts can be cumbersome. For large projects, these charts can fill walls. To assist managers with the size of charts, some prepare PERT networks in levels. They use a master network to show large activities and individual charts to plan and control smaller or subactivities. Some organize their charts based upon the categories used in the WBS. Others are organized by scope. "Higher level" activities are those activities expressed in larger time durations, whereas "lower level" activities show the detail associated with one or more "higher level" activities.

As an evaluation and control system, PERT provides the manager the ability to monitor project activity and assess the impact of project accomplishments. It facilitates timely planning of subsequent activities and provides the manager the dual ability to monitor the micro as well as macro elements of a project.

The Time and Cost Tradeoff

Typically, but not always, a project can be shortened by adding more resources. Embedded in every time estimate is an implicit resource statement. For example, if the activity to modify the clinic site (activity B) is estimated to take 3 weeks, this could imply that it will take 3 weeks with a crew of four working 8 hours per weekday.

$$4 \text{ workers} \times 8 \text{ hours per day} = 32 \text{ worker hours per day}$$

$$32 \text{ worker hours per day} \times 15 \text{ work days} = 480 \text{ worker hours}$$

At $14 per hour, this would equal $6720 for staff time. Consider alternative ways to schedule 480 worker hours, which is the estimated amount of work that must occur regardless of how many workers or days are allotted.

If two workers were scheduled to work the 480 hours, the activity could be completed in 30 work days or 6 weeks (480 hours/2 workers × 8 hours per day = 30 days).

If six workers were scheduled to work the 480 worker hours, the activity could be completed in 10 days or 2 weeks (480 hours/6 workers × 8 hours per day =10 days).

If four workers were used and required to work 12, in contrast to 8 hours per day, the activity could also be completed in 10 days or 2 weeks.

Requiring workers to work 12 hours per day, in contrast to 8 hours per day, would, however, change the expenses related to this activity. Mandatory overtime would have to be paid, usually at a pay rate 50% higher than the base hourly rate (i.e., 480 hours/four workers × 12 hours per day = 10 days).

In this last scenario, the tradeoff between time and cost is very evident. As originally scheduled using four workers at 8 hours per day for 480 hours (15 days), the staff cost was estimated to be $6720. This is found by multiplying 480 worker hours by $14 per hour. Using four workers, 12 hours a day for 480 hours requires some calculation. Having the extra time shortens the number of days needed to 10. This means that for 10 days the four workers will receive $14 per hour for 8 hours and $21 per hour for 4 hours. In total, 320 worker hours are paid at the base rate and 160 worker hours are paid at the overtime rate. The base rate cost is now $4480 and the overtime rate cost is now $3360 for a total of $7840, an increase in our budget of $1120. In fact there are many possible tradeoffs that can occur here relative to the number of workers and the number of hours. Table 12-6 shows the options for some of them.

Inherent in each of these alternatives are key assumptions. One is that each worker contributes equally to project tasks, e.g., that there is enough work to go around infinitely. It is the converse of the law of diminishing returns, which states that as more workers are added, the output provided by each marginal worker decreases, a more likely reality. It is unlikely that an unlimited number of workers could be added to a project, and so estimations need to consider the scope of what is needed. The second is that additional resources are available. Although more workers or equipment could help to move a project time forward, these things are not always available, and so projections again need to be made realistic.

The project manager understands the tradeoff between project time and project cost, and that there are many strategies available to complete specific project activities. Some of these options take more or less time than the time chosen for project planning. Some options involve higher costs. If cost concerns are not a factor, a project can be rescheduled using crash times, which are the quickest time that an activity can be completed given any amount of resources.

Table 12-6 Resource/Cost Tradeoffs

For a project with 480 total worker-hours

Workers	Hours per day	Days	Total cost
1	8	60.0	$ 6720
1	12	40.0	$ 7840
2	8	30.0	$ 6720
2	12	20.0	$ 7840
3	8	20.0	$ 6720
3	12	13.3	$ 7840
4	8	15.0	$ 6720
4	12	10.0	$ 7840
5	8	12.0	$ 6720
5	12	8.0	$ 7840
6	8	10.0	$ 6720
6	12	6.7	$ 7840
7	8	8.6	$ 6720
7	12	5.7	$ 7840
8	8	7.5	$ 6720
8	12	5.0	$ 7840
9	8	6.7	$ 6720
9	12	4.4	$ 7840

assumes $14 per hour and $21 per hour OT

Conversely, to lower project and activity costs, activities and projects can sometimes be lengthened. This will delay project completion. Even though such an action may have a system cost impact (e.g., the cost impact of a delayed opening of a new clinic), it may also lower the cost of the project. Delays may be caused by using fewer workers or less skilled workers who are paid less but require more time to complete the project. Delay may mean using manual labor to accomplish a task, even though the task could be done quicker, albeit more expensively, using an automated process with specific equipment.

The central point is to acknowledge the fundamental relationship between time and costs in project management. Within boundaries, the project manager is able to trade off one against the other.

OTHER PERT METHODS

Multiple Time Estimate PERT

Multiple time estimate PERT provides the project manager with a probabilistic range of estimates of the time required to complete project activities, or the overall project. Using multiple time estimate PERT, the manager can trade off different levels of probability (i.e., the probability of completing an activity in a specified amount of time), which is sometimes referred to as a time/probability tradeoff. Because multiple time estimate PERT utilizes optimistic, pessimistic, and most probable time estimates, there becomes a need for assessing the probabilities that are associated with each time estimate. Given the probabilistic nature of the time estimates used in PERT, other versions of PERT incorporate more formal methods for the project manager to assess time tradeoffs, cost, and the probability of completion success or failure. For most projects, however, the use of multiple time estimate PERT is overly complex and unnecessary.

PERT COST

PERT COST was developed as a companion to PERT. It adds the ability to assess and trade off time and cost at the activity level. It requires each activity to have three costs estimates: an estimate associated with the optimistic time, pessimistic time, and most probable time. Other versions use boundary limits (e.g., crash time cost estimates) as a basis for these multiple cost estimates. PERT COST is a complex system best used in very specific settings. Project managers of major construction and research and development projects use PERT COST to plan, evaluate, and control project activity. By comparing the planned value of work scheduled with the planned value of work accomplished, the project manager is able to extend the use of variance analysis to manage project costs as well as project times. Computer programs exist to develop PERT networks and support a project manager's use of multiple time estimate PERT and PERT COST. The application of these more advanced versions of PERT is usually restricted to large-scale, highly complex projects.

CONCLUSION

PERT remains the premier method to define, plan, schedule, and control a project. It provides the manager with the ability to consider alternative plans and change plans once a project has begun.

The PERT network is the outcome of the combined insight of many. Groups of managers and experts are typically used to construct the WBS for PERT analysis. PERT also provides the ability to do "what if," or sensitivity analyses; for example, what if the project had to be completed in 8 weeks instead of 12? "What ifs" are common questions that project managers consider.

PERT requires comprehensive project planning. During the concept and definition phase of a project, project managers construct and consider many different project approaches using PERT as a basis for moving forward. As circumstances change or develop, the project may need to be adjusted to accomplish its objectives. PERT provides the tools to do this by stressing the interrelation of project activities. It further provides an explicit tool for measuring the time/cost tradeoff inherent in any large-scale project.

EXERCISES

12-1 Using the information in Table 12-7, construct a PERT network and answer each of the following questions:
   a. What is the expected project completion data?
   b. What is the scheduled start and completion date for each activity?
   c. Which activities are on the critical path?
   d. How long can noncritical path activities be delayed without jeopardizing the overall completion date for this project?

12-2 Assess the impact of the following changes to the time estimates provided in question 12-1. Individually, what is the impact if:

Activity	Predecessor	New Time Estimate
O. Advertise for new staff	N	4
P. Interview for new staff	O	6
Q. Select new staff	P	1

Collectively, what is the impact of these changes?

12-3 As project manager for the example included in question 12-1, what would you recommend to preserve the original project completion date if activity A was reestimated to take 8 weeks, not the original 4 weeks? Provide details.

12-4 Develop a WBS and PERT network with no more than 20 activities for each of the following projects.
   a. Buying a car
   b. Screening 1000 school-age children for high blood pressure and reporting the results to the child's physician

Table 12-7 Project to Convert a 20-Bed Unit in a Nursing Home to
Accommodate Patients with Dementia

Activity		Predecessor	Time estimate (weeks)
A	Secure state approval	–	4
B	Identify 20-bed unit to be used	A	1
C	Move existing residents	B	1
D	Clean space	C	2
E	Develop architectural plans	A	9
F	Install new heating and ventilation systems	E	4
G	Install security systems	E	2
H	Move walls; renovate	F	4
I	Identify new equipment	A	1
J	Order new equipment	I	1
K	Unpack and inspect new equipment	J	1
L	Install new equipment	D,K,H	3
M	Reassign staff	A	1
N	Identify new staffing needs	M	1
O	Advertise for new staff	N	3
P	Interview for new staff	O	2
Q	Select new hires	P	3
R	Develop care plan protocols	M	1
S	Train staff	R,Q,M,L	1
T	Modify quality assurance plans	S	2
U	Coordinate with hospital discharge planners	T	4
V	Complete internal audit	U,G	1

Chapter 13

Financial Evaluation of Projects

LEARNING OBJECTIVES

1. To develop skills in evaluating the financial consequences of alternative projects.
2. To understand what comprises a cash flow.
3. To understand the concept of payback as a tool to evaluate the financial desirability of a project.
4. To be able to compute discounted cash flow and to use three tools to evaluate the financial impact of projects (i.e., net present value, internal rate of return, and modified internal rate of return).

REAL WORLD SCENARIO

Eugene Righter is manager of strategy for St. Clement's–Mercy Medical Center in a midwestern city. The medical center is widely regarded for the excellence of its clinical services, in particular its use of cutting-edge technology. At a recent meeting with the organization's clinical directors, three new projects were proposed for development within the medical center over the next 5 years. Any of the three projects would enhance the medical center's image as a progressive healthcare organization, and all of them are consistent with the St. Clement's mission. As manager of strategy, it was Eugene's job to assess the financial attractiveness of all new projects; unfortunately, although all three projects could be supported equally from a clinical perspective, the medical center had the financial resources to undertake only one. Eugene realized that because the projects were each designed to operate for a number of years, it was important to consider the financial attractiveness of each over several years. He recalled from his education that there were a number of financial tools that might be useful to assess this long-term financial attractiveness.

LEARNING OBJECTIVE 1: TO DEVELOP SKILLS IN EVALUATING THE FINANCIAL CONSEQUENCES OF ALTERNATIVE PROJECTS

Note: This is the objective for the entire chapter actually, although specific, more focused learning objectives are discussed throughout the chapter.

The concept of the time value of money was introduced in Chapter 4, including the tools of compounding and discounting. For a healthcare manager, the most important use of these tools is in evaluating potential organizational projects. This chapter provides examples of how to apply these tools in organizational decision making. Any project must compete for organizational approval and for the capital or funding associated with approval. Capital is limited and must be allocated to meet the many goals and objectives faced by the contemporary healthcare organization. New projects need to be designed to be competitive within this context of organizational priorities and realities.

Every project must compete for capital with existing projects, other new projects, and alternative uses of capital such as capital investment opportunities; e.g., certificates of deposit (CDs), mutual funds, money markets, etc. If an existing project needs to be stopped to furnish the capital needed for a new project, the termination expenses associated with stopping the first project must be added as an expense associated with the new project. However, generally new projects compete against other new projects and alternative capital uses, not existing projects.

In well-managed healthcare organizations, a project never competes only against itself for organizational approval. When organizations consider a new project, it is not enough to know how much a project will cost and how much it can be expected to earn. The manager must also compare a given project with other project alternatives and alternative uses of capital. Well-managed healthcare organizations evaluate projects based upon the implications and alternatives associated with the project and the capital needed to support it.

Most situations requiring managers to evaluate the attractiveness of a potential project or investment opportunity involve understanding and building upon the concept of the time value of money. In general, organizations are required to spend money now, an outflow of cash known as the initial investment or present value (PV). In future years the organization will experience a series of cash flows (cf) as a result of the project; these cash flows may be positive or negative, but in either case, by convention they are generally determined at the end of a defined time period, such as a month or a year. The amount of these cash flows is known as the future value (FV). Cash flows may involve either uneven amounts or equal amounts of money. Cash flows of equal size that occur at equal time intervals are known as annuities or payments (PMT).

Recall from Chapter 4 in the discussion of compounding and discounting that the rate at which the value of money grows (going forward in time, known as compounding), or declines (going backward in time, known as discounting), is known as the discount rate, cost of capital or opportunity cost (i). The number of time periods (n) involved in the project or investment is the final factor.

The key variables addressed so far are:

- Present Value: (PV)
- Cash Flow in Time Period n: (cf_n)
- Future Value in Time Period n: (FV_n)
- Annuity (cash flows of equal size separated by equal time periods): (PMT)
- Discount Rate, Cost of Capital, Opportunity Cost: (i)
- Number of Time Periods: (n)

Using the formulas and techniques presented in the discussion of the time value of money it is possible to compute any unknown key variable, given sufficient information regarding other variables. For example, the present value (PV) can be computed, if the future value in time period n (FV_n), the number of time periods (n), and an appropriate discount rate (i) are known.

In this chapter, tools for analyzing and comparing the attractiveness of a potential project or investment are described. These tools, the net present value (NPV), the internal rate of return (IRR), and the modified internal rate of return build upon the concept of the time value of money.

So fundamental are these concepts to management decision making that financial and business calculators have keys for each of the important variables to facilitate computation. In addition, spreadsheet programs, such as Excel, have functions to compute the values. Readers are encouraged to utilize such calculators or spreadsheet programs to assist in financial analysis. This chapter also presents how the calculations actually "work," to provide a better understanding of the nature of the analyses.

LEARNING OBJECTIVE 2: TO UNDERSTAND WHAT COMPRISES A CASH FLOW

Managers of healthcare organizations need to consider many elements when evaluating potential projects. For example, market and competitive factors may influence the effect of the project on market share, the likely impact on the organization's image, and the organization's ability to establish and maintain a competitive distinction. Epidemiology too may influence the effect of the project. Health services managers should assess the likely impact of a project on the health status of the community. Managers must also always be sensitive to the impact of new projects on existing personnel and the organization's ability to attract and retain well-qualified staff. The well-educated and highly trained nature of large portions of the typical health services organization's staff make these factors especially important.

However, among all relevant factors financial issues are usually weighted most heavily by managers. In particular, managers assess a project's impact on the organization's ability to generate cash. This is not surprising, as it is the availability and flow of cash which, in a very real sense "fuel" the organization and its activities. Without an acceptable cash flow, the organization's survival is in question. For this reason, it is critical to consider cash flow.

As the words suggest, a "cash flow" reflects the actual "movement" of funds in to or out of an organization. Revenues generated by a project are cash inflows. Expenses, such as payroll or supply purchases, are cash outflows. The difference between cash inflows and cash outflows is known as net cash flows. For example, if cash inflows for a new patient care service are $100,000 and the cash outflows associated with the project are $95,000, then the net cash flow for the service is $5,000. Net cash flows for any period of time may be either positive or negative.

Most projects involve a series of events that entail either the outflow or inflow of cash. For example, a multispecialty group practice might decide to purchase a new piece of laboratory equipment with the capability of completing multiple blood analyses electronically and much more rapidly than currently available technology. The purchase price of this equipment is $55,000. It is anticipated that the equipment has a useful life of 5 years; i.e., ongoing technological enhancements will make this equipment essentially obsolete in 5 years, and it will need to be replaced. The original vendor has agreed to pay $5000 to buy back the equipment at the time of replacement. This $5000 is known as the salvage value or salvage price. During its 5 years of operation, it is estimated that the equipment will generate revenue through charges associated with its use. Table 13-1 displays estimated net revenue for the equipment.

Net cash flow takes into account both cash inflows and cash outflows. Notice that these numbers refer to actual cash flows. As such, some items recognized as an expense by generally accepted accounting principles are not cash flows. The most noteworthy example of this is depreciation. Depreciation expense is an accounting convention that is used to reflect the gradual erosion of an asset's value because of it use over time. It does not involve any actual flow of cash, however, and thus does not enter into this type of project analysis.

Table 13-1 Estimated Net Cash Flows for Blood Analyzer Project

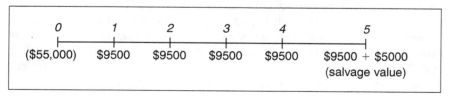

0	1	2	3	4	5
($55,000)	$9500	$9500	$9500	$9500	$9500 + $5000 (salvage value)

Table 13-2 Statement of Income—For Profit Nursing Home (000)

Gross Revenue from Operations		$8,300
Expenses:		
Total except Depreciation	$7,300	
Depreciation	100	
Total Expenses		($7,400)
Net Income Before Taxes		$ 900
Income Taxes @ 40%		($ 360)
Net Income		$ 540

Cash Flow Statement—For Profit Nursing Home (000)

Service Revenue (net of allowances)	$ 8,300
Total Expenses (except depreciation)	(7,300)
Pre-Tax Cash Flows	$ 1,000
Taxes @ 40%	(360)
Net Cash Flow	$ 640

Consider the case of a private, tax-paying nursing facility. The facility's income statement and a statement of cash flows are shown as Table 13-2. According to accounting convention, net income is calculated including depreciation as an expense. However, depreciation is not a cash expense. It is not included in the statement of cash flows. As a result, net income for the facility is $540,000, whereas the net cash flow for the same period of time is $640,000. The difference between the two, $100,000, is depreciation. The relationship between net income and cash flows is shown in Equation 13-1.

Net Income + Depreciation = Net Cash Flow	Equation 13-1

Which Cash Flows Should Be Included in Analyzing Projects?

One fundamental approach to evaluate the attractiveness of a project is to analyze the cash flow's implications associated with it. Certainly, from a financial perspective, projects that generate larger, positive net cash flows are more attractive than other projects with lower positive, or even negative, net cash flows.

By convention, in assessing project opportunities, not all cash flows are included in the analysis. Only those cash flows directly related to the project should be included. The treatment of several major types of cash flows is described in the following paragraphs.

1. Revenues and expenses, other than depreciation, directly related to the project are included in the analysis.
2. The impact of the project on areas of the organization apart from the project itself needs to be considered. For example, a hospital opening a freestanding ambulatory surgery center may experience changes in demand for its existing inpatient or hospital-based outpatient surgical services, most likely reduction in demand for these services as a result of implementing the new center, a process known as "cannibalization." Thus, for the entire organization (in this example, the hospital), some of the revenue realized by the new program is not "new" revenue; rather, it actually represents a shift in revenue brought about by patients using the new center instead of previously existing services. As such, only the "new" or incremental revenue associated with the new venture should be considered in the analysis. In calculating the cash inflows and outflows associated with the project, estimates of the actual incremental impact of the program need to be made. This estimation process, as much an art as a science, requires competence in the forecasting methods as well, as discussed in Chapter 5.
3. Sunk costs (i.e., a cost that has already been incurred or has been committed), are not included in the cash flow analysis. For example, the hospital may have retained consulting services to analyze the feasibility of the freestanding ambulatory care surgery center before analyzing its feasibility. This cost is a sunk cost; whether or not the hospital decides to proceed with the surgery center, the money has already been spent. Therefore, the expenditure does not represent a relevant cash flow for the analysis.

LEARNING OBJECTIVE 3: TO UNDERSTAND THE CONCEPT OF PAYBACK AS A TOOL TO EVALUATE THE FINANCIAL DESIRABILITY OF A PROJECT

A vital analysis completed by managers is an assessment of the net cash flows of a project, taking into account the timing of these cash flows. The timing of cash flows builds upon the concept of the time value of money. For example, a manager may determine that the project being analyzed is projected to generate a series of negative cash flows, followed by a large positive cash flow. This cash flow pattern is not uncommon for a new product or service that builds market share over a period of several years. Table 13-3 displays such a cash flow for a planned health screening program.

The initial investment in the project is $10,000, shown as a negative cash flow in time period 0, which represents the present time. Operations in years 1 to 4 each

Table 13-3 Net Cash Flow—Health Screening Program

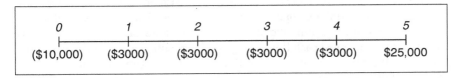

generate a negative cash flow of $3000. Finally, in year 5, a positive cash flow of $25,000 is realized. It is assumed that year 5 is the final year of the project; i.e., no cash flows related to this project, positive or negative, occur after this point.

The question facing a manager is, "As a project, is this a good financial investment?" One way to formulate a response to this question is to assess the project's cash flows.

It might seem intuitive to sum up the positive cash flows (cash inflows) and negative cash flows (cash outflows) associated with the project and make a decision based on whether the resulting net figure is positive or negative. After all, this approach does recognize the importance of cash flows. However, this approach is not adequate as it totally ignores the time value of money.

Alternatively, a manager might calculate what is known as the payback period. This is the length of time it takes to recoup the project's initial investment. In this example, the project's investment is recovered in the fifth year of the project. Based on this knowledge, a decision on whether or not to proceed with the project would be made. Does 5 years represent a reasonable time to recoup an initial investment of $10,000? This is essentially a judgment or value-driven call for the organization.

Although used relatively frequently, calculation of the payback period is also an incomplete approach, incomplete because it does not directly take into account the time value of money. As such, the approach is overly simplistic, and its use is discouraged.

LEARNING OBJECTIVE 4: TO BE ABLE TO COMPUTE DISCOUNTED CASH FLOW AND TO USE THREE TOOLS TO EVALUATE THE FINANCIAL IMPACT OF PROJECTS (I.E., NET PRESENT VALUE, INTERNAL RATE OF RETURN, AND MODIFIED INTERNAL RATE OF RETURN)

Taking into consideration the information on compounding and discounting presented earlier, it should be apparent that "adjustments" must be made to account for the timing of the anticipated cash flows. To assess the financial value of the project, the present value of cash flows associated with the project should be computed.

Recall that in computing this present value, cash flows that are more distant in the future are discounted over more time periods. Thus, cash flows received earlier in the project's life are worth more in current (present) dollars than those received later.

This process of calculating the present value of future cash flows is known as calculating a discounted cash flow. The goal of computing a discounted cash flow is to derive the present value of a project's cash flows. The present value provides a measure of the project's value at the current time (time = 0), so managers can compare present values among various projects; i.e., it creates an "apples and apples" framework for financial analysis. The arithmetic sum of the present value of the project's cash flows is known as the net present value (NPV) of the project.

Determining a net present value requires discounting and involves these steps:

1. Select an appropriate discount rate and use it consistently to discount all future cash flows to the current time (i.e., time = 0).
2. Calculate the net present value of these discounted cash flows.
3. Compare the calculated net present value with a previously stated criterion or compare the net present values of various projects against one another.

In general, the management decision rule is that projects with a positive NPV are attractive, and that projects with larger positive NPVs are more attractive than those with smaller NPVs. Strictly from a financial perspective, projects with a negative NPV are not attractive.

Virtually all projects entail an initial investment, so it is essential that these funds be available at the time they are needed for the project. Regardless of the NPV, if the initial investment required for the project is not available, then the project may not be feasible. It may be possible for the organization to obtain financing (short or long term) to meet the initial investment requirement. The financial impact (in terms of cash flows, ability to take on additional debt, debt service requirement, etc.) would need to be woven into the cash flow analysis as well.

Recall that an important component of discounting is determining the appropriate discount rate. This topic is considered in greater depth later in this chapter. Assume that after careful research, the manager determines that the $10,000 available for investment could be used to purchase a CD for 5 years at an interest rate of 4.5%. Assuming an essentially equivalent level of risk between the CD and a new project opportunity, 4.5% would be an appropriate discount rate to use in calculating net present value. This calculation is depicted on Table 13-4, showing the present value of each future cash flow. The NPV of the potential project is −$702, not an attractive outcome from a financial perspective. Based on this analysis, then, investing in the CD would be more attractive financially.

This simple example is useful to illustrate several concepts regarding NPV as a decision tool. For example, although the project is not financially viable under current conditions, what initial investment would make the project attractive?

Table 13-4 Present Value of Future Cash Flows for Health Screening Program

(assume discount rate of 4.5%)		
Year	*Net Cash Flow*	*PV of Cash Flow*
0	−$10,000	−$10,000
1	−$ 3000	−$ 2871
2	−$ 3000	−$ 2747
3	−$ 3000	−$ 2629
4	−$ 3000	−$ 2516
5	$25,000	$20,061
		NPV = −$ 702

If the project's NPV can be increased to a positive value, then it becomes a viable project; i.e., if the NPV can be increased by over $702. In effect, if any of the cash flows can be modified to result in a positive present value of at least this amount, then the project becomes financially viable. For example, management can determine that if its initial investment (cash outflow in time = 0) can be reduced to less than $9298, the project becomes financially attractive. At an initial investment of exactly $9298, the NPV is equal to 0. If management has defined a philosophy to accept "break even" projects in some circumstances, this project would then be acceptable.

Alternatively, using the cash flows and the discount rate it is possible to compute other changes that would generate a positive NPV. Management can then assess various strategic and tactical options (pricing, marketing, distribution, etc.) to assess whether any such changes are possible. For example, what positive cash flow must be generated in year 5 to result in a positive NPV? This is the same as asking what cash flow, discounted for 5 years at 4.5%, results in a present value of at least $20,763 (the negative discounted net cash flow excluding year 5). By using a hand-held calculator or a spreadsheet program (or working through the mathematics in detail, one cash flow at a time) the answer is $25,874. If the project is able to generate a positive net annual cash flow for year 5 of at least $25,874, then the NPV is greater than or equal to zero.

The impact of the discount rate selected can also be illustrated by this example. Suppose the discount rate used were 3% instead of 4.5%. With the new discount rate (Table 13-5), the net present value is $414.

Table 13-5 Present Value of Future Cash Flows for Health Screening Program

(assume discount rate of 3.0%)		
Year	Net Cash Flow	PV of Cash Flow
0	−$10,000	−$10,000
1	−$ 3000	−$ 2913
2	−$ 3000	−$ 2828
3	−$ 3000	−$ 2745
4	−$ 3000	−$ 2665
5	$25,000	$21,565
		NPV = $ 414

Annuities: A Particular Series of Cash Flows

Cash flows may occur in a variety of patterns. As in the examples presented earlier, the initial investment is followed by a series of uneven cash flows; i.e., the net annual cash flows differ among years. When this is the case, calculating the discounted present value of these cash flows involves a discounting calculation for each time period.

Other projects may generate equal cash flows. For example, Table 13-6 shows a project that generated net annual cash flows of $9,500 for each of the next 5 years. This pattern of cash flows is known as an annuity. An annuity is a series of equal

Table 13-6 Project with Equal Cash Flows—an Annuity

Year	Net Cash Flow
0	−$40,000
1	$ 9500
2	$ 9500
3	$ 9500
4	$ 9500
5	$ 9500

cash flows occurring over time at equal intervals. In this example, $9500 is received every year; both the amount and the timing of the cash flow are fixed and equal. An annuity is simply a specific pattern of cash flows. The cash flows involved with an annuity can be either net cash inflows or cash outflows. By convention, and for use with business or financial calculators or spreadsheet applications, cash flows associated with annuities are known as payments (PMT).

There are two types of annuities that differ only in the timing of when the payment takes place. If the payment occurs at the end of the time period specified, the annuity is referred to as an ordinary annuity. If the payment takes place at the beginning of the time period specified, the annuity is an annuity due. The majority of annuities are ordinary annuities.

Table 13-7 is an example of an ordinary annuity in which the purchaser will receive a series of $500 payments after each of the next 5 years. This is spoken of as a 5-year ordinary annuity. Notice that the first payment of $500 is received at the end of year 1, the second payment at the end of year 2, and so on for 5 years. A typical question that arises is, How much should an individual be willing to pay now for this annuity?

It should be clear that this question is a version of the present value computations already discussed. As always, the individual needs to determine an appropriate discount rate or cost of capital. Suppose an alternative investment is identified, i.e., a 5-year CD with an interest rate of 6%. As described, this represents the opportunity cost of purchasing the annuity. This problem becomes one of discounting each annual cash flow of $500 at the rate of 6% to determine the present value.

The calculated present value of $2106 is the purchase price at which the individual should be financially indifferent between the two investments; i.e., there is no financial advantage in purchasing one over the other. Obviously if the annuity

Table 13-7 Pattern of Cash Flows in an Ordinary Annuity—Payment Received at End of Period Indicated

Year	Net cash flow
0	−$2000
1	$ 500
2	$ 500
3	$ 500
4	$ 500
5	$ 500

is priced at less than $2106 it becomes a more attractive investment; prices over $2106 are less attractive.

Many standard calculators have a "PMT" key, which enables the user to enter the amount of the annual payment once along with the number of time periods of the annuity, rather than having to enter the same cash flow amount (the payment) for each year of the annuity. This computational function is not only convenient, but it also protects against the risk of entering data incorrectly. Common examples of an annuity are a home mortgage or a car loan, both of which typically involve a series of equal payments (the annuity).

Often, situations arise in which there is an annuity embedded within a series of annual cash flows (Table 13-8). This cash flow has a series of 6 payments of $750 each from years 3 through 8 of the project. Assume a discount rate of 7%, what is the present value of this project (i.e., what is the most that should be invested in this project)?

There are two ways to go about solving this problem. The long way is to calculate the discounted present value of each annual cash flow and determine the NPV. This approach requires that each cash flow be entered individually.

A second, somewhat shorter, way to solve this problem is to utilize the fact that there is an annuity embedded in the cash flow stream. In effect, the cash flow stream is divided into multiple parts, those included in the annuity and those separate from it. The steps to solve this problem using the embedded annuity are described below and illustrated in Table 13-9.

Table 13-8 Pattern of Cash Flows with an
Embedded Annuity (Years 3–8)

Year	Net cash flow
0	
1	$ 1000
2	$ 500
3	$ 750
4	$ 750
5	$ 750
6	$ 750
7	$ 750
8	$ 750
9	$ 500
10	$ 100

Table 13-9 Calculation of Net Present Value including Cash Flow Stream with an Embedded Annuity (Discount rate = 7%)

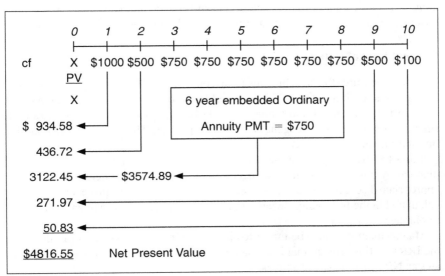

1. Calculate the present value of the discounted cash flow for those periods not included in the annuity; i.e., years 1, 2, 9, and 10. Calculated present values are:

Year 1:	$934.58
Year 2:	$436.72
Year 9:	$271.97
Year 10:	$ 50.83

2. Calculate the present value of the embedded annuity. For this computation, the payment is $750, the interest rate is 7%, and the number of periods is six, the length of the annuity. This calculation yields a present value for the annuity of $3574.89. However, the annuity cash flows have been discounted only to the end of time period 2, the point at which the embedded annuity begins, not time period 0. Therefore, this calculated value must be discounted for an additional two periods to arrive at a present value at time 0. The calculated value of the embedded annuity portion of the cash flow stream at time = 0 is $3122.45.

3. Total the calculated present values to arrive at the NPV for the project. This amount equals $4816.55 for this example. The organization should be willing to invest no more than $4816.55 in this project.

Obviously, either approach to solving the problem should arrive at the same NPV. Viewing the project as an annuity simplifies the calculation somewhat. If the annuity is embedded in the middle of a cash flow stream, care must be taken to ensure that the cash flow of the annuity is fully discounted to the present time.

Internal Rate of Return

The NPV measures the present value of discounted cash flows for a project, assuming a particular discount rate. This is useful input for organizational decision making. On the other hand, the manager might be interested to know what rate of financial return is, in fact, generated by the project. This rate is known as the internal rate of return (IRR).

Table 13-10 displays the anticipated cash flows for a large respite care program planned by a nursing facility. Management of the facility has determined that an appropriate discount rate for this project is 6%. The NPV of the project is $5103, as calculated in the following. Because the NPV is positive, the organization decides to pursue the project.

Management may also be interested in calculating the actual rate of return (i.e., the IRR) for this project; that is the same as determining what discount rate generates an NPV of zero. Using a financial calculator with an IRR key to accomplish this computation, the IRR is 9.9%. As a check, the NPV is computed using a discount rate of 9.9%. As shown in Table 13-11, the NPV using these data is ($3), a value essentially equivalent to zero. This indicates that the calculated IRR is correct.

Managers, particularly in industries other than health care, speak of something known as the "hurdle rate," which refers to the minimum rate of return required

Table 13-10 Internal Rate of Return

Year	Net cash flow	PV (discounted at 6%)
0 (initial investment)	($40,000)	($40,000)
1	$ 5000	$ 4717
2	$10,000	$ 8900
3	$10,000	$ 8396
4	$15,000	$11,881
5	$15,000	$11,209
Net Present Value		$ 5103

Table 13-11 Estimated Cash Flows and NPV for Respite Care Program at Discount Rate = 9.9%

Year	Net cash flow	PV (at 9.9%)
0 (initial investment)	−$40,000	−$40,000
1	$ 5000	$ 4550
2	$10,000	$ 8280
3	$10,000	$ 7534
4	$15,000	$10,283
5	$15,000	$ 9356
	NPV =	$ −3

for a project to be accepted or pursued by the organization. Hurdle rates may be established formally by boards, committees, or management teams, or they may be informal expectations of an organization. Suppose the formally established hurdle rate of the nursing facility is 10%. This means that it is willing to pursue only projects with an IRR greater than 10% (i.e., 10% is the financial return hurdle that must be "cleared" by the project).

Based on the information presented, independent from other nonfinancial considerations, the proposed respite care program would not be pursued, because the IRR is less than the approved hurdle rate. If the IRR exceeds the hurdle rate, then the project exceeds the required minimum return, and all other things being equal it is financially acceptable to the organization. As stated, there are always nonfinancial factors, such as community need and impact on health status, that must be considered before making a final decision on health services projects.

Modified Internal Rate of Return

Taking a closer look at IRR, it should be apparent that what is being done in calculating the IRR is that each future cash flow is, in effect, being compounded at the IRR percentage. In the respite care example this amounts to compounding at a rate of 9.9%. That is, an assumption is being made that funds could be invested and generate a return of 9.9%. Although the mechanics of the calculation may be clear, this IRR rate may or may not be an appropriate (or available) interest rate.

The question is really one of whether money could actually be invested at this rate; i.e., it may be higher than or lower than the actual financial rate of return that could be obtained. To reflect this discrepancy, the IRR is frequently modified or adjusted to take into account any disparity between the IRR and the rate of financial return actually available in the financial market. This new measure can be referred to as the modified IRR.

Determining the modified IRR involves what is known as the *terminal value*. The terminal value is the value (taken at the final or terminal year of the project) of all cash flows compounded to this terminal year at an appropriate cost of capital. The specific steps to complete to determine the modified IRR are:

1. Determine an appropriate cost of capital or discount rate.
2. Compound all net cash inflows forward to the terminal year using this cost of capital. This compounded value is known as the terminal value. Compute the sum of the terminal values in the terminal year.
3. Use the cost of capital to discount all cash outflows back to year 0 of the project. Frequently, there may be only one cash outflow, the initial investment. Because this outflow takes place in year 0, no discounting is required.
4. The modified IRR is the discount rate that equates the present value of the terminal value to the present value of cash outflows.

Table 13-12 displays the discounted and compounded cash flow values for the respite care project. For this example, management has determined that 7% is an appropriate cost of capital (step 1). That is, 7% is the rate of return actually available for this project.)

Table 13-12 Modified Internal Rate of Return for Respite Care Program (000)

0	1	2	3	4	5	Terminal value @ 7%
−$40						
	$5					$ 6554
		$10				$12,250
			$10			$11,449
				$15		$16,050
					$15	$15,000
					Net Terminal Value	$61,303

Table 13-13 Timeline for Mammography Center

0	1	2	3
−$25,000	$7000	$10,000	$20,000

The terminal value of each cash flow is computed by compounding each cash flow by the cost of capital 7%. For example, the terminal value of the $5000 cash flow projected for year 1 is the future value of this amount compounded for 4 years at 7%, or $6554. The sum of terminal values for the project is $61,303. The only cash outflow in this example is the initial investment of $40,000 which takes place at time 0, so it need not be discounted.

The modified IRR is the discount rate which equates the present value of the terminal value to the present value of the cash outflows. In this example, the adjusted IRR is the discount rate that "equates" $61,303 with $40,000. Taken another way, it is the compounding factor that grows an investment of $40,000 to a value of $61,303 in 5 years. The adjusted IRR is 8.91%.

To illustrate another example, suppose a group of hospitals and several physicians are considering developing a state-of-the-art mammography center. To participate, hospital A needs to contribute $25,000 now. Its anticipated net cash flows over the next 3 years are $7000, $10,000, and $20,000, respectively. The board of trustees of hospital A has identified 14% as the organization's hurdle rate for this type of project. The chief financial officer has identified an opportunity cost of 7%. Based only on financial factors, should hospital A participate in the project?

Table 13-13 displays the timeline for this project. Using a PV or initial investment of $25,000, and the net cash flows anticipated, an IRR of 18.6% is computed. Using 7% as the discount rate or cost of capital yields an adjusted IRR of 15.7%.

Both the IRR and the modified IRR exceed the hurdle rate of 14%, so hospital A should pursue the mammogram project.

CONCLUSION

This chapter presents three tools to assist in analyzing projects: the net present value, the internal rate of return, and the modified rate of return. In actual practice, the internal rate of return is the most frequently used tool. Discussions regarding hurdle rates are not uncommon in finance and executive management meetings. Although in some respects the modified IRR is a more accurate assessment of the return of a project, it is infrequently encountered in management suites or boardrooms. NPV falls somewhere in between in terms of frequency of use. Capable healthcare managers should be equally competent in the use of all three tools, and in fact, it may be useful to compare the outcomes of the three approaches in arriving at a final determination regarding a potential project.

Determining the Discount Rate, and a Brief Look at Risk

From the material presented in this chapter it should be apparent that the determination of an appropriate discount rate (alternatively known as the cost of capital, or opportunity cost) is an important element of financial evaluation of projects. Choosing a rate that is either unrealistically high or low may result in poor management decisions; e.g., missed opportunities or poor returns on projects.

Determining the discount rate is not a precise science; rather, it is an excellent example of a manager's use of reasoned judgment. As described, probably the most appropriate approach is to use the rate of return of an alternative investment. This is the opportunity cost.

In earlier examples, interest rates on bank passbook accounts and CDs were used. A bank account interest rate is an example of a relatively risk-free investment (assuming the amount of the account is less than the limit of federal deposit insurance). In the context of finance, risk refers to the probability that actual future returns will be less than expected returns. For a bank savings account, in most cases, the depositor is guaranteed the stated interest rate; i.e., the risk is low. Various investment offerings of the federal government are also examples of virtually risk-free investments; e.g., treasury bills, notes, and bonds. In fact, government treasury bonds (t-bonds), long-term investment vehicles requiring investments of over $1000, are often considered the benchmark for risk-free investments. Other investments are more risky, although all investments have some level of risk, however minimal.

Different types of risk exist; some are associated with business uncertainty (e.g., the level of variation between actual and forecast utilization levels of a new project), and some are associated with changes in the broader economy (e.g., the effect of inflation). Many theoretical approaches have been developed to attempt to estimate levels of risk. For a more thorough discussion of elements associated with risk and approaches to estimate it, the reader is encouraged to review any of the general finance texts cited in the list of suggested readings. For the purposes of this book, readers need to be aware that risk is a factor in all projects, levels of risk may vary among projects, and it is incumbent on the manager to take the relevant risk into account when evaluating projects.

EXERCISES

13-1 A representative of a reputable financial services company has approached you as manager of a four-person group of anesthesiologists with an opportunity to purchase a 10-year annuity due for each member of the group. The annuity due would pay $40,000 each year beginning 5 years from now (i.e., at time = 5). What is the most you would be willing to pay now, per each physician, for this investment? Assume an appropriate discount rate of 7%.

13-2 The hospital's marketing and finance departments have just provided you, as chief financial officer, with pro forma income statements for your proposed sonogram center. These statements appear in the following.

Pro forma Income Statement
(000)

Time	$t + 1$	$t + 2$	$t + 3$	$t + 4$
Service Revenues (net)	$425	$500	$580	$700
Expenses	$400	$450	$525	$600
Depreciation Expense	$ 35	$ 35	$ 35	$ 35
Net Income	($ 10)	$ 15	$ 20	$ 65

What is the project's IRR? Assume an initial investment of $175,000 and an appropriate discount rate of 6%. The hospital is operated as a not-for-profit facility.

13-3 The chief operating officer (COO) of a small, not-for-profit community hospital has to make a recommendation to the board of trustees on choosing among two project options for an unrestricted gift of $250,000 that has just been received. The board has established a time horizon of 5 years on this project. The options are described in the following.
a. Purchase the practice of a young physician (the hospital's third highest admitter). Estimates of projected cash flows for the practice (post-purchase), are:

Probability of Cash Flow

Time	60%	20%	20%
$t + 1$	$ 40,000	$20,000	$ 60,000
$t + 2$	$ 60,000	$30,000	$ 80,000
$t + 3$	$ 75,000	$40,000	$100,000
$t + 4$	$100,000	$50,000	$125,000
$t + 5$	$100,000	$50,000	$125,000

b. Purchase an upgraded analyzer for the laboratory. Based on forecasts of laboratory utilization, the net cash flows for this project are:

Time	Net Cash Flow
$t + 1$	$75,000
$t + 2$	$75,000
$t + 3$	$50,000
$t + 4$	$50,000
$t + 5$	$50,000

Which investment should the COO recommend and why?

13-4 What are some of the factors that can influence the riskiness of projects (investments) in healthcare organizations?

Chapter 14

Quality Analysis

LEARNING OBJECTIVES

1. To describe how statistical process control can be used to monitor and improve the services provided by healthcare organizations.
2. To describe the use of total quality management and continuous quality improvement methods and models to enhance system performance.
3. To analyze service systems using run charts and control charts.

REAL WORLD SCENARIO

A multispecialty group practice is striving to serve its patients promptly. It has defined a late patient as one who is brought into a medical examination room more than 5 minutes after the scheduled appointment. Patients who wait in the waiting room more than 5 minutes after the scheduled time of their appointment are late patients. The practice has collected the following data over a 10-day period (Table 14-1).

Number of Patients Who Waited

It should be noted that this multispecialty group practice gives approximately the same number of available appointments each day. Based on this, does the clinic need to redesign its patient care systems to better serve its patients? Is there a problem? If yes, describe it and recommend an approach. If no, explain your logic.

LEARNING OBJECTIVE 1: TO DESCRIBE HOW STATISTICAL PROCESS CONTROL CAN BE USED TO MONITOR AND IMPROVE THE SERVICES PROVIDED BY HEALTHCARE ORGANIZATIONS

This chapter calls attention to the methods and models to monitor, diagnose, and improve the outcomes associated with healthcare service systems. Quality analysis requires the analyst to define quality, gather data related to measures

271

Table 14-1 Number of Patients Who Waited
(Data: Clinic Records for June)

Day	Number of Patients Who Waited
1	12
2	16
3	26
4	4
5	8
6	17
7	13
8	16
9	22
10	18

Mean = 15.2
Standard Deviation = 6.40
Median = 16.0

used to quantify quality, and analyze the data to arrive at conclusions related to the quality of system outcomes. These conclusions then become the basis for system change.

As indicated in Figure 14-1, service system outcomes are the product of the conversion of inputs (e.g., skills, resources) in accordance with a specific protocol. Skills and resources are used in accordance with some form of protocol to achieve desired outcomes. However, all outcomes may not be desired because of the malapplication or misapplication of the inputs. This is the classical systems model.

Every healthcare organization is a series of interrelated and interlocked service systems. Outcomes associated with one system are inputs for other systems. For example, the meals served by a hospital's dietary department can be considered the outcome

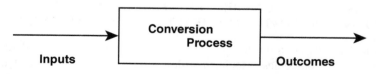

Figure 14-1 General Systems Framework

associated with the dietary subsystem in the hospital. When we look at the patient care subsystem, the meals served are one input that (should) contribute to intended patient care outcomes. The outcomes of one system are the inputs in other subsystems.

For our purpose, *quality* is defined as an intended system or subsystem outcome. It is the outcome intended by the service system and can be influenced by a change in the inputs and/or processes (e.g., protocol) used to convert inputs into the intended outcome. This is an important point as it is based on the premise that quality (or lack of quality) is a product of the inputs and processes used to convert inputs into system and subsystem outcomes.

Quality has many dimensions. What constitutes quality to patients may be different from what constitutes quality to physicians, nurses, therapists, and technicians. Quality analysis defines quality in measurable terms, monitors and measures it, and then subjects these data and information to analysis to improve quality.

Although quality has many dimensions, to manage and analyze quality requires that it be defined in measurable terms. In other words, the methods used to analyze quality require measurable definitions. Some refer to these as quality characteristics. For example, patients entering a clinic for an appointment to see their primary care physician do not want to wait. When they wait, they may ascribe less quality to their appointment than when they do not wait. We are able to count this quality characteristic (the expectation of not waiting). We can count those patients who do wait and do not wait as well as count waiting time, the time a waiting patient waits.

The first step in quality analysis is to identify quality indicators based on quality characteristics, such as waiting for an appointment. This identification must define these indicators in sufficient detail so they can be measured and counted.

Once the quality indicators are specified, data need to be collected. Because these data will be the basis for conclusions regarding the service system, the data acquisition must be reliable, valid, and include an appropriate amount of data gathered using scientific rules of sampling.

Statistical process control provides the manager with the tools needed to monitor, diagnose, and (potentially) improve the outcomes associated with healthcare service systems, such as systems involving patient care, general administration, or both. These methods are most commonly found associated with continuous quality improvement (CQI) and total quality management (TQM) methods and initiatives. These methods call attention to processes used to convert inputs into outcomes. Instead of focusing on who does what (e.g., job descriptions) in what order to create an intended outcome, these methods focus on the "overall conversion process" and the outcomes associated with current systems.

Systems and subsystems do not always produce the same outcome. Again, this is a very important point. Outcome variability occurs in any system or subsystem. As such, even though we define quality as the intended system or subsystem outcome, we recognize that outcomes will vary. A certain amount of variation in system outcome is natural and expected. This leaves the analyst with the responsibility to discern whether any outcome variability is natural variability or (conversely) a signal of the system producing outcomes that fail to meet expectations.

Statistical process control recognizes that all systems produce variation in their outcomes to some degree. The vital analytic task is to discern whether the variation is within acceptable limits (of variation), or an indication that the system used to create the intended outcome needs to be revised. In this regard, statistical process control provides analytic approaches to assist the analyst to decide whether outcomes are within acceptable limits and whether the variation constitutes appropriate grounds for system modification or is a false-positive—a potentially false signal that system modification may be needed.

Once appropriate quality measures are identified, statistical process control provides the basis to statistically describe actual measurements and compare actual measurements with intended goals. It also provides the context to monitor and evaluate outcome variations. This gives the analyst the ability to identify natural system variation and variation that signals the need for formal intervention.

LEARNING OBJECTIVE 2: TO DESCRIBE THE USE OF TOTAL QUALITY MANAGEMENT AND CONTINUOUS QUALITY IMPROVEMENT METHODS AND MODELS TO ENHANCE SYSTEM PERFORMANCE

CQI and TQM are methods used to diagnose and improve systems performance. They focus on adapting inputs and conversion processes to realize new or revised system outcomes. These methods and models must be a part of the repertoire of the quality analyst.

CQI and TQM focus on what is done (i.e., tasks), by whom (i.e., responsibility), and in what sequence (i.e., process). They identify modification that will improve the system outcome. The names CQI and TQM demonstrate their orientation to "quality," even though both can be used to improve service efficiency and effectiveness as well as service quality. The use of these techniques in health care has been influenced by many factors, including quality improvement as an accreditation requirement in hospitals and other healthcare providers. In some instances, corporate healthcare systems have adopted TQM as the company-wide approach to identify and improve patient care in all aspects of operations. They are very appropriate techniques to improve systems that involve many servers.

In health care, TQM represents a significant change in orientation involving the provision of clinical care and may represent a true management innovation. It focuses the attention of clinicians and managers on the *total process* of providing patient care. It de-emphasizes focus on specific individuals and departments in the functionally organized bureaucracy. It recognizes the responsibilities assigned to specific individuals as part of the total process or system. It is a systems-oriented model that builds the capacity to analyze, design, or redesign and implement with some important modifications and considerations.

TQM acknowledges the difference between clinical quality and service quality and offers methods to examine the processes used to provide services to patients. Quality is viewed as a *system outcome* that can and must be controlled and managed. As a management method, it forces systems to specify indicators of quality, monitor themselves against these indicators, and identify and correct extreme variations. TQM strives to improve the quality of patient care from both a clinical and service perspective.

TQM is a formal methodology designed to improve the operation of a system. It focuses on outcomes and strives to identify strategies to change conversion processes to improve service outcomes. As such, the quality of service can be improved using TQM. Efficiency can be improved using TQM. In other words, TQM is a systems improvement methodology. As methods to analyze and design systems, TQM is based upon specific concepts and skills. TQM has a specific language and requires users and those required to train and support users to be able to use specific techniques.

Brainstorming

Using TQM requires all workers to think, manage, and work. It does not segregate by level or role within the organization. Brainstorming is a technique used to facilitate group thinking. It is frequently used with a facilitator. Brainstorming is the process of collecting ideas from all members of a group without rendering any judgment or evaluation of the ideas. Participants are free to offer anything either new or something that builds upon the comment of others. Brainstorming usually separates discussion of the ideas from the presentation of the ideas. Group process techniques suggest that results be recorded on a neutral space, such as a flip chart. Participants should focus on the neutral space to guard against any negative or positive reaction to any specific idea. This includes individual reactions that may involve subtle body language. Brainstorming can be used to identify problems and develop solutions to problems. A typical question could be, "How could we improve the quality of service rendered to our patients?"

Consensus Building Techniques

Brainstorming puts ideas on the table for the group to consider. Different perspectives often conflict. Processes to identify ideas can only be considered successful when the process facilitates and builds consensus and ownership of the ideas. Consensus building techniques are used to avoid individualized argument and confrontation, maintain the substance of the ideas as the focus of the process, and identify those ideas that the group can agree are important and relevant. Under the heading "nominal group techniques" a manager can find numerous techniques and games a facilitator can use to build and identify group consensus. Consensus is not total agreement or the agreement of a simple majority. It is the willingness of the group to own the idea. This is a very important distinction. Typically, nominal group processes use multiple rounds of voting and discussion until the group (not just a majority in the group) is comfortable that their ideas have been heard and the group's ideas are ones that they can own and embrace. As discussion evolves, it is sometimes necessary to halt activities and add to the group representatives from other parts of the organization. It is essential that the group include experts from those parts of the organization included or implied in the desired improvement. The membership of the group as well as the facilitator's ability to insure a neutral environment is essential for the success of brainstorming.

Force Field Analysis

Force field analysis (FFA) is used to create group consensus as well as to examine problems and issues the group feels merit improvement. It requires the group to identify "driving forces" that the group believes are causing the need to change or "the problem." It also requires the group to identify the "restraining forces" that are impeding the ability to change. Users generally believe that working to eliminate a restraining force is more successful than enhancing a driving force. The group then lists the desired improvement at the top and then identifies "driving forces" and "restraining forces." Typically, specific driving forces are linked with specific restraining forces. The technique forces participants to broaden their thinking about a specific improvement and begin to identify and build a strategy (Figure 14-2).

Force field analysis is problem oriented. It requires the group to specify the problem and list the forces that are causing the problem (driving forces) and those forces that are preventing it from being solved (restraining forces). It is important that the group concentrate its attention on forces that are under the control of

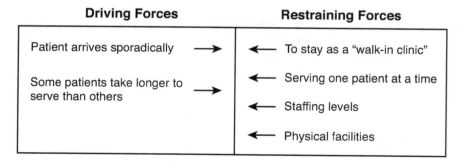

Figure 14-2 Example of Force Field Analysis

the organization. As a technique it can elicit many or a small number of forces. Unlike the fish bone chart discussed in the following, which imposes a classification approach on the group, a force field analysis provides the group the ability to analyze a problem from many perspectives.

The Fish Bone Chart

Often referred to as a cause-and-effect diagram, the fish bone chart is used to portray the group's thinking of the factors that are contributing to a specific problem or current operation. Fish bone charts force comprehensive thinking and a comprehensive diagnosis of the problem. Groups prepare fish bone charts as part of the process used to analyze the problem. Unlike force field analysis, which identifies driving and restraining forces, a fish bone chart portrays all the factors related to a specific outcome. Two common frameworks exist. One arranges the factors that contribute to the problem using the four categories: Equipment and Supplies, Procedures, Policy, and People. The other framework uses the four categories: Methods, Machinery, Manpower, and Materials.

Using one of these frameworks, the quality analyst indicates the specific factors, such as a specific policy or work procedure that could be the cause of the problem. Some may see the fish bone chart as a comprehensive causal map that indicates the factors that are combined to create a specific outcome. The previous figure indicates that the purpose of the analysis is to "identify the amount of time a patient waits before being seen by an attending physician." The fish bone chart identifies the factors that influence this outcome, using four categories:

1. Procedures
   Procedures of New Patient Processing
   Procedures for Existing Patients
   Procedures for Medically Ordered Return Visits
2. Equipment and Supplies
   Computer Systems and Appointment Software
   Medical Record
   Telephone
3. People
   Job Description and Role of the Receptionist
   Job Description and Role of the Nurse
   Job Description and Role of the Physician
4. Policy
   First In First Out (FIFO) Patient Processing
   All Medicaid Patients Referred to Local Emergency Department
   Ability to Pay Determined before Service
   Policy on Serving Patients with Outstanding Bills

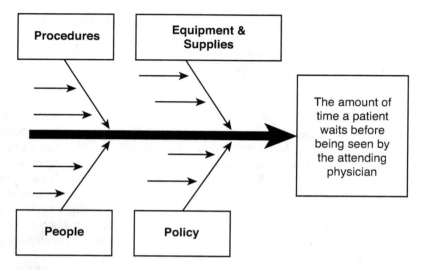

Figure 14-3 Example of a Fish Bone Chart

Although this list is not comprehensive, each of these factors contributes to the outcome listed in Figure 14-3. Used appropriately, the fish bone chart depicts the factors that influence the specified outcome. Stated another way, the specified outcome would not occur unless all the factors listed in the fish bone chart interacted to cause it.

Fish bone charts are used to break a problem into its component parts. They focus the attention of the group on the problem and require the group to construct a comprehensive diagnosis of the problem. They force the group to consider the many potential causes of the problem, not just a few that may quickly come to mind. Starting with the outcome, they create a retrospective map of the factors that make the outcome. By accomplishing this, the fish bone chart calls attention to specific factors that can be changed to change the outcome.

Pareto Charts

A Pareto chart is a vertical histogram that lists the most common problems or problem causes in descending order from the leftmost margin of the chart. Pareto charts are based upon the belief that, in general, "80% of the trouble comes from 20% of the problems." The purpose is to focus on the major problems or the major causes of the problem (Figure 14-4).

Like all histograms, these charts are efficient approaches to visually present relative frequencies of events. They are easy to read as long as the number of bars is kept to a minimum and labels are used to present the scale, the title, and the legend for each individual bar.

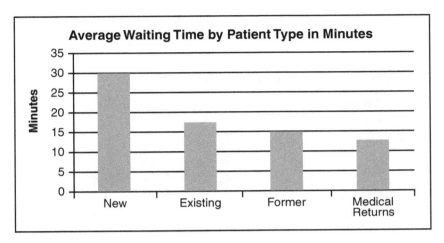

Figure 14-4 Example of a Pareto Chart

Run Charts and Control Charts

Run charts are used to illustrate patterns of data collected over time. They are intended to indicate patterns. Run charts can be used to monitor a system over time and plot occurrence against the average or desired average or desired level of service to monitor performance. They are also used to identify when a system is not in compliance with a desired outcome or process indicator. Over the long term, the run chart provides a data image of the system in operation. Such a chart can indicate when the system is functioning within acceptable limits and when the overall average changes. In general, functioning systems should yield data points above and below the average. When a system begins to consistently yield data points above the average, this may mean that the average is shifting up. Conversely, when the system begins to demonstrate a pattern of data points consistently below the average, this may mean that the average is shifting down.

Run charts are used to monitor systems. They report the status of a system as well as trends that have or may be developing. When desired levels of service are added (in place of the average), run charts provide the ability to visually inspect and evaluate the system. Control charts take the approach one step further. A control chart adds to the data plot control limits. In some instances these limits are based on standard deviation. When standard deviations are used, a line that represents $+1.96$ and -1.96 standard deviations is added to the chart. Deviations beyond this line represent, by definition, abnormal events. Consider the following data in Table 14-2.

Table 14-2 Data for a Control Chart Number of Medically
Complicated Births, Durham Hospital

Month	Number of Medically Complicated Births
January	19
February	27
March	20
April	16
May	18
June	25
July	22
August	24
September	17
October	25
November	15
December	17
Total	245
Mean	20.4

In this example (see Figure 14-5), the bold horizontal center line is the plot average (i.e., 15.2 patients). The solid lines at the boundary of the data are the 95% confidence interval (i.e., average $+1.96$ and -1.96 standard deviations; 1 standard deviation for these data is 6.4 patients).

The Flow Chart

A general systems flow chart is used to describe and analyze work processes. Such charts create an image of the steps used in a work process and the decisions that create branches in the work processes. Chapter 3 provides instructions and examples of general systems flow charts.

In a TQM environment, the general systems flow chart is used to describe what is the current process and system. A second chart is then prepared by the group to describe how the system or process should function. The two charts are then compared to indicate what changes must be made. As with

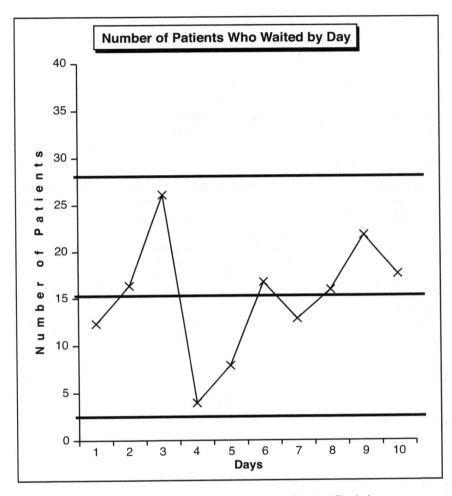

Figure 14-5 Example of Control Chart Using Standard Deviations

most applications of general flow charts, the chart is used for analysis as well as design or redesign. Other types of flow charts are also used. A workflow analysis chart is used to describe each step in a work process by workstation. For example, a patient's bill is followed between and among the many desks or workstations in the business office. A workflow analysis chart is used to identify redundant operations and to develop work flows that are natural loops through a well-arranged office. Typically, a simple chart is drawn to indicate how an office is physically arranged. Flow lines are added to indicate how work flows between desks.

A development chart is used to assign or analyze responsibility for different process steps in the overall work process. Typically such a chart lists the name of the worker across the top horizontal axis of the chart. Under each name is the list of responsibilities each work is assigned in the process. The chart is used to analyze current responsibilities as well as revise work assignments.

The Scatter Diagram

Scatter diagrams are used to illustrate the relationship between two variables or process characteristics. At best, such charts can suggest associative properties. Such charts provide no basis to conclude a casual relationship. Any scatter diagram should report the correlation coefficient between the two variables.

Scatter diagrams create a cloud of data. The cloud can suggest a negative, positive, or no correlation between the two variables or characteristics. By providing a picture, they are very efficient at calling attention to the relationship between variables. Consider the following example of a scatter diagram (Figure 14-6).

This chart indicates the graphical relationship between the total number of visits and the total number of patients who waited over a 20-day period.

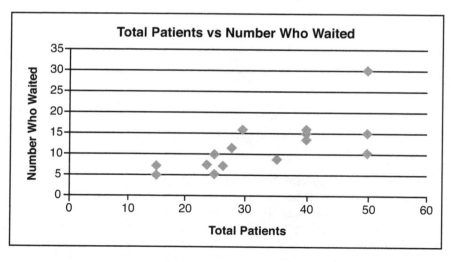

Figure 14-6 Example of a Scatter Diagram

The previous eight items constitute the primary methods and language of TQM. Each technique provides a unique ability. To reiterate:

Technique	**Use**
Brainstorming	To generate ideas
Consensus Building Techniques	To create group ownership and consensus
Force Field Analysis	To help create group consensus
Fish Bone Chart	To determine the components of a problematic outcome
Pareto Chart	To illustrate frequency of outcomes
Run and Control Charts	To illustrate trends over time
Flow Charts	To illustrate steps and sequence
Scatter Diagram	To illustrate (potential) relationships

TQM is a collection of formal management methods, concepts, and models. Many practical guides indicate different steps to follow to use TQM. In general, all can be subsumed under the following approach.

Prepare the Organization for Total Quality Management

The organization must state the purpose of TQM as being to improve the quality of services rendered to patients. If TQM is perceived as a negative or punitive process, employees will resist its use. All must be prepared to use TQM and understand its language and methods. TQM is not something others do in the organization. Success requires that TQM methods become the quality management approach used throughout the organization.

Assign Responsibilities

As a management method, TQM is only as good as the teams that use it. Teams are assigned responsibility for a specific problem or outcome. The membership of each team must be comprehensive to ensure that the team possesses sufficient expertise to understand and address its responsibility.

Identify Indicators of System Processes and Outcomes

Under this step teams are required to analyze specific processes of the organization, define what is meant by "quality," and develop measurable indicators of system performance. To develop indicators, teams must know and express the goals of "their" system and be able to assess the degree to which these goals are being achieved. Indicators are quantitative. They are the product of counting.

Teams use brainstorming, consensus building techniques, flow charting, and force field analysis to develop their understanding of the system being studied.

Fish bone charts may be prepared to develop understanding of the factors that contribute to a specific indicator or outcome. For example, hospital-wide indicators could be:

- Average length of stay by diagnosis
- Hospital readmission rate within 30 days
- Expenses per patient day
- Revenue per patient day
- Uncompensated care per patient day
- Appropriateness of posthospital placement
- Number of patients awaiting transfer to a nursing home
- Full-time equivalent (FTE) personnel per patient day

For specific subsystems in a hospital, indicators could be the number of:

- Surgical deaths
- Postoperative surgical infections
- Units of blood used
- Medication errors
- Medical records awaiting signature by attending physician
- Imaging procedures repeated
- STAT laboratory tests
- Meals served per patient day
- Hospital bills unresolved after 30, 60, 90, and 120 days
- Safety incidents

Indicators should be specified by the team responsible to diagnose and enhance system quality. Management should not mandate indicators. The team should be composed of individuals who possess the expertise to know the best and most appropriate indicators of system performance.

Collect Data on the System or Work Process

At this phase in the TQM process, data are collected to indicate system performance. Frequency and level are important. Pareto charts are constructed. Run and control charts illustrate trends over time. Scatter charts illustrate relationships. Flow charts describe how the system currently functions. In some instances, the team develops a questionnaire or data protocol to be used to collect data. For example, in analyzing surgery, the TQM team authored the following questionnaire:

1. Does the patient arrive ready for surgery? If no, what does the patient need?
2. Is the surgical suite ready when the surgical team is scheduled to occupy it? If no, what is preventing their use of the room?
3. How long do patients have to wait?

4. Is the surgical team performing the surgery in keeping with existing time estimates? If no, is there a problem with materials, machinery, manpower, or materials?
5. What are the problems?

These questions could be the product of a previous force field analysis or analysis of the problem using the fish bone chart. Sometimes historical records may yield data. In other instances, the TQM team arranges to have the data collected.

Evaluate the System or Work Process: Formal Evaluation Begins

The team, based upon its previous work and data, evaluates the operation of the current system or work process using the chosen measurable indicators. Throughout, the team considers many ways to improve the system or work process. Those parts of the system or work process that cause the most problems are focused upon. Pareto charts are used. Control charts are used to evaluate system performance against averages and determine whether performance is changing and/or is within acceptable limitations.

Improvements Are Designed and Implemented

Teams design improvement strategies. Fish bone charts may be used. Flow charts may be used to identify exactly where the improvement should be made and the specific improvement to be made.

Evaluation Continues to Determine Whether the Change Worked

Once begun, TQM is a continuous process of modification and evaluation followed by modification and evaluation. When a team has completed one set of responsibilities, the responsibilities of the team can be revised and enlarged.

Overall, TQM provides a formal approach to analysis, design, or redesign and implementation within a systems context. Numerous methods exist to facilitate TQM. By focusing the attention of the team "on the system," TQM is a formal management method designed to use the expertise included in the team to analyze the current system and recommend improvements. In principle, TQM is not revolutionary. It is a recognized best practice associated with systems management. It provides a formal method for analysis, design, and implementation. It focuses attention on goals and indicators of performance. It requires teams of first-line experts to analyze a system or work process before suggesting a fix or improvement. By focusing on process, TQM does reorient management in most healthcare organizations. Most healthcare organizations are organized based upon function (e.g., laboratory, medical records, nursing, rehabilitative services, housekeeping, etc.). Labor has been divided by a common expertise. Most healthcare organizations are not organized by service or product line (e.g., maternity care, cardiac care, etc.). As such, TQM enhances the ability to coordinate services that require the coordinated interplay of many service stations located in many functionally organized departments. TQM focuses on the process of providing service. Under TQM, the needs of the department are secondary to the needs created by these processes. Lastly, as a philosophy, TQM challenges everyone to always do better. It holds everyone responsible to look for ways to improve services and provides an outlet for their input and wisdom. Whether TQM dilutes the authority, power, and prerogative of senior management is an open question. It clearly empowers work groups to analyze and improve system performance.

TQM is based upon the actions of the group or team. TQM is not done alone in the privacy of an office facing a computer screen. It requires the ability to work effectively with groups. Frequently these groups have diverse backgrounds, values, and perspectives. Some professions seem to always argue, even on the TQM team. The ability to use TQM and help others use TQM requires the skill to work within a diverse group and facilitate a group. TQM can also require the ability to analyze, display, and present data. Use of statistics can become important. As TQM has become popular, many have presented different twists and subtle refinements. Whether significant difference exists is a matter of belief and perspective. For example, CQI stresses that TQM is a continuous process of improvement. It also stresses the need to change the culture of the organization. Whether CQI and TQM are significantly different is a matter of opinion.

In the process of collecting and analyzing data, TQM teams are doing a form of applied research. In some instances, they are using data from a sample, not a population. When this is the case, teams may need advice concerning the appropriate way to extract a sample from a larger population and how to generalize the sample to the population. However, TQM is not scientific research. For example, a TQM team found that in 100 surgeries randomly selected out of 1145 done in a month, 32 began more than 30 minutes late. The results were disputed by the surgeons as being based upon too small a sample taken from only 1 month. The dispute and the results both have merit. It is beyond dispute that the 32 cases actually did begin more than 30 minutes late. The 32 late cases are a reality. They occurred. As such, there is an opportunity to improve the process of surgery. This is beyond dispute. Whether 32% of all surgeries began or will begin 30 minutes late, however, as a general conclusion or interference based on this data, may require additional studies with larger samples. However, fixing the system to correct for late surgeries remains an opportunity. The only point of dispute is the severity of the problem. There should be no debate as to the existence of late-starting surgeries. Remember a cardinal principle of TQM, "If it ain't broke, improve it anyway."

LEARNING OBJECTIVE 3: TO ANALYZE SERVICE SYSTEMS USING RUN CHARTS AND CONTROL CHARTS

This section addresses how to use basic time series analysis, run charts, and control charts as methods to monitor outcomes associated with either patient care or management systems.

Time Series Analysis

A time series analysis is a chart that presents a specific occurrence over a period of time. In a time series analysis, "time" is always the horizontal axis on the chart. The purpose of a time series analysis is to show the amount and direction of change over the time period included in the analysis. For example, consider the data in Table 14-3.

Presented as a traditional time series analysis, these data demonstrate month-to-month variation (Figure 14-7).

Table 14-3 Number of Medically Complicated Births with Moving Range, Durham Hospital

Month	Birth	Moving Range
Jan	19	
Feb	27	8
Mar	20	7
Apr	16	4
May	18	2
Jun	25	7
Jul	22	3
Aug	24	2
Sep	17	7
Oct	25	8
Nov	15	10
Dec	17	2
Sum	245	60
Average	20.4	5.5

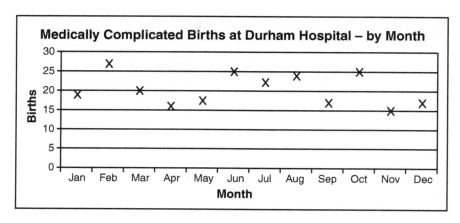

Figure 14-7 Example of Time Series Analysis I

Example of Time Series Analysis I

As stated, time series analysis is used to describe how occurrences change over a period of time. Time can be presented in any unit, such as days, weeks, months, quarters of years, and years. Time series analyses help to describe occurrences and portray the variation in the occurrences. For example, Figure 14-7 demonstrates the number of medically complicated births at a hospital over a 12-month period. Medically complicated births ranged from a low of 15 in November to a high of 27 in February. On average, using the mean, 20.4 medically complicated births occurred at this hospital over this time period.

Although this average describes the pattern of occurrence, it does not indicate that the hospital experienced 20.4 medically complicated births every month. The average of 20.4 medically complicated births indicates that during these 12 months, on average, the hospital experienced this number of medically complicated births. Averages only describe the middle of a data distribution.

Using traditional statistical approaches, the next step is to describe the data in Table 14-3 with its calculated 95% confidence interval using standard deviations. We know that in most distributions 95% of the data lie between the mean or average $\pm$ 1.96 standard deviations. In this case, our (sample) standard deviation is 4.1 births. As such, to further describe these data, we indicate that 95% of the time the number of medically complicated births was between the average (20.4) and + and − 8 births (e.g., standard deviation of 4.1 $\times$ 1.96). Expressed this way, our 95% confidence interval is 12.4 and 28.4 medically complicated births per month.

When this 95% confidence interval is added to the time series analysis, it can be seen that the number of medically complicated births reported in each month falls within

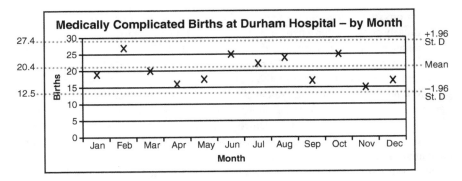

Figure 14-8 Example of Time Series Analysis II

this 95% confidence interval. All values were either more than 12.4 births or less than 28.4 births. In no month during this time period did the number of medically complicated births fall outside the range of the 95% confidence interval (Figure 14-8).

Example of Time Series Analysis II

When time is involved, a time series analysis reveals more than traditional statistics (e.g., averages, standard deviations, and 95% confidence interval) about the occurrences being reported in the data. The calculated statistics (e.g., mean, standard deviation) can hide a very critical feature of the original data. The statistics alone can hide the month-to-month variation in the data. If there were no month-to-month variation in the data, however, then either approach would be acceptable. If variation is present, the time series analysis is the more accurate presentation. It preserves the evidence of the data. Preserving the evidence of the data is one of the strongest attributes of a time series analysis.

Analytic Methods: The Run and Control Chart

In an ideal world there would be zero medically complicated births. In the real world, however, medically complicated births do occur. As such, a hospital must be prepared to respond to their occurrence. If, using the previously cited data, the hospital prepared to respond to 20.4 medically complicated births, for some months the hospital would have been prepared and for other months would have been underprepared. The occurrence of medically complicated births, as described in the time series analysis, varies by month. It is not a steady state.

Too often, it is assumed that any month that had more than 20.4 medically complicated births was a "bad" month, and any month in which there were fewer than 20.4 medically complicated births was a "good" month. However, these assumptions do not recognize the *natural variation* that characterizes the number of medically complicated births per month. The run and control charts systematically describe this month-to-month variation and provide the ability to deduce specific conclusions based on the pattern of variation around a mean value.

To respond efficiently and effectively, the quality analyst must be able to respond to individual occurrences and the pattern in which they are encountered. As such, variation is very important to managers. As stated, period-to-period variation is a natural characteristic of most occurrences presented in a time series analysis. Although traditional statistics do provide a measure of this variation—the variance and standard deviation—these statistics provide no way to describe the actual month-to-month variation in the data. They mask it. As also stated, TQM is based upon the premise that variation is a natural phenomenon and should be used, not masked, as we strive to improve the systems we manage. From this perspective, variation is an expected characteristic of any process, and we need an approach that will help us analyze the variation inherent in any process. A certain amount of the expected variation of occurrences is random; it happens by chance. There is nothing we can or should do to try to control this type of variation except to build into our management and clinical systems the ability to respond to it. As managers, we should expect this natural amount of variation. Another amount of this variation, however, may represent a signal that a fundamental change or shift is occurring, requiring a change in the process. The critical term here is "signal."

The primary challenge is to differentiate validly between the natural or random variation expected in all occurrences examined over time (e.g., time series analyses) and variation that constitutes a signal of a fundamental positive or negative change requiring management action. TQM tells us that variation is natural and we need to learn from the variation about the systems or processes that produce these occurrences. We must redesign systems only when the variation signals us that fundamental negative change is occurring. TQM is also telling us that random variations cannot be described or analyzed using traditional statistics because the (random) variation does not adhere to the requirements of the Central Limit Theorem and the Standard Normal or Beta or Gaussian Probability distributions. In other words, traditional averages or means, standard deviations, and 95% confidence intervals are irrelevant. These statistical tools cannot be used to describe and analyze variation. More importantly, they cannot help to discriminate between natural variation and variation that signals a fundamental change.

The Run Chart

The run chart is a time series analysis. Its horizontal axis is time and its vertical axis is the data axis. The chart is a data plot; it usually includes a minimum of 12 observations. The data points are connected.

An Example of a Run Chart

The center line of the run chart distinguishes this chart. The center line is the median value of the data. In Figure 14-9 the median is 14. The median is used to represent the middle of the data distribution. The mean is not used because a mean can be overly influenced by a small number of very low or high data values.

A run is defined as one or more consecutive data points on the same side of the median. Data points on the center line are ignored. The run chart allows the quality analysts to draw specific conclusions about the data based on the number of runs presented by the data. Once a run chart is prepared, the analyst:

1. Counts the number of appropriate data points (ADP). This equals the total number of data observations minus the number of observation on the median line on the run chart. In Figure 14-9, the ADP is 17. Seventeen of the data points are not on the median line.
2. Estimates the lower level (LL) and upper level (UL) number of runs using the following formula:

$$UL = (0.59 \times ADP) + 2.70$$
$$LL = (0.41 \times ADP) - 1.78$$

In Figure 14-9, ADP = 17,

$$\text{then the } UL = (0.59 \times 17) + 2.70$$
$$= 12.73 \text{ or } 13$$
$$\text{then the } LL = (0.41 \times 17) - 1.78$$
$$= 5.19 \text{ or } 5$$

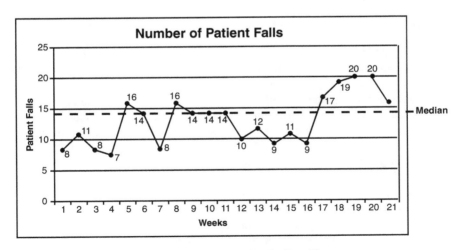

Figure 14-9 An Example of a Run Chart

3. Counts the number of runs (R), defined as the number of one or more consecutive data points on the same side of the median. Figure 14-9 demonstrates eight runs.

4. If the number of Rs is lower than the LL or greater than the UL, the variation is based upon a change in the process and warrants additional and detailed analysis. If the R is between the UL and LL, the variation is considered natural, and further analysis is not needed.

5. The LL for Figure 14-9 has been calculated as 5, and UL as 13. If the number of runs is less than 5 or greater than 13, then a fundamental change has occurred that warrants further detailed analysis and potential system change. Because the data in Figure 14-9 indicates eight runs, the analyst would conclude the variation in the number of falls is within natural limits and no systematic change is needed.

6. Other points to consider signals of process variations that warrant additional analysis include:

   a. If any one run presented by the data has 7 (when ADP is less than 20) or 8 (when ADP is 20 or greater) data points.

   b. If any one run has 14 points that consecutively zigzag the median.

   c. If any run, including the data points on the median, have 6 or more consecutive increasing or decreasing values.

The run chart provides analysts with a systematic approach to assess variation. This assessment of variation is the basis for additional analysis using TQM tools and techniques.

The Control Chart

Run charts and time series analyses can be used to describe the variation in occurrences. More important, control charts can be used to analyze this variation. A control chart tracks variation to determine whether it occurs within predetermined boundaries or limits (natural limits). These charts also provide the ability to draw certain analytic conclusions based upon whether the variation crosses the threshold boundaries used on a control chart. When the variation crosses the control chart's boundaries, fundamental change in the system's outcomes has occurred. Variation across or near a boundary is a signal to analyze the underlying system and potentially redesign it.

The concept of control charts is simple. It involves taking a time series analysis and adding appropriate boundaries, called control limits. The control limits represent the band of natural variation inherent in the time series analysis. When these natural variation boundaries are crossed, the analyst should look for fundamental change in the underlying process that creates the occurrences and (potentially) change the system. Given this approach, the challenge is to find an approach that can be used to establish the appropriate boundaries of the control limits. A control chart is created when these limits are added to a time series analysis.

Control charts provide analysts the ability to assess the variation in occurrences and use the variation as a signal that an intervention is needed. They are based on the fundamental premise that variation is a natural, not abnormal, characteristic examined over a period of time. Control charts accept this natural variation inherent in processes and systems and tell us when we need to act and when the variation being reported is natural and beyond the control of the organization and the manager.

There are many types of control charts based on whether the data are continuous or discrete. The following two provide the analyst with a starting point to use control charts.

1. Time series for moving ranges, also known as a range chart and a moving range chart
2. Time series for individual values, also known as an X chart

Control Limits for Control Charts

Control limits are the threshold boundaries that are added to a time series analysis to create a control chart. These limits, expressed as an upper limit and lower limit, are intended to provide managers an interpretative context. As stated, when the variation remains within the control limits, the variation is natural. No organizational response is appropriate. The underlying process or system is acting naturally and producing a natural level of variation. Natural variation occurs within the control limits. We always find natural variation. When the variation exceeds control limits and/or presents related characteristics involving these limits and the center line, then the quality analyst must act. The variation is no longer a natural property. It represents a dramatic signal that a fundamental change has occurred in the process or systems underlying the occurrences being examined. Again, notice the use of the term "signal." The preceding two statements are the fundamental concepts underlying the appropriate generation and use of control charts.

When time series analyses present individual values, not averages or subgroup averages, the average moving range can be calculated and used to establish threshold values. The moving range is calculated by determining the absolute between a preceding and succeeding month (Table 14-4). For example, the number of medically complicated births in January was 19, and in February was 27. The moving range calculation is the difference between January and February, or 8.

Table 14-4 Number of Late Surgeries

Month	Number of Surgeries	Number of Late Surgeries
January	435	112
February	401	129
March	572	186
April	409	103
May	577	89
June	329	67
July	467	156
August	301	94
September	235	89
October	325	127
November	378	156
December	444	124
Total	4873	1432

In March the number of medically complicated births was 20. The moving range, expressed as an absolute number, for February–March is the absolute difference or 7, not −7. A chart can be used to examine the moving ranges, the month-to-month variation that may be occurring.

Calculate the moving range by time interval (e.g., month), sum the differences, and then divide this sum by the number of range calculation. In the example, divide by 11 to determine the *average moving range*. For the example, the average moving range is 5.5 births.

The upper control limit for a moving range chart (of individual values) is the average moving range × 3.27—3.27 is a constant, just as 1.96 is the constant used to calculate a 95% confidence interval when we use the central limit theorem.

In our example, therefore, the upper control limit for the moving range chart is:

Average Moving Range = 5.5 × (the constant) 3.27 = 17.985

For this control chart, 17.985 is the upper threshold limit used to evaluate the variation presented in the time series analysis we have been using involving medically complicated births. It is the upper boundary or control limit. Given the nature of this chart there is no lower limit.

The center line for a moving range chart (of individual values) is the actual average moving range. When the change from one month to another is more than 17.985, a value outside the boundary of values established by upper control limits, then interpret this change as sufficient to justify some type of additional attention involving more detailed system analysis, design, and/or implementation.

When we use control charts, we also must use a time series for individual values, known as an X chart. To prepare an X chart:

1. Present a time series analysis that presents individual values over time.
2. Add to this time series analysis chart a center line based upon the average of all values. For our example, the average of all values is 20.42 medically complicated births.
3. Add to the chart lines indicating the upper and lower natural process limit. These limits equal the average of all values $\pm$ 2.66 times the average moving range. For our example, the upper natural process limit is:

Average of all values: 20.42 medically complicated births +
2.66 $\times$ (average moving range of 5.5) = 35.05

For our example, the lower natural process limit is 5.79. Rounded, the upper and lower natural process control limits for the X chart are 35 and 6.

Interpreting Control Charts

Use the following rules to interpret X charts and moving range charts. It is imperative that both types of control charts are prepared from the same data. Each type of chart presents different characteristics associated with the variation. An intervention is warranted when:

1. A single monthly value falls beyond a control limit. This constitutes a signal that a fundamental change may be occurring.
2. At least three out of four consecutive values are closer to one of limits than they are to the center line. This also constitutes a signal that a fundamental change may be occurring.

These two preceding signals constitute warning signals that a change may be occurring.

1. Whenever eight or more successive values fall on the same side of the central line, fundamental change in the underlying process or system has occurred.
2. Whenever three or more successive values fall outside of the control limits, a fundamental change has occurred in the underlying process or system.

The occurrences being analyzed and the limit being violated (i.e., upper or lower) indicate whether the change is positive or negative.

Analysts need the ability to identify and quantify measures of quality, establish systems to monitor quality, and analyze quality use using scatter, run, and control charts. When signals indicate that variation is not natural, the analyst must employ diagnostic tools such as flow charts, fish bone diagrams, force field analysis, and Pareto charts. To develop system revisions and/or to enhance the quality of outcomes, analysts also use brainstorming and consensus building techniques as well as general systems flow charting.

EXERCISES

14-1 Do a force field analysis (FFA) on the driving and restraining forces that influence your ability to do well in a specific academic course. One driving force may be "your desire to learn." One restraining force may be "your need to devote time to other work."

Table 14-5 Number of Student Complaints by Complaint Type

Complaint Type	1	2	3	4	5	6	Total Visits
September	34	38	16	45	13	103	824
October	23	24	7	40	9	56	956
November	14	50	11	20	26	34	1167
December	67	40	12	17	34	9	1034
January	13	31	10	12	15	45	645
February	20	60	4	13	9	6	1645
March	23	97	18	23	4	3	1432
April	43	31	3	14	13	0	745
May	4	25	0	12	16	1	456
Total	241	396	81	196	139	257	8904

Complaint
1. The quality of service received
2. Waiting time was too long
3. Follow-up care was not available
4. Clinic was hard to find in the building
5. The medical care/treatment took too long
6. They could not find my medical record

14-2 Using the following data, prepare a run chart, scatter chart, and control chart. A late surgery is defined as any surgical operation that was started more than 30 minutes after its scheduled time (Table 14-4).

14-3 The ambulatory health service at a university is experiencing an increased number of student complaints concerning the services it offers in its walk-in urgent care clinic.

The Basis of Complaint

Type 1   The quality of service received
Type 2   Waiting time was too long
Type 3   Follow-up care was not available
Type 4   Clinic was hard to find in the building
Type 5   The medical care/treatment took too long
Type 6   They could not find my medical record

Using these data, select a complaint for analysis. Your analysis must include a fish bone chart as well as other types of charts and techniques you deem necessary to appropriately analyze this data (Table 14-5). What do you recommend and why?

SECTION V

An Application of Quantitative Methods

Chapter 15

Quantitative Analysis in Strategic Planning

Healthcare organizations must evolve to thrive, and this evolution is more likely to succeed if guided by a strategic plan. Quantitative analysis is essential for strategic planning. In this chapter, examples of the application of quantitative tools will be discussed in the context of creating a strategic plan for a healthcare organization.

LEARNING OBJECTIVES

1. To differentiate and define various types of planning.
2. To define the service area for an organization.
3. To identify key elements of a strategic plan, and to use quantitative analytic techniques to develop a useful strategic planning database.

REAL WORLD SCENARIO

Groveland Clinic is an independent group practice comprised of 27 physicians in several specialties, including internal medicine, pediatrics, obstetrics/gynecology, cardiology, endocrinology, neurology, and sports medicine, as well as three physician assistants, and numerous ancillary health services. The clinic was incorporated approximately 15 years ago and is currently the largest independent practice association in the state. Facing substantial changes in the community as well as increased competition from other providers locally, Brent Callcraft, the administrator of the clinic, has been charged by the board of directors to develop a strategy for the organization to enhance its competitive position for the next 5 to 10 years. Callcraft knows that he must consider many factors to devise such a strategy, and that it will be a significant undertaking. Meeting with Dr. Wanda Wells, the clinic's medical director, Callcraft is asked to assemble a small working group to identify critical data elements that must be compiled, and to undertake the analysis.

301

LEARNING OBJECTIVE 1: TO DIFFERENTIATE AND DEFINE VARIOUS TYPES OF PLANNING

Planning is a systematic approach to achieving predetermined targeted future results or outcomes by making resource allocation decisions and identifying activities or actions to be completed. There are different types of planning, including community, operational, business, master or facility/space, and strategic, which differ in terms of their objective, unit of analysis, and time horizon.

Community planning is oriented toward identifying strategies and programs for communities or population groups. Generally speaking, this type of planning has a relatively long time horizon (10 years), because a lot of community programs take many years to evolve and become sustainable.

Operational planning is oriented toward the organizational or even suborganizational level (e.g., a department within a hospital). This type of planning has a short time frame, usually less than 1 year, and is focused on the day-to-day activities that must be completed to implement strategy.

Business planning can be thought of as a blueprint designed to guide a program, initiative, or business through a period of about 5 years. Typically, business plans are developed to frame a startup activity, outlining its purpose and objective, as well as marketing and financial strategies. Business plans include statements, known as pro forma statements, which project the expected financial results for the activity over the plan's time horizon. Business plans should be developed for all startup activities and are typically required when seeking capital investment from outside the organization (e.g., obtaining a business loan).

Planning that focuses on the physical space, such as buildings, is known as *master*, *facility*, or *space planning*. This type of planning takes into account the amount and type of space required for particular activities, and also deals with issues related to proximity among physical spaces. For example, a master plan would consider how much space is needed for an emergency department within a hospital, what special equipment or physical capabilities might be required in that space, and where that space should be located in the hospital (e.g., first floor, relatively proximate to the radiology department, with easy access to the surgical suite, etc.). The time horizon for this type of planning is governed by the length of time the space is likely to be useful; in many cases this can be quite long (e.g., 10–20 years), although updated master plans will certainly be required.

Strategic planning is used to articulate an organization's mission, goals, and objectives, and to define a set of activities to achieve these goals and objectives, over a time horizon of approximately 5 to 10 years. The activities are based on a reasoned, evidence-based approach to allocating resources. If an organization is fortunate enough to have unlimited resources, strategic planning decisions

Table 15-1 Major Types of Planning

Type of Planning	Major Focus	Time Horizon
Community	Community or population group	10 years
Operational	Organization or sub-organization—day-to-day	1 year
Business	Organization or sub-organization—assess sustainability and use to acquire external funding	5 years
Master	Space issues, including proximity among units in facility	10–20 years
Strategic	Organization or sub-organization resource allocation decisions to achieve goals, objectives	5 years

would not need to be made. Obviously, such an organization does not exist. A simple way of defining strategic planning is to think of it as answering three questions:

1. Where do we want to be?
2. Where are we now?
3. What's the best way of getting from where we are to where we want to be?

This chapter deals primarily with strategic planning, although aspects of the other types of planning are also touched upon. Table 15-1 differentiates among the essential types of planning.

LEARNING OBJECTIVE 2: TO DEFINE THE SERVICE AREA FOR AN ORGANIZATION

It is particularly important for a healthcare organization to identify who uses or might potentially use the organization's services in the future. This process is known as defining the service area. Many attributes can be used to define a service area for a healthcare organization. For example, a pediatric practice typically serves patients under the age of 18, obstetrics/gynecology specialists provide care for women, cardiologists focus on conditions pertaining to the heart, etc. In each of these instances the principal population served by the clinician is defined by the patient's age (pediatrics), gender (obstetrics/gynecology), or body system (cardiology).

However, in a more general sense the service area of a healthcare organization, program, or service may be defined geographically. For most organizations or services, the majority of clients or patients come from a definable area. This area includes those communities that are important to the healthcare organization in that they account for a substantial portion of the organization's business, as well as those communities that are especially dependent upon the healthcare organization for services. Identifying this service area is important for an organization, because it must make sure that the needs and interests of the population comprising the service area are met. In the next several paragraphs an approach for defining a service area is presented.

Determine the Relative Importance of Each Community to Your Organization

Healthcare organizations must determine where their patients or clients are coming from, a process known as patient origin analysis. For example, suppose you are completing a patient origin analysis for a physician group, Gladwell Medicine. In this case, you would analyze where the patients who utilize the group reside, for example, by zip code. Table 15-2 displays the number and percentage of total patient visits using Gladwell Medicine, arrayed by zip code in descending order.

According to these data, more than 22% of Gladwell's patients come from XXXX1, nearly 19% from XXXX2, etc. Using the setting of a physician practice, the formula for computing patient origin is:

$$\frac{\text{Patient Origin for}}{\text{Community A}} = \frac{\text{Patient Visits to Your Organization from Community A}}{\text{Total Patient Visits to Your Practice}}$$

Obviously, it is critical for Gladwell to know where its patients are coming from and to identify and serve the needs of this group.

There is no percentage that is used strictly to define an organization's service area. However, generally the service area is considered to account for 60% to 75% of the total patient activity. For Gladwell, four zip codes account for more than 70% of patient visits. In addition, notice that there is a relatively large dropoff in percentage between zip codes XXXX4 and XXXX5. This drop–off, or natural "breakpoint," frequently occurs in patient origin analyses. This suggests that there is a notable difference between these two zip codes in terms of the percentage of

Table 15-2 Patient Origin Analysis for Gladwell Medicine, by Zip Code (FY 2007–2008)

Zip Code	Number of Patient Visits	Percentage of Total Patient Visits	Cumulative Percent of Total Patient Visits
XXXX1	234	22.4%	22.4%
XXXX2	196	18.7	41.1
XXXX3	174	16.6	57.7
XXXX4	129	12.3	70.0
XXXX5	80	7.6	77.6
XXXX6	74	7.1	84.7
XXXX7	41	3.9	88.6
XXXX8	19	1.8	90.4
XXXX9	14	1.3	91.7
OTHER	85	8.1	99.8
TOTAL	1046	100	

patients contributed. By convention, we would include the zip codes above the breakpoint in the service area. Taken as a whole, the patient origin analysis suggests that the first four zip codes represent a substantially more important area to Gladwell than the others.

Determine the Relative Importance of Your Organization to Each Community

Not only is it essential to assess how important each community is to your organization, but it is also important to assess your organization's relative importance to the communities. For example, a zip code with a relatively low population may contribute a small percentage of your business; however, the majority of the population may look to you for care. This analysis is known as market share analysis. Again using the example of the Gladwell practice, the formula for computing market share for community A is:

Market Share of Community A =

$$\frac{\text{Patient Visits to Your Organization from Community A}}{\text{Patient Visits to All Organizations of Your Type from Community A}}$$

Table 15-3 displays the utilization data of the main zip codes from which Gladwell patients are drawn.

Note: the XXX in columns for providers A, B, and C indicate that these providers treat patients from other zip codes beyond the nine being analyzed. However, these data are not pertinent to completing a market share analysis for Gladwell.

Evaluating Table 15-3, we see that residents of zip code XXXX1 made 528 visits to physician offices in the last fiscal year. Of this total, 234 or 44.3% were to Gladwell. We say that Gladwell's market share of zip code XXXX1 is 44.3%. Table 15-4 displays the market share for Gladwell in each of the zip codes of interest.

Based on these data it is apparent that Gladwell Medical is a very important healthcare resource for residents of zip code XXXX7, where it holds a market share of 44.6%.

It is important for a healthcare organization to include in its service area those communities (or other population groupings) for which the organization's services are important, as well as the communities that are important to the organization, both of which may be measured by utilization patterns. Typically there is substantial overlap between these categorizations. That is, organizations in which we are "important," as reflected by a high market share, typically also account for relatively high percentages of our business. As with patient origin analysis, there is no minimum market share level above which a zip code would be included in

Table 15-3 Visits, by Provider and Zip Code (FY 2007–2008)

		Patient Visits			
Zip Code	Gladwell	Provider A	Provider B	Provider C	Total
XXXX1	234	119	65	110	528
XXXX2	196	28	145	682	1051
XXXX3	174	109	35	72	390
XXXX4	129	59	131	7	326
XXXX5	80	541	129	74	824
XXXX6	74	59	365	291	789
XXXX7	41	15	7	29	92
XXXX8	19	55	198	704	976
XXXX9	14	29	577	308	928
OTHER	85	XXX	XXX	XXX	XXX

Table 15-4 Marketshare of Gladwell Medical, by Zip Code (FY 2007–2008)

Zip Code	Gladwell Patient Visits	Gladwell Marketshare
XXXX1	234	44.3%
XXXX2	196	18.6
XXXX3	174	44.6
XXXX4	129	39.6
XXXX5	80	9.7
XXXX6	74	9.4
XXXX7	41	44.6
XXXX8	19	1.9
XXXX9	14	1.5

the organization's service area; however, it is generally wise to take a conservative approach to defining the area (i.e., it is more prudent, strategically, to err on the side of including more communities, rather than excluding them). As a general guideline, if the organization has a market share of more than 15% in a community, the community should be included in the service area. It should be noted that in urban areas with dense populations and multiple providers, market shares will be substantially lower than the levels shown in this example; this fact must be taken into account.

For Gladwell Medical, based on the patient origin and market share analyses, the service area would be defined to include at least the following zip codes: XXXX1, XXXX2, XXXX3, XXXX4, XXXX7.

In addition to the quantitative approach used in patient origin and market share analyses, several qualitative or subjective analyses must be completed in defining service area. The first of these qualitative factors takes into account the relative location or proximity of zip codes. The preliminary service area for Gladwell, as defined by patient origin and market share, is shown in Figure 15-1.

Note that most of the preliminary service area zip codes, indicated by shading, are contiguous (i.e., they touch). Notice zip code XXXX5. It is surrounded by zip codes included in the preliminary service area for Gladwell, although it does not qualify to be included itself, based on insufficient patient origin and market share data. In effect, zip code XXXX5 is somewhat of an island in the middle of a sea of service area counties. There might be several reasons why this pattern has occurred. For example, perhaps the zip code has an extremely low population, has relatively poor access to Gladwell, or has a very specialized population

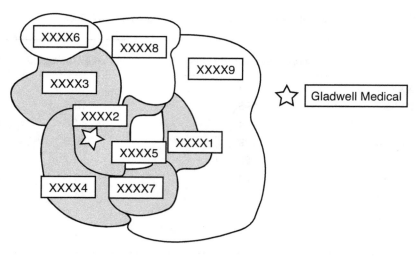

Figure 15-1 Preliminary Service Area of Gladwell Medical

(e.g., a military base or university), which has distinct healthcare needs and frequently dedicated healthcare resources. Whatever the reason, however, because of the proximity and contiguity of zip code XXXX5 relative to other service area zip codes, we would choose to include it in Gladwell's service area.

Another qualitative factor that must be taken into account in defining a service area is the referral activity/practice among providers, which may result in unusual utilization patterns. For example, a provider may establish a specialty clinic or program off of its principal site. This program would likely attract patients from a geographic area different from its principal service area. In defining the organization's service area, these program-focused, specific service areas would be included in the overall service area.

A final factor that must be taken into account when defining service area is the notion of barriers. Barriers come in different types. Some, such as geographic (rivers) or topographic (mountains), may create physical barriers that can impede access or use of a facility. Therefore, although a geographical area may be relatively close to the healthcare provider, the physical barrier makes it extremely difficult or even impossible to actually use the program. Other barriers, although not physical in nature, may be equally daunting to surmount. Individuals may elect to use or not use a particular provider because of differences in values, beliefs, or simply based on tradition or longstanding habits. The impact of such barriers, somewhat more "psychological" in nature, may affect use patterns as much as any physical barrier. As a result, in establishing service area, attention must be paid to these barriers.

LEARNING OBJECTIVE 3: TO IDENTIFY KEY ELEMENTS OF A STRATEGIC PLAN, AND TO USE QUANTITATIVE ANALYTIC TECHNIQUES TO DEVELOP A USEFUL STRATEGIC PLANNING DATABASE

Organizations do not exist in a vacuum; rather, they function as a part of a "living," evolving environment. As such, they are affected (and can affect) several factors that exist both inside and outside the organization. In creating a strategic plan, both internal and external factors must be considered. This section identifies and describes several key external factors, many of them with quantitative components. A number of internal factors, such as governance and management team, organizational structure, provider capabilities, information system, financial health and stability, etc., but they are not discussed here. In differentiating between external and internal factors, generally the clearest distinction is that the organization has greater degrees of control over internal versus external factors. For example, the size and age distribution of the population, certainly important to a healthcare organization's strategy and activities, are not controllable by the organization (i.e., they are external factors).

In addition to the distinction between internal and external factors, both quantitative and qualitative factors must be taken into account, although the former aspects are discussed in greater detail in this section of the book. This focus is not to minimize the importance of qualitative factors, which can, on occasion, be the overriding strategic consideration. For example, political factors, both within and outside the organization, can be the final criteria by which a decision is made whether or not to pursue a particular strategy.

What are the key factors that must be considered in developing a strategic plan? The key is to identify those factors that influence the need for and utilization of healthcare services. There are several of these factors. First, identify the most important external elements, introduced by the acronym SHEEPED, each letter of which corresponds to an area that must be carefully evaluated. In each case, the data analyzed should include current as well as historic data for at least 5 to 10 years.

SHEEPED: A Framework for Analyzing External Factors in Healthcare Strategic Planning

Socioeconomic Factors

The relationship between the need for healthcare services and the level at which these services is utilized, and various socioeconomic factors is well established. For example, an individual's income level can have a substantial impact on the amount and type of healthcare services used. Individuals with a higher income utilize greater levels of most healthcare services. Some of this is tied to the fact that higher income levels are typically associated with employment status and availability of health insurance programs. Moreover, individuals with higher income levels have more discretionary income that can be used to obtain healthcare services not covered by insurance plans. An exception to this general rule is that individuals with lower income levels tend to use emergency department services at greater levels than those with higher income.

Other socioeconomic factors that must be taken into account in strategic planning include race, gender, education level, marital status, size of household, and availability of health insurance coverage. Each of these factors needs to be analyzed in terms of past socioeconomic status of the community, as well as forecasts of such information in the future. For example, changes in the ethnic composition of the U.S. population are likely to have an impact on the delivery of healthcare services in the future, particularly in evolving urban areas, requiring healthcare providers to implement translation services and perhaps print healthcare information in multiple languages.

Healthcare Resources and Utilization

Existing health and social service organizations within the service area must be identified and evaluated in light of potential competitive and/or collaborative opportunities. At a minimum, an inventory of such programs and services should be developed, including descriptions of the programs offered, detailed information on available technology, with a particular focus on specialized or unique capabilities such as specialized imaging devices or cutting-edge clinical approaches. This resource inventory should be mapped geographically. In addition to the inventory, quantitative information should be gathered and analyzed regarding utilization of healthcare resources in the service area. For example, in terms of hospital resources, the analysis would include at least the following:

1. Availability statistics
   a. Number and location of hospitals
   b. Number of beds, by service
   c. Outpatient capabilities and capacity
   d. Educational programs or services
2. Utilization statistics
   a. Number of admissions (These data can be combined with service area population data to determine service area utilization measures, such as admissions per 1000.)
   b. Average length of stay
   c. Program or service utilization statistics

By recognizing the interrelationship among the data elements cited in the preceding, several very additional useful measures can be computed. Examples of this were introduced in Chapter 5, including Equation 5-3, which is used to compute the number of patient days. Here, we also introduce a second Equation 15-1, which uses patient days to determine the percentage occupancy for a facility.

1. Patient days: By combining the number of admissions by the average length of stay, the number of patient days of care can be calculated. This statistic is particularly useful in analyzing hospital utilization, determining bed occupancy rates, likely demand for hospital inpatient ancillary and support services such as laboratory tests, imaging examinations, meals served, pounds of laundry handled, etc.

$$\text{Patient Days} = (\text{Hospital Admission Rate per 1000 people}) \times (\text{Number of People (in 1000s) in the Service Area}) \times (\text{Average Length of Stay}) \quad \text{Equation 5-3}$$

2. Average annual percentage occupancy: Knowing what percentage of a healthcare organization's beds is occupied is important to plan for the emergency needs of a community, as well as staffing and other programmatic needs.

$$\text{Average Annual Occupancy Rate} = \frac{\text{Patient Days Used}}{\text{Patient Day Capacity}} = \frac{(\text{Number of Admissions}) \times (\text{Average Length of Stay})}{(\text{Number of Beds Available}) \times (\text{Days in Year})} \quad \text{Equation 15-1}$$

The examples provided in the preceding refer only to institutional healthcare resources such as a hospital or a nursing home. It is important to evaluate individual healthcare provider resources as well. Physicians are a particularly important individual healthcare resource, and their availability and utilization must be monitored carefully. The physician assessment for a community should at least include the following:

- Number of physicians, by specialty and age
- Number of physicians by office location
- Physician activity levels, e.g., admissions, revenue generated, referrals, etc.

Epidemiologic Factors

Epidemiology is the study of the distribution and determinants of disease, and there are several quantitative measures of great interest to health planners. In terms of planning, epidemiologic data break down into three major categories: natality—pertaining to birth; morbidity—pertaining to disease; and mortality—pertaining to death. Each of these categories includes several indicators of interest as they reflect health status and need. Examples of pertinent indicators are introduced in Chapter 5, and they are repeated here to place them in the context of strategic planning.

- Natal statistics:
  - Number of births.
  - Birth rate: Relates the number of births to the total population, usually expressed as the number of births per thousand.
  - Fertility rate: Takes into account the ages and gender distribution of the population, expressing the number of births per thousand women aged 15 to 44.
  - Low and very low birth weight births: Usually expressed as the percentage of total births considered low birth weight (less than 2500 g) or very low birth weight (less than 1500 g).
  - Premature births.
  - Percentage of Caesarian births.
- Morbidity statistics:
  - Incidence rates of various diseases: Incidence refers to the occurrence of an event, in this case a new case of a disease. So populations are assessed relative to the number of new cases per 1000 or 100,000 population.
  - Prevalence rates of various diseases: Prevalence refers to existing cases of a disease, so populations can be assessed relative to the number of existing cases of a disease per 1000 or 100,000 population.
- Mortality statistics:
  - Crude mortality rate: This is a measure of the total number of deaths in a particular geographical area, divided by the population of the area, so the rate is usually referred to in terms of the number of deaths per 100,000.
  - Age-adjusted mortality rate: This rate takes into account that populations differ in terms of their age distribution, and that difference will, of course, have an effect on the number of deaths that occur. This rate adjusts for different age distributions and is usually referred to as the number of deaths per 100,000.
  - Cause-specific mortality rate: This statistic measures the number of deaths from a particular cause, such as cardiovascular disease, in relation to the population. It is usually referred to as the number of deaths from a specific cause per 100,000.
  - Infant mortality rate: Many analysts use infant mortality rate as a particularly important proxy measure of the quality of a health system. The measure indicates the number of deaths of infants (under the age of 1 year) per number of live births. It is usually referred to as the number of deaths per 1000 births.

Economic Factors

The economic vitality of the country as well as the local community can have a considerable impact on healthcare need and use. Rising unemployment rates will lead to decreases in the number of people covered by employer-based health insurance, and probable increases in coverage by government programs, such as Medicaid. These patterns will undoubtedly have an impact on the type and level of health services used. Similarly, the rate of inflation has an influence on purchasing decisions, including healthcare services. It is instructive to evaluate the employers of the local community. Are they in industries which typically offer rich employee benefit packages, including health insurance or is the workforce provided with very limited benefits? Are local employers in growth industries, as categorized by standard industrial classification (SIC) categories? Are local industries high-risk employers, such as agriculture, lumbering, and fishing?

Political Factors

One area of external analysis, although primarily qualitative in nature, will be included here because of its particular importance to healthcare planning. The area's political environment (e.g., limited government intervention/free market orientation versus more regulation and increased levels of government involvement) can have a significant impact on a healthcare organization's future strategy and its ability to carry out this strategy. For example, requirements related to a certificate of need program, if relevant, will certainly have an impact on an organization's ability to enter a market, or modify its programmatic offerings. Some states have imposed temporary moratoria on development of particular healthcare services, such as nursing home or acute beds. Local issues, such as zoning regulations, can also have a substantial impact on strategic decisions.

Environmental Factors

Healthcare need is affected by environmental conditions in the service area. Aspects such as water and air quality must be monitored to identify existing and potential health risk factors. For example, areas in which the local air quality is demonstrably compromised, based on emissions data, would suggest the likelihood of increased levels of pulmonary-related morbidity. It is also important to monitor the location of toxic waste disposal sites, either suspected or documented.

Demographic Factors

Demography is the study of the population, and perhaps the most basic area of quantitative analysis pertaining to demographic characteristics. This area of quantitative analysis relates quite closely with the socioeconomic characteristics described earlier. The two most important demographic factors to consider are:

- Total population size: Healthcare resources are used by virtually everyone, so while the particular type of services used will vary depending on the characteristics of the population, all other things being equal, larger populations will require more healthcare services.
- Population by age: Healthcare utilization varies by age, with the younger (less than 5 years old) and older (over 65 years old) using more healthcare services; the type of services used will also vary by age. Healthcare planners need an understanding of the age distribution of the population to identify future healthcare needs.

In addition to analyzing past and current demographic data, it is especially important to develop forecasts of future population levels. Approaches to complete such forecasts are presented in Chapter 6.

EXERCISES

15-1 Using the following data set on hospital admissions, define the service area for Hospital A, based only on quantitative factors (Table 15-5).

15-2 Compute the target bed capacity of Cheswick Community Hospital 10 years from now, based on the following information:

Assume current population of Cheswick Community Hospital's service area = 145,000

Assume projected population increase of 8% in service area over the next 10 years.

Table 15-5 Hospital Admissions, by Community

Community	Hospital A	Hospital B	Hospital C	Other Hospitals
North	45	64	76	123
South	159	324	12	521
East	65	24	137	311
West	145	68	95	113
Central	32	56	78	159
Upper	29	84	45	814
Lower	37	14	8	57

Assume a future admission rate per 1000 of 102.

Assume average length of stay of 4.7 days in 10 years. Assume a target occupancy rate of 78% in 10 years.

15-3   Newgroveton is a community of 445,000. In the most recent year, there were 750 new cases of disease A in the community. Assume the expected incidence rate for disease A is 245 per 100,000 people. Was the community's experience better or worse than expected? Explain your answer.

15-4   The population of South Winslet is 358,000. Assume the following physician distribution by specialty in the community (Table 15-6).

Assume that one half of physicians retire at the age of 65 and all physicians retire at age 70.

How many physicians, by specialty will we must recruit in 5 years? Ten years?

Table 15-6   Exercise 15-4

Specialty	Number of Physicians	Number Currently Aged 60–65
General Practice	90	18
Pediatrics	38	6
General Surgery	41	2
OB/GYN	50	6

Assume the following target ratio of physicians per 100,000 people.

Specialty	Target Physician Ratio per 100,000
General Practice	31
Pediatrics	18
General Surgery	13
OB/GYN	14

INDEX

317

CPSIA information can be obtained
at www.ICGtesting.com
Printed in the USA
FSHW020631200421
80629FS